I0894512

Proliferation of Open Government Initiatives and Systems

Ayse Kok
Bogazici University, Turkey

A volume in the Advances in Electronic Government, Digital Divide, and Regional Development (AEGDDRD) Book Series

IGI Global
DISSEMINATOR OF KNOWLEDGE

Published in the United States of America by
IGI Global
Information Science Reference (an imprint of IGI Global)
701 E. Chocolate Avenue
Hershey PA, USA 17033
Tel: 717-533-8845
Fax: 717-533-8661
E-mail: cust@igi-global.com
Web site: http://www.igi-global.com

Library of Congress Cataloging-in-Publication Data

Names: Kok, Ayse, 1979- editor.
Title: Proliferation of open government initiatives and systems / Ayse Kok, editor.
Description: Hershey, PA : Information Science Reference, [2018]
Identifiers: LCCN 2017034506| ISBN 9781522549871 (hardcover) | ISBN 9781522549888 (ebook)
Subjects: LCSH: Transparency in government. | Electronic government information.
Classification: LCC JC598 .P76 2018 | DDC 352.8/8--dc23 LC record available at https://lccn.loc.gov/2017034506

This book is published in the IGI Global book series Advances in Electronic Government, Digital Divide, and Regional Development (AEGDDRD) (ISSN: 2326-9103; eISSN: 2326-9111)

British Cataloguing in Publication Data
A Cataloguing in Publication record for this book is available from the British Library.

All work contributed to this book is new, previously-unpublished material.
The views expressed in this book are those of the authors, but not necessarily of the publisher.

For electronic access to this publication, please contact: eresources@igi-global.com.

Advances in Electronic Government, Digital Divide, and Regional Development (AEGDDRD) Book Series

ISSN:2326-9103
EISSN:2326-9111

Editor-in-Chief: Zaigham Mahmood, University of Derby, UK & North West University, South Africa

MISSION

The successful use of digital technologies (including social media and mobile technologies) to provide public services and foster economic development has become an objective for governments around the world. The development towards electronic government (or e-government) not only affects the efficiency and effectiveness of public services, but also has the potential to transform the nature of government interactions with its citizens. Current research and practice on the adoption of electronic/digital government and the implementation in organizations around the world aims to emphasize the extensiveness of this growing field.

The Advances in Electronic Government, Digital Divide & Regional Development (AEGDDRD) book series aims to publish authored, edited and case books encompassing the current and innovative research and practice discussing all aspects of electronic government development, implementation and adoption as well the effective use of the emerging technologies (including social media and mobile technologies) for a more effective electronic governance (or e-governance).

COVERAGE

- Knowledge Divide, Digital Divide
- Electronic Government, Digital Democracy, Digital Government
- E-Government in Developing Countries and Technology Adoption
- ICT Infrastructure and Adoption for E-Government Provision
- Frameworks and Methodologies for E-Government Development
- E-Citizenship, Inclusive Government, Connected Government
- Adoption of Innovation with Respect to E-Government
- ICT within Government and Public Sectors
- Online Government, E-Government, M-Government
- Emerging Technologies within the Public Sector

IGI Global is currently accepting manuscripts for publication within this series. To submit a proposal for a volume in this series, please contact our Acquisition Editors at Acquisitions@igi-global.com or visit: http://www.igi-global.com/publish/.

The Advances in Electronic Government, Digital Divide, and Regional Development (AEGDDRD) Book Series (ISSN 2326-9103) is published by IGI Global, 701 E. Chocolate Avenue, Hershey, PA 17033-1240, USA, www.igi-global.com. This series is composed of titles available for purchase individually; each title is edited to be contextually exclusive from any other title within the series. For pricing and ordering information please visit http://www.igi-global.com/book-series/advances-electronic-government-digital-divide/37153. Postmaster: Send all address changes to above address.

Titles in this Series

For a list of additional titles in this series, please visit:
https://www.igi-global.com/book-series/advances-electronic-government-digital-divide/37153

Handbook of Research on Women's Issues and Rights in the Develping World
Nazmunnessa Mahtab (University of Dhaka, Bangladesh) Tania Haque (University of Dhaka, Bangladesh) Ishrat Khan (University of Dhaka, Bangladesh) Md. Mynul Islam (University of Dhaka, Bangladesh) and Ishret Binte Wahid (BRAC, Bangladesh)
Information Science Reference • ©2018 • 452pp • H/C (ISBN: 9781522530183) • US $245.00

Handbook of Research on Sociopolitical Factors Impacting Economic Growth...
Suleyman Ozdemir (Bandırma Onyedi Eylül University, Turkey) Seyfettin Erdogan (Istanbul Medeniyet University, Turkey) and Ayfer Gedikli (İstanbul Medeniyet University, Turkey)
Information Science Reference • ©2018 • 472pp • H/C (ISBN: 9781522529392) • US $275.00

Urbanization and Its Impact on Socio-Economic Growth in Developing Regions
Umar Benna (Benna Associates, Nigeria) and Indo Benna (Muhammad Al-Mana College of Health Sciences, Saudi Arabia)
Information Science Reference • ©2018 • 404pp • H/C (ISBN: 9781522526599) • US $195.00

Sustainable ICT Adoption and Integration for Socio-Economic Development
Charles K. Ayo (Covenant University, Nigeria) and Victor Mbarika (Southern University, USA, and ICT University, USA)
Information Science Reference • ©2017 • 264pp • H/C (ISBN: 9781522525653) • US $180.00

Digital Media Integration for Participatory Democracy
Rocci Luppicini (University of Ottawa, Canada) and Rachel Baarda (University of Ottawa, Canada)
Information Science Reference • ©2017 • 259pp • H/C (ISBN: 9781522524632) • US $200.00

Digital Governance and E-Government Principles Applied to Public Procurement
Rajesh Kumar Shakya (The World Bank, USA)
Information Science Reference • ©2017 • 323pp • H/C (ISBN: 9781522522034) • US $185.00

For an enitre list of titles in this series, please visit:
https://www.igi-global.com/book-series/advances-electronic-government-digital-divide/37153

IGI Global
DISSEMINATOR OF KNOWLEDGE

701 East Chocolate Avenue, Hershey, PA 17033, USA
Tel: 717-533-8845 x100 • Fax: 717-533-8661
E-Mail: cust@igi-global.com • www.igi-global.com

Table of Contents

Preface xii

Section 1
Policy Barriers to OGI

Chapter 1
Open Government and Bureaucratic Secrecy in the Developing Democracies: Africa in Perspective 1
Luke Amadi, University of Port Harcourt, Nigeria
Prince Igwe, University of Port Harcourt, Nigeria

Chapter 2
A Privacy Perspective of Open Government: Sex, Wealth, and Transparency in China 29
Bo Zhao, University of Tilburg, The Netherlands

Section 2
Technical Barriers to OGI

Chapter 3
Open Mexico Network in the Implementation of National Open Data Policy 50
Rafael Valenzuela, Autonomous University at Juarez City, Mexico
Alberto Ochoa, Autonomous University at Juarez City, Mexico

Chapter 4
Open Government Data (OGD) Initiative in India: An Empirical Analysis 68
Rupak Chakravarty, Panjab University, India

Section 3
Financial Barriers to OGI

Chapter 5
Openness of Public Financial Management: Assessing an Emerging Economy.92
Salah Uddin Rajib, Jahangirnagar University, Bangladesh
Mahfuzul Hoque, University of Dhaka, Bangladesh

Section 4
Legal Barriers to OGI

Chapter 6
Prospects and Challenges of E-Government in Black Africa: A Comparative Study of Nigeria and Cameroon 111
Floribert Endong, University of Calabar, Nigeria

Chapter 7
Data Organization as Structure for Collaborative Governance: The Case of Implementation of Employment Guarantee Legislation in Rural India........ 132
Sharadindu Pandey, IIFM, India
Dhwani Sharma, Bhopal School of Social Science, India

Section 5
Organisational Barriers to OGI

Chapter 8
Conceptualizing Cyber-Security From EU Perspective........ 143
Ayse Kok, Bogazici University, Turkey

Chapter 9
A Discussion Paper on Cybersecurity Policies........ 155
Ayse Kok, Bogazici University, Turkey

Related References........ 166

Compilation of References........ 206

About the Contributors........ 228

Index........ 230

Detailed Table of Contents

Preface xii

Section 1
Policy Barriers to OGI

Chapter 1
Open Government and Bureaucratic Secrecy in the Developing Democracies: Africa in Perspective 1
Luke Amadi, University of Port Harcourt, Nigeria
Prince Igwe, University of Port Harcourt, Nigeria

Despite the widespread assumption that open government (OG) has emerged as a critical apparatus of governance, its institutionalization in the developing democracies remains contestable. Studies in open government suggest transparency and accountability in public office. This typically depends on the development of OG data and use of the same for effective and efficient governance choices and decision making. Although open government initiatives have recently proliferated to remedy transparency and accountability deficiency in governance in various ways, while it succeeds in fostering the culture of governance accountability in the developed societies, it has failed to fully resolve the difficulties associated with bureaucratic secrecy in the developing democracies, particularly in Africa. This chapter builds on content analysis to review and analyze salient issues raised on bureaucratic secrecy in Africa and in particular provides evidence of the effects of bureaucratic secrecy on the advancement of OG initiatives.

Chapter 2
A Privacy Perspective of Open Government: Sex, Wealth, and Transparency in China 29
Bo Zhao, University of Tilburg, The Netherlands

Open government and freedom of information are key values in today's democracy, rule of law, and public governance. Their further development may have to be equally taken into consideration with other important public interests, such as state secret, public security, and other individual rights including reputation and privacy. In particular, there is the need to consider how individual privacy can be protected in the digital era in which both the concept and practice of open government may claim more territory. Taking China as an example, this chapter tries to reveal the complex, dynamic relationship between open government (transparency) and privacy protection, in particular by studying two specific privacy-related issues: the disclosure of official's public interest-related private life and the disclosure of family asset. In the sense that they can be regarded as the benchmarks to measure the level of open government and FOI development in a community, both can reflect the cultural and political complexities that affect such developments.

Section 2
Technical Barriers to OGI

Chapter 3
Open Mexico Network in the Implementation of National Open Data Policy 50
Rafael Valenzuela, Autonomous University at Juarez City, Mexico
Alberto Ochoa, Autonomous University at Juarez City, Mexico

The objective of the chapter is to identify some barriers to accessing public data through the study of one of the pillars of Mexico's national open data policy, the Open Mexico Network. Based on the exploratory analysis of the "Mexico Abierto network" and the description of a case study in northern Mexico, an attempt is made to answer the following question: Does Mexico's national open data policy generate timely data and have efficient access to data? and the final question, Is it easy for citizens to obtain? The study identifies major problems from the design of the national policy of open data, such as not having foreseen the creation of positive incentives for local governments to update the databases in the "México Abierto network."

Chapter 4
Open Government Data (OGD) Initiative in India: An Empirical Analysis........68
Rupak Chakravarty, Panjab University, India

Open Government Data (OGD) is a relevant discussion concerning transparency in governmental procedures. The chapter examines how India has followed up on the open data policy and constituted the Open Government Data (OGD) Platform and National Data Sharing and Accessibility Policy (NDSAP) to ensure that citizens can access data generated from public-funded governmental activities. The author has conducted an empirical examination of the status of the Open Government Data initiative in India, its scope, how the programme ranks against other countries, and has evaluated the same against the parameters of Democracy Index (33 out of 165), Open Data Barometer (43 out of 100) of Open Government Data and webometric analysis. India has taken proactive steps towards releasing government data to public domain. This can be seen in the rising growth in contribution of datasets and increase in OGD literature. The NDSAP and OGD Platform can be applauded as a healthy step on the part of the Government of India towards transparency and encouraging public participation in governance.

Section 3
Financial Barriers to OGI

Chapter 5
Openness of Public Financial Management: Assessing an Emerging Economy.92
Salah Uddin Rajib, Jahangirnagar University, Bangladesh
Mahfuzul Hoque, University of Dhaka, Bangladesh

This chapter reviews the open government model and assesses the position of public financial management (PFM) of an emerging economy, Bangladesh. Open government (OG) is an emerging issue that is identified as the prerequisite of ensuring the accountability and transparency. From different research platforms, OG is suggested to pertain to the development goals of the country as well. Therefore, it has an importance to the emerging economy. This chapter investigates the openness of public financial management (PFM) through the theory of accountability, transparency, and open government model in Bangladesh. It seems that though the ease of accessibility of government data is demanded in the developing economy for accountability, transparency, and development, the situation of public financial management is far reaching from the demand in Bangladesh. The open government data platform and different PFM agencies are disclosing very little information regarding the public finance. The chapter argues to strengthen the basic structure of opening up the PFM.

Section 4
Legal Barriers to OGI

Chapter 6
Prospects and Challenges of E-Government in Black Africa: A Comparative Study of Nigeria and Cameroon 111
Floribert Endong, University of Calabar, Nigeria

Most scholars' perspectives on e-government development in Africa have tended to be monolithic. This has been irrespective of the fact that African nations have been adopting relatively different approaches to e-governance. Though the dominant tendency among them has been to struggle to have a certain amount of web presence through the creation of e-government web portals, each African country has designed its own (customized) e-government initiatives. It will therefore be very interesting to explore the extent to which the prospects and challenges of e-governance in

Africa have been varying across countries. This chapter attempts to fill this gap in knowledge through a comparative study of e-government implementation in Nigeria and Cameroon. The chapter is divided into three main parts. The first part provides a conceptual definition and a brief history of e-government. The second part explores the phenomena of ICTs and e-governance in Africa while the last part provides a comparative perspective on the implementation of e-government in Nigeria and Cameroon.

Chapter 7
Data Organization as Structure for Collaborative Governance: The Case of Implementation of Employment Guarantee Legislation in Rural India.............132
Sharadindu Pandey, IIFM, India
Dhwani Sharma, Bhopal School of Social Science, India

NREGA is an employment guarantee legislation promulgated for the rural workers of India. It provides 100 days of employment in a year with a provision of unemployment allowance by implementing agencies. To monitor the legislation, a collaborative platform has been developed that is customized to the requirement of the multiple stakeholders (e.g., different governments, village bodies, beneficiaries, public, work engineers, etc.). A large amount of the data is generated on the platform. Despite this, it takes lot of time in complaint redressal and mostly it is done manually. The chapter attempts to explore ideas of how the collaborative platform could be made more effective by organizing the data such that the requirement of field-based variability can be minimized.

Section 5
Organisational Barriers to OGI

Chapter 8
Conceptualizing Cyber-Security From EU Perspective....................................143
Ayse Kok, Bogazici University, Turkey

If the aim of the EU is the establishment of deeper cooperation with other nations within the context of cyber security in the future, platforms (e.g., the Task Force) should create an effective agenda that reflects the differences between the EU (soft power) and other countries such as China or Russia (hard power). Yet, there should not be any compromise in the principles and norms of these countries with regard to their Internet policies. Although this may sound too difficult to accomplish, it is not impossible given EU's increased emphasis on cybersecurity along with its evolving cybersecurity strategy.

Chapter 9
A Discussion Paper on Cybersecurity Policies 155
Ayse Kok, Bogazici University, Turkey

This chapter presents various reasons for the insufficiency of externalities in terms of the inference of market failure with regard to the field cybersecurity policy, which is claimed to be necessary for government intervention. The main argument of this chapter is that cybersecurity market failures are much smaller than initially assumed, and as a result, more harm might be done by trying to correct them through naïve government regulation.

Related References 166

Compilation of References 206

About the Contributors 228

Index 230

Preface

INTRODUCTION

In recent years, a number of open data movements sprung up around the world, with transparency and data reuse as two of the major aims. To mention a few, there is the Public Sector Information (PSI) Directive in 2003 in Europe (Arcelus et al., 2012), U.S. President's Obama open data initiative in 2009 (Bogdanovici et al., 2014), the Open Government Partnership in 2011, and the G8 Open Data Charter in 2013. Open government data portals resulting from such movements, such as data.gov.uk, data.gov, and data.gov.sg, provide means for citizens and stakeholders to obtain government information about the locality or country in question (3). While not being the only motivation, initially corruption was one of the main issues that prompted the founding of open government data initiatives such as the above (Dos Santos, et al). 2014. Corruption is a global issue that seriously harms the economy and society as a whole, affecting people's lives and often infringing fundamental human rights. The democracy of many countries around the world is undermined by deep-rooted corruption, which also affects the economic development. While the total economic costs of corruption cannot be easily calculated, the 2014 European Commission Anti-Corruption Report states that corruption can be estimated to cost the European Union. (Mercado et al., 2014)

Challenges

In places where there is widespread belief that corruption prevails, the people end up losing faith and trust in those entrusted with power. As the Global Corruption Barometer 2013 (Zuiderwijk et al., 2014) shows, corruption can be identified running through the democratic and legal process in many countries. This results in people losing trust in key institutions such as political parties, the judiciary and the police. While transparency cannot be regarded as an end, it can be regarded as a means to act as a disincentive to corruption. Collectively, there are three main reasons for opening government data (Zuiderwijk et al., 2014):

1. **Transparency:** In order to have a well-functioning, democratic society, citizens and other stakeholders need to be able to monitor government initiatives and their legitimacy. Transparency also means that stakeholders not only can access the data, but they also should be enabled to use, reuse and distribute it. The success to achieve transparency results in a considerable increase in citizen social control;
2. **Releasing Social and Commercial Value:** Governments are one of the largest producers and collectors of data in many different domains. All data, whether addresses of schools, geospatial data, environmental data, transport and planning data, or budget data, has social and commercial value, and can be used for a number of different purposes which are different than the ones originally envisaged. By publishing such data, the government encourages stakeholders to innovate upon it, and create new services; and
3. **Participatory Governance:** Through the publishing of government data citizens are given the opportunity to actively participate in governance processes, such as decision-taking and policy-making, rather than sporadically voting in an election every number of years. Through open government data initiatives such as portals, stakeholders can also be more informed and be able to make better decisions.

The above motivations, while not being the sole ones, are the foundations for most open government data initiatives. The latter act as a preventive policy and give stakeholders the opportunity to scrutinise and reuse the available information in a number of ways, including identifying patterns in the data and creating new services. This results in an increased accountability that in turn hinders corruption. Besides, by the creation of new services based on open government data, users add value to the latter, which can also be commercialised. The participation of citizens in decision-making processes is also a very important aspect of opening governmental data, as it empowers citizens and thus enables governments to be more citizen-centred. However, citizen participation is not only limited to the decision-making process. Open government initiatives may also allow stakeholders to provide feedback on government actions or collaborate in policy-making.

Overcoming Barriers

Although the number of public entities seeking to publicly disclose their data has seen a drastic increase, it is still a major challenge to achieve the full potential of open government data and support all interested parties with the publication and consumption of this data. A number of barriers, including technical, policy and legal, economic and financial, organisational, and cultural barriers, also contribute to this challenge. Yet, a major stumbling block for the full exploitation of open government initiatives remains the heterogeneous nature of data formats used by public administrations, which include anything from images, PDF and CSV files and Excel sheets, to higher structured XML files and database records. This heterogeneity is a technical barrier to both data providers and data consumers, and hinders society from realising government data transparency. Open government data portals also suffer from the large number of diverse data structures that make the comparison and aggregate analysis of government data practically impossible. The diversity of tools to present, search, download and visualise this government data is also nearly as diverse as the number of existing portals. Past efforts have sought to overcome this situation by creating comprehensive and connected European transparency portals such as publicdata.eu. However, the diversity of transparency standards across Europe, which proved to be a bottleneck, highlighted the need that platforms beyond the state-of-the-art also need to be more than just direct entry points to government data analysis. They also need to provide a platform for advocacy towards common transparency standards at the highest level across several jurisdictions.

Government data portals also experience a number of cultural obstacles which hinder them from reaching their full potential. For example, public entities might be unwilling to publish their data. This may be so for a number of reasons, including the perception that it requires a lot of resources and effort, or that the release of government data might backfire. This disposition is, however, slowly changing world-wide, mostly due to advocacy of civil society initiatives.

This book aims to explore the state of open government data initiatives, as well as existing tools and approaches. The book discusses different aspects of such open government initiatives, including the above-mentioned barriers, their impact upon all the different processes within the open government data life cycle, any proposed standards, and challenges impeding the efforts. In In this book, the aim is not to provide new interpretations of existing literatures. Thus, it gives an overview of existing interpretations, and provide an integrated and unified model that covers the relevant concepts, terminology, initiatives, challenges, and guidelines, therefore portraying how each element forms part of the bigger picture. The book starts by providing an overview of policy barriers when it comes to the implementation of OGI initiatives in developing countries. In Section 2, the open government data life-cycle as envisioned by authors has been provided which is followed by Section 3 with an overview of open government data initiatives, including assessment frameworks, evaluations and challenges. The book proceeds with discussing different challenges of publishing and consuming open government data in Section 4, whereas in Section 5 the authors identify the various impacts that publishing government data has on different stakeholders.

ORGANIZATION OF THE BOOK

The book is organized into nine chapters. A brief description of each of the chapters follows:

Chapter 1 reviews studies in open government and suggests that although open government initiatives have recently proliferated to remedy transparency and accountability deficiency in governance in various ways by fostering the culture of governance accountability in the developed societies, it has failed to fully resolve the difficulties associated with bureaucratic secrecy in the developing democracies particularly in Africa.

Chapter 2 provides a discussion on open government and freedom of information as key values in today's democracy, rule of law and public governance. This chapter reveals the complex, dynamic relationship between open government (transparency) and privacy protection, in particular by studying two specific privacy-related issues: the disclosure of official's public interest-related private life and the disclosure of family asset by taking China as an example. The paper concludes how both of these issues can reflect the cultural and political complexities that affect such developments.

Chapter 3 identifies some barriers to accessing public data, through the study of one of the pillars of Mexico's national open data policy, the Open Mexico Network. Based on the exploratory analysis of the Mexico Abierto network and the description of a case study in northern Mexico, an attempt is made to answer the following question: Does Mexico's national open data policy generate timely data and have efficient access to data? easy to obtain from part of Citizens? The study identifies strong problems from the design of the national policy of open data, such as not having foreseen the creation of positive incentives for local governments to update the databases in the "México Abierto network."

Chapter 4 provides examines how India has followed up on the open data policy and constituted the Open Government Data (OGD) Platform and National Data Sharing and Accessibility Policy (NDSAP) to ensure that citizens can access data generated from public-funded governmental activities. The author has conducted an empirical examination of the status of Open Government Data initiative in India, its scope, how the programme ranks against other countries, and has evaluated the same against the parameters of Democracy Index (33 out of 165), Open Data Barometer (43 out of 100) of Open Government Data and webometric analysis. The chapter concludes how the NDSAP and OGD Platform can be applauded as a healthy step on the part of Government of India towards transparency and encouraging public participation in governance.

Chapter 5 reviews the open government model and assesses the position of public financial management (PFM) of an emerging economy, Bangladesh. This chapter investigates the openness of public financial management (PFM) through the theory of accountability, transparency and open government model in Bangladesh. It seems that though the ease of accessibility of government data is demanded in the developing economy for accountability, transparency and development, the situation of public financial management is far reaching from the demand in Bangladesh.

Chapter 6 explores the extent to which the prospects and challenges of e-governance in Africa have been varying across countries. This chapter attempts to fill this gap in knowledge through a comparative study of e-Government implementation in Nigeria and Cameroon. In comparison to other monolithic approaches adopted by related studies on Africa so far, it explores the phenomena of ICTs and e-governance in Africa while the last part provides a comparative perspective on the implementation of e-Government in Nigeria and Cameroon.

Chapter 7 attempts to explore ideas how a collaborative platform could be made more effective by organizing the data in a way so that requirement of field based variability can be minimized. It takes as an example a platform in India, 'NREGA', which is part of employment guarantee legislation promulgated for the rural workers of India. To monitor the legislation, this collaborative platform has been developed which is customized to the requirement of the multiple stakeholders e.g. different governments, village bodies, beneficiaries, public, work engineers etc. It sheds light on the time-taking procedures in complaint redressal which is mostly done manually.

Chapter 8 provides a conceptual discussion on cybersecurity from EU perspective. It claims that if the aim of the EU is the establishment of deeper cooperation with other nations within the context of cyber security in the future, platforms (e.g: the Task Force) should create an effective agenda that reflects the differences between the EU (soft power) and other countries such as China or Russia (hard power). Yet, there should not be any compromise in the principles and norms of these countries with regard to their Internet policies. Although this may sound as being too difficult to accomplish it is not impossible given EU's increased emphasis on cybersecurity along with its evolving cybersecurity strategy.

Chapter 9 provides a theoretical discussion on cybersecurity. Cybersecurity policy entails interesting set of cases in which research shows that the market failure is much smaller than it seems to be at first glance, if it exists at all. Inappropriate government regulation, whether it is in the form of being too stringent or just misapplication, can result in significant welfare costs that are as real as those occurring due to market failure. The possibility of "government failure" should not be ignored by policy analysts. The chapter concludes that the following evidence should be provided by those who prefer an intervention into the Internet economy: an evidence of the existence of actual market failure rather than observable externalities and a regulatory solution that is likely to do more good than harm. None of these appear to have been provided yet.

As the Prophet Mohammed said (s.a.w.w), "The best of men is the most beneficent of them to others." With this book, we hope to have been beneficient for both practitioners and scholars involved in the field of open government initiatives.

REFERENCES

Arcelus, J. (2014). Framework for useful transparency websites for citizens. *Proceedings of the 6th International Conference on Theory and Practice of Electronic Governance*, 83–86. http://doi.acm.org/10.1145/2463728.2463749

Bogdanovi'c-Dini'c, S., Veljkovi'c, N., & Stoimenov, L. (2014). How open are public government data? an assessment of seven open data portals. In M. P. Rodríguez-Bolívar (Ed.), *Measuring E-government Efficiency, Public Administration and Information Technology* (Vol. 5, pp. 25–44). Springer New York. doi:10.1007/978-1-4614-9982-4_3

Dos Santos Brito, K., Silva Costa, M., Cardoso Garcia, V., & Romero de Lemos Meira, S. (2014) Experiences integrating heterogeneous government open data sources to deliver services and promote transparency in brazil. Computer Software and Applications Conference (COMPSAC), 2014 IEEE 38th Annual, 606–607.

Mercado-Lara, E., & Gil-Garcia, J. R. (2014). Open government and data intermediaries: The case of aiddata. In *Proceedings of the 15th Annual International Conference on Digital Government Research* (pp. 335–336). ACM. http://doi.acm.org/10.1145/2612733.2612789

Zuiderwijk, A., & Janssen, M. (2014a). Barriers and development directions for the publication and usage of open data: A socio-technical view. In M. Gascó-Hernández (Ed.), *Open Government, Public Administration and Information Technology* (Vol. 4, pp. 115–135). Springer New York. doi:10.1007/978-1-4614-9563-5_8

Zuiderwijk, A., & Janssen, M. (2014b). The negative effects of open government data - investigating the dark side of open data. In *Proceedings of the 15th Annual International Conference on Digital Government Research* (pp. 147–152). ACM. http://doi.acm.org/10.1145/2612733.2612761

Section 1

Policy Barriers to OGI

Chapter 1
Open Government and Bureaucratic Secrecy in the Developing Democracies:
Africa in Perspective

Luke Amadi
University of Port Harcourt, Nigeria

Prince Igwe
University of Port Harcourt, Nigeria

ABSTRACT

Despite the widespread assumption that open government (OG) has emerged as a critical apparatus of governance, its institutionalization in the developing democracies remains contestable. Studies in open government suggest transparency and accountability in public office. This typically depends on the development of OG data and use of the same for effective and efficient governance choices and decision making. Although open government initiatives have recently proliferated to remedy transparency and accountability deficiency in governance in various ways, while it succeeds in fostering the culture of governance accountability in the developed societies, it has failed to fully resolve the difficulties associated with bureaucratic secrecy in the developing democracies, particularly in Africa. This chapter builds on content analysis to review and analyze salient issues raised on bureaucratic secrecy in Africa and in particular provides evidence of the effects of bureaucratic secrecy on the advancement of OG initiatives.

DOI: 10.4018/978-1-5225-4987-1.ch001

INTRODUCTION

Transparency in government remains central to inclusive and participatory development. It exposes hidden agenda in government which could run counter to development as it largely promotes accountability. Since the end of the Cold War a key issue has been how to make governance more transparent, inclusive, participatory and open. This has resulted in recent proliferation of the term 'Open Government'.

The 'phrase Open Government (OG) was first used in the United States in the 1950s in the debates leading up to passage of the Freedom of Information Act'(Yu & Robinson,2012). Open Government (OG) had re- emerged in most advanced societies since the triumph of liberal democracy. The term however had a novel turn particularly in the 2000s .This was largely influenced by the emergence of the Obama administration in the United States . This include the pattern and dynamics of inclusive government in which transparency and accountability could be an integral component of government and decision making . A central supposition of OG includes openness which encompasses availability of official data or OG data .

As one of the most commonly deployed terms in the neo liberal governance (Lathrop & Ruma, 2010). Open Government (OG) has become a major term within divergent spheres of governance. Recent decades suggest terminological shifts in the use of the term as it becomes increasingly linked to open technology. As the later suggests, the sharing of data through the internet networks involving relevant stakeholders. There is "Open Government Data" (OGD) which implies making government data available to the public who may have need for them.

Thus, the term "open government data" might refer to data accessibility of government information or public accountability including official disclosures(Yu & Robinson,2012).

Policy initiatives that promote or reinforce this trend have been described as "open government" projects. Such initiatives often encompass provision of data, increase overall governmental transparency(Yu & Robinson,2012).The basis for data availability in OG initiative is primarily for improved and informed decision making of both the government and the governed.

Beyond this, both the private and public sector individuals, agencies and related institutions who are stakeholders are expected access to government data to make informed choices and decisions for the overall development of the society. Information is key to development administration such as technology based government including e-governance, use of mobile apps, e-administration, visibility and accessibility of key government decisions suggesting a sense of evidence based administration.

In development contexts OG forms part of the function of modern government and provides useful insights including recent trends and changes aimed at overall economic growth. For instance, in the ongoing globalization there is proliferation of OG initiatives including new media, social networking, building online alliances and praxis etc.

Despite its robust offshoot, OG has perhaps been less emancipatory among the poor societies . This is replete with a number of evidence based trends that suggest the poor disclosure of government or inclusiveness in decision making process .Thus, the manifold relevance of OG initiative not -withstanding, its actualization has been less effective as government data in the developing societies are rarely made available for public awareness and use. How this challenge which falls under bureaucratic secrecy encompassing bottlenecks and similar confidentiality could be surmounted in the developing democracies forms part of the primary objective of this chapter.

While liberal scholars and proponents see OG as a tool for advancing democracy and transparency, including OG data sets, it has largely been contestable in most developing democracies where a number of challenges are at variance with open government. Particularly, King (2006) has been rather critical of the dynamics of openness identifying 'Openness and its discontents', the aim is to explore a number of complexities and contradictions surrounding OG.

The growing interest on OG suggests its policy and scholarly relevance since the end of the Cold War and need for institutionalization of transparency and accountability in government. In particular, this points out the potential of government transformation in the neo liberal order . Regular discussions on OG since the 2000s at local and international summits including the United Nations General Assembly, point to the saliency of OG in modern government .

However, sustained debates that theorize OG as transparent and moves 'openness' from the margins to the centre of bureaucracy in developing societies remains rare. The scant study is largely reflective of the paucity of scholarship interrogating bureaucratic secrecy. In particular, the contradictory images of OG in Africa despite its proliferation suggests challenge to the emancipatory claims of OG. This has also been part of debates pointing out the impossibility of open society in the liberal order(De Cock, & Bohm, 2007).

This chapter examines some of the salient issues surrounding the dynamics of bureaucratic secrecy in Africa within the context of political space created by democracy to identify whether African bureaucracy is attuned to a more liberalized order. The chapter is interested in bureaucratic openness in Africa, in line with the OG initiatives. The aim is to move bureaucracy in Africa to the centre of government beyond the paradigm of bureaucratic secrecy.

The objective of the paper is to re-examine some of the salient conceptual and theoretical issues raised on bureaucratic secrecy in Africa as a barrier to OG initiative —bureaucratic bottleneck, red tape, favoritism, corruption, informal rules of engagement, patrimonial relationship etc. It argues that the evidence suggesting how bureaucratic inefficiency constricts OG initiatives has been less studied. This does not serve as an inclination to vitiate bureaucracy in Africa, rather it is a critical engagement to advance knowledge on bureaucracy in post 1990 Africa and an effort towards strategic institutional overhaul of Africa's bureaucracy for inclusive governance and development.

In particular, the chapter posits that reliance on technological advancement alone which recent OG initiatives provides such as the internet culture will hardly institutionalize bureaucratic openness. Rather strategic overhaul and reform of the bureaucracy along ethical guidelines is suggested.

To this end, this chapter revisits existing view points on OG and bureaucracy in Africa on the grounds that a number of critical issues regarding bureaucracy have not been adequately addressed such as public accountability, transparency, responsive and responsible government. The chapter offers a way of looking at the concept of bureaucracy in line with OG initiatives as it seeks to provide answers to some salient questions regarding bureaucratic secrecy in Africa: How does bureaucracy in Africa transparently address formal needs of the people?.In what ways are official data made open to public scrutiny,?. How is government data made accessible in real time contexts to the people.?. How are government data generated in terms of inclusiveness and participatory governance?.

This chapter may not be able to sufficiently answer all these questions. Rather it explores the main principles, concepts and criteria framing OG data initiatives and challenges which affect their implementation. The chapter argues that while the OG initiative and the data it provides may offer researchers, technocrats, the citizenry and policy makers useful insights on the patterns of conduct of the business of governance, there have been the challenge of data transparency in government in most African societies resulting in bureaucratic secrecy. The rest of the chapter is structured as follows; theoretical framework, methodology, conceptual Issues, bureaucratic secrecy in Africa, recommendations, further research direction and conclusion.

Theoretical Framework

Institutional theory mirrors trends generally present in theorizing about social structure and action from the classical to contemporary theorists (Alexander, 1983). This chapter builds on the liberal institutional theory to examine patterns of interaction between the bureaucracy (an institution) and the wider social space within a liberal system. Liberal institutionalists such as Robert Keohane, Joseph Nye, Joh Muelle, K J Holsti and Richard Rosecrance define institutions to include organizations, practices and permanent rules that guide international role behavior. Even though the nation -state remains primary, intergovernmental organizations such as the United Nations,

Figure 1. Geographical structure of Africa 1999. Note: Sudan consists of South Sudan. Source: World Bank, 1999

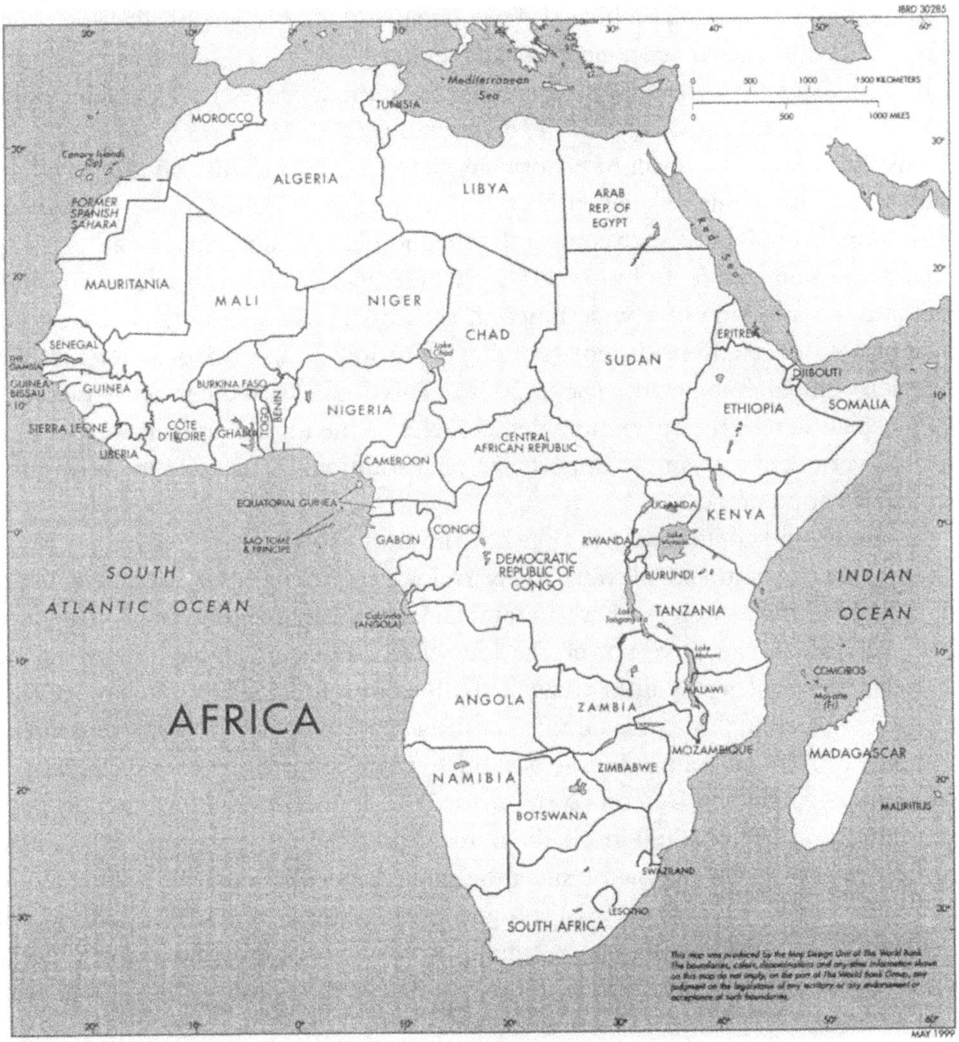

Figure 1

its specialized agencies, the European Union, and the IMF have wielded extensive influence since the Second world War (Andrain & Apter,1995).

What makes a political society healthy or otherwise is whether individual citizens are content with the working of their public institutions. Institutional economic theorists equally attempt to incorporate theory of institutions into economics to understand dynamics and patterns of interactions of formal institutions with the society (North, 1993). Horowitz (1994) pointed out that although democratization is a worldwide phenomenon, it is neither universal nor uniform in places where it exists. A significant element of institutionalizing democracy centers on "consolidation of democracy". Linz and Stephan(1996)argue that democracy consolidation is not connected with "liberalized nondemocratic regimes", or "pseudo-democracies", or " hybrid democracies" where some democratic institutions coexist with nondemocratic institutions outside the control of the democratic state.

Institutions are the result of historical struggles over prevailing understandings and rules of the game (Thelen, 1999). The empirical evidence of the primacy of institutions in explaining such comparative economic development is overwhelming (Acemoglu,Johnson & Robinson,2001). Contemporary institutional theory has captured the attention of a wide range of scholars across the social sciences and is employed to examine systems ranging from micro interpersonal interactions to macro global frameworks (Scott,2004). This includes themes on democracy which spans across the developing democracies of the third world such debates as open government inform the importance of institutional structures in driving the democratization process.

Scholarly and popular writers alike have traditionally depicted "Africa as a place where formal institutional rules are largely irrelevant. Although every African country has a constitution as well as a body of laws and administrative procedures that place formal limits on executive power, the long-held consensus among observers has been that these rules play little role in actually constraining leaders' behavior. This view is reflected in the "personal rule" or "Big Man" paradigm that has dominated the study of African politics for the past thirty years" (Posner & Young 2007:127). Similarly, Stephan and Dercon (2009) made cogent remarks on the contradictions of capitalist institutional failures in the third world. They quite properly pointed out that the historical developments since the mid-nineteenth century have tended to belie this 'optimistic', 'progressist' prognosis, in that the capitalist penetration of the 'third world' through trade and capital investment not only has failed to carry with it capitalist economic development, but has erected positive barriers to such development.

Institutional variation debate contends that institutions are endogenous due to variations on a number of issues including formal versus informal institutions. Other factors such as geography, ecology, climate, culture etc, affect exogenous component of productivity or technology .In a related theoretical account, Acemoglu & Robinson (2010)argue that the historical dynamics of institution in Africa have been different and that the processes of State formation seem to have been less delayed compared to Euroasia. And that State institution appear to be absolutist and patrimonial. They argue that institutional failure is largely responsible for Africa's poverty. In an empirical study they examined the primacy of institutional capacity failure to provide comparative development (Acemoglu, et al; 2001).

This chapter explores, OG through the liberal institutionalist theory. Liberal institutionists explore the interaction of the people within the ambit of institutional freedom, equality, transparency, accountability and in a distinct manner the guarantee of institutional apparatus that makes for fairness . Such interactions within the liberal order include openness, accessibility, transparency etc. This creates a culture of inclusiveness devoid of bureaucratic secrecy.

Methodology

The chapter is a content analysis which reviews and analyzes salient theoretical and conceptual issues raised on both OG and bureaucratic secrecy with reference to Africa. Content analysis is a method for reviewing and analyzing any form of content by examining various aspects of the content. Such interpretations of social discourse centres on critical evaluation of 'content' of social interactions (Amadi & Imohita, 2017). Lasswel (1948) argues that content analysis is integral to a critical review of any content. He identified the core questions that guide the analysis of every content which include "Who says what, to whom, why, to what extent and with what effect?"._Holsti (1969, p.14) offers a broad definition of content analysis as, "any technique for making inferences by objectively and systematically identifying specified characteristics of messages".

Regarding the specific methodology deployed to select the reviewed data on "Open Government" and "bureaucratic secrecy", the study adopted a dual research exploration approach in which a sample of relevant articles were drawn on both terms. A scholarly review was firstly conducted with a search on key academic journals in relevant data bases including the Proquest and Ebsco. The search which yielded a number of useful data guided both the analysis and review of the relevant literature while the literature that did not address the core themes of the study were discarded.

Further content check was made to deepen the search to identify previous studies on OG studies in Africa and to identify possible gaps in literature. This additional search yielded a total of 180 relevant literature. The aim is to examine "Open Government" policies among African counties and in particular for the acquisition of a solid body of evidence that could ultimately lead to mapping initiatives across these societies and developing a common set of metrics to consistently assess impact and value creation on issues associated with bureaucratic secrecy.

The central research question is; has democracy resurgence across Africa impacted the culture of bureaucratic openness, if it has what chain of causes or events suggest such openness, if it has not, what could be done to institutionalize bureaucratic openness?

This chapter builds on extensive review of related data in the field of open governance and advances a new knowledge while identifying the bureaucratic rigor which undermines OG in Africa and opens the study for further research.

Conceptual Issues

The concept of bureaucratic secrecy and open government have gained novel scholarly relevance since the triumph of liberalism in the 1990s.Conceptual clarification is important to enrich the ongoing debate.

As a widely used concept, bureaucracy has in recent scholarship proved useful to the success or otherwise of government. Its linkages with responsive and responsible government points to its saliency in modern government. Bureaucracy needs to be understood both as an institution, governance apparatus, a platform of formal value system, practice and a paraphernalia of government. It is increasingly constitutive of socio-political and economic measures. Understanding bureaucracy as a platform of formal value system, suggests the basis for accountability, transparency and openness against secrecy. This underscores and underpins the complexity and procedural dynamics of bureaucracy.

A critical bureaucratic theory explores bureaucracy as a space where complex endeavors are engaged within divergent interests and political power(Weber,1968). Effective coordination and resistance to a singular dominating interest makes bureaucracy efficient.

Although a number of studies have examined aspects of bureaucratic secrecy such as bottlenecks in the developing societies with emphasis on bureaucratic corruption (Gould& Mukendi, 1989; Mbakun,1996; Amadi & Ekekwe,2014), institutional failure (Acemoglu & Robinson,2010) and bureaucratic personalization (van Loom & Wittington,1981).

The concept of bureaucracy was popularized in the Writings of Marx Weber (1968) who provided an ideal bureaucracy. Although bureaucracy is a long used term in both government and organizations, it has often been associated with the formal sector within the public domain particularly with pejorative features as inefficiency, red tape, depersonalization, secrecy, slow pace of policy execution. This does not imply that bureaucracy does not perform highly useful and specialized functions.

Bureaucracy is a form of organization with precise structural characteristics (van Loom & Wittington, 1981).While bureaucracy can be used to apply to governmental and non-governmental organizations alike, in common usage in the discipline of political science the term refers specifically to the *public service* or to the *administrative branch* of government (van Loom & Wittington, 1981).

Bureaucratic structure in the developing societies perhaps do not aptly fit into the ideal type of Weber. Such classical descriptions appear to have been confronted with a number of barriers in practical contexts. Bureaucracy as a concept has been examined from a number of conceptual perspectives. There is abundant literature contesting transparency of bureaucracy in Africa (Mbakun 1996; Amadi &Ekekwe,2014). From the pejorative strand bureaucracy is closely associated with the term secrecy which include "official secret," as a "specific invention of bureaucracy" (Weber, 1968, p. 992). Moynihan (1999) examined the term "symbolic secrecy"—to underscore secrecy that serves no actual purpose other than to advance state power as an end in itself. The "public or open secret" include those issues that are in public domain or open glare but may not be disclosed.

Bureaucratic secrecy has often been deployed to maintain stability and some level of control mechanism. It equally privileges the holders of the information to the exclusion of those who do not have access to information. Secrecy as a social practice, invokes some level of 'clique' in which an informal relationship emerges within a Bureaucracy.

This contradicts formal bureaucratic principles and hierarchy (Simmel,1950). Such contradictions have been the basis of investigating bureaucratic institutional structures that foster such secrets rather than the direct challenges associated with the secret itself.

Thus, secrecy forms part of the bureaucratic control dynamics that perhaps pose barrier to OG. It involves the exclusive possession of official data or knowledge which others may not have access or restricted to. With such privileges, secrecy implicitly "elevates the value of the thing concealed" (Luhrmann, 1989, p. 161). Bureaucracy's political and economic as well as developmental potentials, are undermined by secrecy linked to public corruption (Amadi & Ekekwe,2014). This lies in the non-formal power structure and relations created by bureaucrats to subvert categorical oppositions and hence to create the conditions for informal proclivity including the diversion of public resource for private gains (Amadi & Ekekwe,2014). These limitations not- withstanding, bureaucracy in the developing societies perform a number of distinct functions which include policy implementation and some level of coordination of key governmental principles.

The concept of open government on its part has often been used as a synonym for public accountability. Karl Popper (1962) was among the early scholars who used the concept "open society" to explore dynamics of resilience and response to its trajectories. Open Government is part of America's post Second World War peace dividend as "the federal bureaucracy generally was not eager to have its activities and operations disclosed to the public, the press, or other governmental entities" (Relyea & Kolakowski, 2007; Yu & Robinson, 2012).

OG took on a bold new direction in the wake of the liberal movements that emerged in the West in the mid -2000s and made more strides within the globalizing world as it is linked with technological advancement including the internet culture, e-governance, e-administration, e-data etc. Thus, debates on OG re-emerged in the 2000s in the United States under the Obama administration. Speaking in the United Nations General Assembly in September 2010, former U.S. President Barack Obama emphasized the collective call for open government pointing out that "the strongest foundation for human progress lies in open economies, open societies, and open governments" (Obama,2010). He further argued that "we should bring specific commitments to promote transparency; to fight corruption; to energize civic engagement; to leverage new technologies so that we strengthen the foundations of freedom in our own countries, while living up to the ideals that can light the world" (Obama,2010).

In the context of universality of the OG initiative resulting in the quest for deploying more 'open" and 'transparent' approaches in government, the initiative became almost simultaneously proliferated across the United States, Europe and North America. Grounded in accountability in governance, these early response on OG initiative became primarily concerned with the notion of "making government work" particularly in the context of "governance for all and by all". This perceived inclusiveness in governance was imbedded in guaranteeing freedom, equality, public opinion etc which are the core ideals of liberal democracy.

OG initiative among others, have some salient goals which include transparency, participation, accessibility etc. Several studies and cross country initiatives have employed the term to describe various aspects of governance including the ecosystem of Open Government, dynamics of e-governance, OG data initiatives, the internet culture, e-administration, OG capabilities, ethical considerations in OG etc (King, 2006; Lathrop, & Ruma, 2010; Lessig, 2005) .In particular, the OECD created OURdata, an index that assesses governments' efforts to implement OGD in three critical areas: Openness, Usefulness and Re-usability. Open Government Partnership (OGP) which is a multi-stakeholder initiative (MSI) has been part of this recent leap.

In September 2011, in New York – OGP was launched with the endorsement of the Open Government Declaration by the governments of Brazil, Indonesia, Mexico, Norway, Philippines, South Africa, United Kingdom, and the United States. There have been increasing scholarly attention on delineating 'the politics of open government' from the "technologies of open data" (Yu & Robinson, 2012). The argument is that technology can make public information accessible in various ways 'but technology alone will not resolve debates about the best priorities for civic life, and enhancements to government services are no substitute for public accountability" (Yu & Robinson, 2012).

Beyond its several goals, it is argued that it is only recently that OG has gained visibility in non-liberal democracies. Part of the contention is that since its robust emergence, little has been done to impact the poor societies in the context of access to information (Diallo & Calland, 2013). This perhaps obscures the implicit universal claim of OG. In critical studies on governance are debates which link OG to aspects of the "authoritarian liberal construct" a term deployed to dissuade the alleged equality proclivity of liberalism. Critiques have attacked the OG initiatives and argue instead that the initiatives have been largely a Western construct as its overall analysis centers on modalities to improve Western governance and societies (Kendall, 1960;'King, 2006). For instance, Kendall (1960) has been critical of the "open society" thesis pointing out its "fallacies'. This discourse has perhaps centered on the basis of failure of democracy to guarantee requisite openness. Thus, OG could be seen as an additive to the search for openness in government within a liberating current of democracy. It remains an important dimension of neo liberal values itching for relevance in most developing countries of Africa, Latin America and parts of Asia. Among the Asian Tigers and the emergent 'network states' such as Hong Kong, Taiwan etc., there have been implicit relevance of OG dynamics replicated in e-governance.

There are conceptual debates which posit that OG is premised on the interest of neo liberals who seek to propagate their vested interest abroad in the guise of "openness" as they rather re-inscribe imperialism and economic domination, in particular distinguishing a "great society "and the "open society" (Vernon, 1976; Stiglitizt,1999).

De Cock and Bohm (2007) argue on the impossibility of open society, linking such ideals to the 'Liberalist fantasies". They emphasize OG's ability to undermine initiatives of domestic governments and rather point to imperialism and appropriation of resource through the instrumentalities of globalization. Stiglitz (2016) affirms that, "there could be possibilities of economic appropriation that could emerge in the guise of openness reflective of a new form of imperialism, this has been part of the alleged 'new discontents of globalization' embedded in trade and unequal relationship or the emergence of a culture of "postcolonial contra-modernity" (Bhabha, 1994:6) or the rise of "oppressive assimilationist technologies …linked to 'the social imaginary of both metropolis and modernity". Thus, the post modernity scholarship re-emphasize the tendency of OG initiatives toward re-inscription of Western modernization and multiculturalism (Apperdurai, 1996; Ferguson, 2006)

Conceptual issues raised on OG have equally pointed to an appraisal of the theoretical basis of globalization as both complex, contradictory and often disaggregated (Rosenau,1996; Appadurai, 1996; Giddens, 1999; Tomlinson, 1999; Stiglitz, 2004; Ferguson, 2006; Pieterse, 2010).

The increasingly contentious categories in the capitalist system which underscores inequality evidently critiques OG as both enervated and superficial in fostering equality (Muller, 2013). Jerry Muller provides a profound and rather systematic exploration of capitalism, one grounded in inequality. Thus, in line with OG debate, this underscores a way of rethinking the theoretical basis of OG as a superficial category in an increasingly unequal world. The particular experience with dimensions of inequality in America is identified in the recent works of Thomas Piketty (2014) who argued that inequality in the United States had taken critical and perverse dimensions in recent times. Birdsal (2005) re-focuses attention on the complex matrix of indicators across material, socio-cultural and economic spheres of inequality and argues that inequality has resulted in a divided globalized world.

Kitchin (2013) provides similar critiques when he argued that "Open data lacks a sustainable financial model; promotes a politics of the benign and empowers the empowered; lacks utility and usability; and facilitates the neo-liberalization and marketisation of public services". Open government data initiatives and the issues challenging their implementation underlines the opportunities that could be unduly deployed for various uses.

In particular, OG had emerged as a useful term for conceptualizing global/local policy articulations. Within the context of rural/urban dichotomy necessitated by relative limited access to information. Diallo & Calland (2013) considers "limited access to information" among the rural peoples particularly in the poor African societies linked to the legal system, culture. These are aspects of challenge to OG initiatives despite its alleged "inclusiveness".

In policy debates, several industrialized societies have advanced useful OG data initiatives while the poor societies are marginalized from such initiatives notably e-governance or e-administration. For instance, the OECD recently devoted an entire line of research on the OECD Open Government Data project which aims to progress international efforts on OGD impact assessment. This widespread use of OG initiatives have attracted divergent responses particularly from critics who largely equate aspects of the OG initiatives to globalization, clamoring for transparency, suggesting restraint and caution by the less developed societies (Stigitz,1999).

These cautionary perspectives are primarily an attribute of Western-centric notion of OG. This is largely conceived as both elitist and less lucid, in the context of transformation in government.

In effect, OG is confronted with complex dilemma in most developing societies. This includes the alleged notion of non-emancipatory undertone of OG. This creates some level of resilience among leaders of developing societies in making disclosures such as Africa. For instance, Panama papers reports how several governments of the West have been accomplice in corruption scandal involving leaders of developing societies(Garside, Harding, Watt, Pegg, Bengtsson, Bowers, Gibson & Hopkins,2016). This contradictory picture and similar illicit transactions create some level of pessimism on the plausibility of OG .

A related dilemma centres on the indistinct boundary of OG, thus what are the limits to openness in OG initiatives within the liberal order?. Gómez-Peña (1996), had argued on the rather figurative undertone of the 'new world border' as a substitute to that of the 'new world order'. This suggests that OG as the dominant characteristic of the 'new' liberal system, has some limitations largely arising from its 'open nature'.

Thus, the OG initiative can be deployed by different persons with different meanings. Since its essence is transparency, its uses could be divergent, complex and limitless. In particular, it may entirely exclude people who do not have sufficient access to such openness. These contradictory features have become avenues for critics who argue that OG initiative advances the economic and political interests of the powerful nations against the poor resulting in hegemonic influence and control.

A particular perspective argues that beyond its seemingly eclectic stance, OG is largely elitist. Wedel (2009) recounts the elitist nature of power brokers in the West and how it undermines democracy.

This points out that OG may not be strictly bidding on both the government and the governed.

Some conceptual debates suggest that OG has had a less revolutionary potential despite its proliferation since the 2000s.This is partly because of its linkages with capitalist exploitation since it emanates from the industrialized West. In real contexts, openness in government among the industrialized societies of the West remains contestable.

The use of OG has thus been criticized as a socio-political and economic intruder, a cultural mixture, economically suspicious as it purportedly lends credence to governance at a technological hypertext reflective of imperialism. Yu & Robinson(2012) argue that "Open government" used to carry a hard political edge: It referred to politically sensitive disclosures of government information. But over the last few years, that traditional meaning has blurred, and has shifted toward open technology.

A related critique of the concept of OG lies on the discourse surrounding its linkages with multiculturalism. The contention is that OG is conceived as a strategy of cooption deployed by the powerful states in defense of the disappearance of border framed within globalization scholarship(Appadurai, 1996; Werbner & Moddod, 1997). This is encapsulated in masquerading the OG initiatives to foster economic advancement and information flow at different levels among States fostering information imperialism(Straubhaar,1991).

The underlying assumption of the critics of OG reinforces the often disputed undertone of the concept. However, critics merely describe the contradictory posture of OG, and fail to engage substantially with its provisions in practical terms particularly in the business of transparency in government. Beyond this, the resurgent fascination with OG conceals such elusive paradox. In the industrialized societies OG is promoted as indispensable for a free and transparent governance .It is increasingly conceptualized both in social and policy circles as a routine for inclusive government . Gurstein, (2011)argued whether Open data could provide effective data use for everyone or "empowering of the empowered".

On the contrary, Chiara-Ubaldi (2015) provides insightful understanding of OG as useful in advancing an inclusive government. In a debate that advances similar perspective, Pollock, (2006), Huijboom and Van der Broek (2011), Janssen (2012) and Yiu (2012) argue that "Open data are synonymous to democratic discourse as they are both participatory, citizen driven and inclusive. This as they contend leads to transparency and accountability.

Kichin(2013)argues that "these critiques do not suggest abandoning the move towards opening data", rather contends that "open data initiatives need to be much more mindful of what data are being made open, how data are made available, how they are being used, and how they are being funded". Following these trends, it is useful to advance a conceptual model that distinctively represents OG as both participatory and inclusive. Having emerged as an integral component of neo liberal government open data has formed part of a wider policy and scholarship suggesting access to government data and inclusive policy framing at all levels of government .

Rethinking this implicit shortcomings of OG unmasks its hegemonic feature and suggests alternative practice. This is critical because, the propagation of the ideals of liberalism should be truly inclusive, non-discriminatory and pro poor. Thus, theoretical exploration of OG which is indeed 'open' is sought. This should offer 'explicit access to relevant data'. These are some of the novel theoretical contributions and advancement of knowledge on OG particularly in North /South dichotomy contexts in which censored information remains a key policy thrust of most advanced societies. Thus, a critical theory of OG in the context of inclusiveness must redress prevailing restriction or denied access to information by the high income societies for a lucid conceptual edge.

Against the background of the raging conceptual debates and critiques, there is no singular dominant theoretical perspective on OG .Theoretical debates on OG thus remains difficult as they do not conform to any fixed criteria of analysis .Beyond the contention that OG has the potential for accountability, it is irrefutably a Western-centric model. The conceptualization of OG and power particularly hegemonic power often renders the contextual policy drive of OG less receptive among the poor societies. This allows for the understanding of the context and basis of mutual mistrust constitutive of the lethargic stance of leaders of most developing societies. Much of this is partly informed by the contextual hegemony that explicates Western institutions such as the CIA and transnational corporations as agents of Western imperialism in which OG and its transparency could be critiqued in global development contexts.

Perhaps more importantly, an inter-contextual theory of OG would examine the relationship between affluent societies of the North and the poor societies of the South or importantly, provide a dialectical articulation of patterns and dynamics of economic relationships of the high and low income countries on the basis of efforts to advance the economic wellbeing of the later by the former through equitable and open government.

OG appears to be a viable option for a virile government aimed at responsible, accountable and responsive initiatives. Such coherence appears devoid of any viable alternative that could adequately capture government and accountability dialectics. Although both pejorative and commemorative perspectives are necessary for a balanced theoretical and conceptual debate, in particular as "openness" makes the concept of OG vulnerable to capitalist appropriation .The theoretical challenge to inclusive and participatory government thus resides in a number of repeated questions: Under what condition does OG, as a governance paraphernalia, justify its progressive potential in non- Western societies?. In what contexts do Western imperialism and capitalist interests subvert OG initiatives in the developing societies?. In the liberal order, what chain of features could provide a measurable indices of the success of OG in both governance and in development contexts. In other words, what theory will allow us to render OG a model of social inquiry or practice that could provide a mapping of the working of government including Western hegemony and global power asymmetry?.

In specific terms, how can OG be suitably theorized in an asymmetrical capitalist international system?. Some of these salient conundrum have been the underlying driving thinking to redress the capitalist order where OG initiatives could thrive on social equality and responsively. Thus, a clear understanding of the interest OG truly serves is important in both government and development. This will largely help policy makers both in developed and developing societies to avoid superficial use of the term. These questions remain central to this chapter.

Bureaucratic Secrecy in Africa

In several decades of post- Cold War Africa following overt democracy resurgence and an end to autocratic one party rule which bolstered some form of accountability in public office, there appears to be evidence of non- bureaucratic reform. Bureaucratic secrecy perhaps has been one of the core challenges constricting open government among the developing democracies although this is not exclusive to the developing societies.

OG both in the developed and the developing societies have proliferated in recent decades as explicated. Despite the volume of scholarship and discourses, bureaucratic practices in most developing societies such as Africa appear to have been shrouded in official secrecy. Although issues of bureaucratic process are not directly constitutive elements of OG, bureaucracy is conceived as largely necessary for the formulation and implementation of policies such as the propagation of OG initiatives. Recent debates have provided a number of useful evidence, from case studies, comparative analysis and empirical studies (Hyden, et al;2003) linking bureaucratic performance to OG initiatives.

Generally African countries are poorly governed and this remains a key problem to OG. By 1998, although Africa still ranked as the region with the worst policies on the World Bank ratings, it was also the region with by far the greatest policy dispersion (Collier & Gunning,1990). This results in persistent local conflicts notably Somalia, Burundi, South Sudan, Boko Haram terrorist insurgency in north-eastern Nigeria, deep ethno religious divisions, poverty, poor resource control, weak regulatory dynamics, ineffective representative democracy, bureaucratic corruption etc.

Debates on bureaucratic secrecy in Africa have provided divergent explanations. It was alleged that after 1960 Africa was increasingly free of colonialism, with the potential for governments that would be more responsive to domestic needs(Collier & Gunning,1999).However the more perverse challenge of post -colonial influence remained germane(Young,2000).African bureaucracy is a colonial invention with complexities and divergences along Francophone and Anglophone administrative traditions. Collier & Gunning (1999:6) have emphasized domestic policy factors such as poor public service delivery. They contend that African governments have typically been less democratic and more bureaucratic than their Asian and Latin American counterparts.

During the 1970s both political and economic matters in Africa deteriorated. The leadership of many African nations hardened into autocracy and dictatorship(Collier & Gunning,1999).The authoritarian one party system was closely associated with bureaucratic secrecy as formal rules of governance was subverted for patrimonial autocracy. It is important to explore some of these salient factors since the end of the Cold War in the 1990s.

Mbakun(1996)had argued that throughout Africa, from Algeria to Zaïre, bureaucrats and politicians promote perverse economic policies, which while impoverishing most of society, provide concentrated and significant benefits to the national elites and interest groups.

The pattern of public employment in Africa account for non- transparency of the Bureaucracy . This includes a situation in which formal rules are subverted through favoritism and parochial sentiments. There are situation in which marginalized or ill-paid public sector became the arena in which ethnic groups struggled for resources(Collier & Gunning,1999) . For instance in the oil rich Niger Delta, Nigeria a large number of unemployed youths took to the creeks as militants and directly involved in vandalization of oil pipelines by Multinational oil corporations(MNOCs) and abduction of expatriate oil workers. This is informed by the content and character of the Nigerian State which has remained elitist, discriminatory and often coercive. Leaving the oil bearing communities poor and marginalized.

Similarly, in the Ghanaian public sector, the locally dominant ethnic group received a wage premium of 25 percent over other groups after controlling for worker characteristics, and cognitive skills were completely unrewarded (Collier & Garg, 1999). The combination of low wage levels and payment structures, which rewarded social connections rather than skill, made it difficult for managers to motivate staff, and the difficulties of service delivery were compounded by the low ratio of non-wage to wage expenditures. As a result, Africa experienced a paradox of poor public services despite relatively high public expenditure (Pradhan, 1996; Collier & Gunning,1999).

Poor service delivery remained at issue affecting the patterns of bureaucratic performance. For example, manufacturing firms in Zimbabwe need to hold high levels of inventories, despite high interest rates, due to unreliable delivery of inputs tied to poor transportation infrastructure (Fafchamps et al., 1998;Collier & Gunning,1999). A survey of Ugandan firms found that shortage of electricity was identified as the single most important constraint upon firm growth; indeed, the provision of electricity by firms for their own use was almost as large as the public supply of electricity (Reinikka & Svensson, 1998; Collier & Gunning,1999). Acemoglu and Robbinson(2010)argue that institutional failure in Africa partly accounts for the inability of political and economic institutions to evolve in Africa resulting in poverty and systemic failure. The bureaucracy as an institution remained emasculated into the dominant power structure. Chong and Calderon (2000)provide similar data sets suggesting the relevance of institutional quality to economic growth.

Perhaps key defining features of bureaucratic secrecy in Africa are “absolutism”or “partrimonialism’.The former implies a situation in which the power of the ruler is absolute and not constrained by institutional rules. Patrimonial system is a situation where there is no distinction between the person of the ruler and the State(Weber, 1968:pp231-232; Acemoglu & Robbinson, 2010:3).A patrimonial state is equally one in which there are few institutional rules and universalistic criteria are not employed(Acemoglu & Robbinson, 2010:3).African bureaucracy in this context deploy ascribed rather than achieved criteria.

Bratton and Van de Walle(1997:62) reinforced this in their debate on neopatrimonial rule in post 1990 Africa as they argue that the right to rule in a neo patrimonial system is ascribed to a person rather to an office despite the existence of a written constitution. They argue that neopartimonial relationship pervades formal political and administrative system and leaders occupy bureaucratic offices less to perform public service than to acquire personal wealth and status.

Joseph(1997) argues that the essence of neo patrimonialism is the award by public officials of personal favors, both within the state(notable public sector jobs) and in society(for instance, licenses, contracts, and projects).In return for material rewards, clients mobilize political support and refer all decisions upward as a mark of deference to patrons.

Goran Hyden, Julius Court & Ken Mease(2003) create salient linkages between bureaucracy and governance when they argue that bureaucracy, however, should not only be studied in the context of implementation of individual policies, but also in terms of governance . They identified 'bureaucratic arena' to refer to all state organizations engaged in formulating and implementing policy as well as in regulating and delivering services. Hyden, et al;(2003) contend that substantial literature argues that the weakness of bureaucracy in Africa helps explain the poor development performance of many countries on the continent .They argue that this includes understanding 'the importance of the rules that determine procedures in the bureaucracy, whether formal or informal, as especially important for public perceptions of how the state operates' (Hyden, et al;2003:3).

Bureaucratic secrecy in Africa has also been at variance with the poor whose voices are insulated from government policy formulation and implementation(Narayan, et al;2000) .This points out the challenge of inclusiveness which is less internalized in African bureaucracy. This has been reflective of the present South African government in which key bureaucratic decisions are shrouded in secrecy resulting in alleged corruption and diversion of public funds in the Zuma administration.

The case of South Africa is especially intriguing, interesting and important as Sandy Africa(2009) recounts that despite the discrimination and secrecy that characterized apartheid South Africa, post -apartheid South African experiences have not demonstrated a marked difference. She argued that . "in the current dispensation, it has emerged into the broad daylight of being subject to public scrutiny, transparency, and democratic accountability. However, that this changed reality should not mask the persistence of awkward dilemmas, tensions and ambivalences in law, policy and practice.

In Nigeria there have been incidence of bureaucratic secrecy linked to massive fraud and looting of State treasury associated with the President Goodluck Jonathan administration. Mbakun(1996) reinforces this debate and contends that Nigeria is not the only country in Africa in which the apparatus of government has become an instrument for the enrichment of members of the politically dominant group. South Africa, long regarded by many scholars in the West as a bastion for free enterprise in Africa, has for many years promoted laws that allowed the white minority to use the redistributive powers of the state to enrich itself while sentencing the black majority to perpetual poverty and deprivation. Similar trends are evident in the African Great Lakes region.

Crawyford Young (2000) recounts that 'in more than a dozen of Africa's 53 states, governments failed to pass the Weberian test of stateness: an effective monopoly of the means of coercion within their territorial domain'. In their analysis of effective bureaucracy, Hyden, et al; (2003)identified a number of indicators which in line with performance which include: (1) Influence, (2) Meritocracy, (3) Accountability, (4) Transparency, and (5) Access. However Africa's bureaucracy do not fall within the categorization. For instance, in Togo. President Eyadema's long-standing rule – himself a military officer politicized public policy-making to a point where professional expertise was no longer valued. Diallo and Calland(2013)have examined access to Information in Africa within the context of law, culture and practice, in particular, argue that Africa has made limited advances in guaranteeing the right of citizens and others to access State information with particular emphasis to countries such as Zimbawe, Sudan and South Sudan,Kenya, Mali,Congo DR, Uganda etc. Such restriction within Africa's bureaucracy is what they termed, 'Access to information' (ATI) is critical of the quest to re-examine bureaucratic secrecy in the era of open government. Only Botswana and perhaps Mauritius have been able to provide a bureaucracy that is institutionally responsive with what falls within the categorization of a developmental State(Acemoglu & Robinson, 2010;Amadi & Ekekwe, 2014).

Beyond the internal dynamics, a number of external factors are discernible. Brian Klaas(2016)had identified "How the West Is Aiding and Abetting the Decline of democracy"

This recognition gives credence to materialist critics who accuse proponents of OG of complicity with the claims and goals of propagating Western capitalism through illicit means namely corruption.

In this regard, OG is framed in an attempt to contrive an avenue for global access to information .The internet and transnational information flow occurs in a context in which the Western societies have become increasingly active in the global arena. These transnational

corporations control both information structures and access. Equally these transnational corporations largely control the worldwide web and information flow. However, as nearly two decades of scholarship on OG suggests, there is inequality riddled in Western information flow to the non -Western societies of the South. This dichotomy demonstrates implicit limitation to the alleged OG initiatives, including technology divide and denial of access to information.

. The OG initiative thus operates to increasingly foreclose certain information which is contrary to its alleged "openness", putting the entire information and communication chain under the influence and control of Western capitalism. This results in denial of access, restrictions and censured information and limited data flow to non -Western societies.

RECOMMENDATIONS

The foregoing suggests that there are a number of barriers to OG in Africa some of which include; corruption in electronic government which suggests that the reliance on technology alone may not provide the much expected openness in OG, there is need for ethical considerations in which active citizenship participation could be fostered. For instance, e-Governance as explicated is useful for free and transparent bureaucracy in Africa, however this is not an end in itself. It should be backed with ethical guidelines. This is aimed at institutionalizing sanity and ethical considerations in the conduct of the business of governance. Clearly the views of the citizen must count in OG initiatives. Such perceptions will serve as a guide to improve the level of citizenship response to OG.

The value for open government should be institutionalized as an integral component of inclusive governance through evidence based data fitness for general access and use. This points to OG capabilities or capacity for open governance which measures the level of response to OG initiatives.

Arguments in Evans &Rauch(1999), are insightful as they posit that "replacing patronage systems for state officials by a professional bureaucracy is a necessary (though not sufficient) condition for a state to be developmental. Much of African society have not been developmental, thus there is urgent need for strategic overhaul of the bureaucracy strictly in line with development ideology.

The Development Portfolio Management Group(2017)identified three "critical elements for catalyzing and sustaining progress on open government reforms" which include building high-level political commitment, empowering government reformers and supporting effective engagement by civil society organizations.

Policy attention is drawn in this direction as bureaucratic reform has been a common ground to efficiency linked to OG. This can only be effective where democratic institutions are fully implemented. Thus, responsive, inclusive and participatory democracy have been indispensable in actualizing the OG initiatives .Our analysis suggest the absence of such features with less clear boundaries and criteria as institutional structures set aside for bureaucratic efficiency. The point the chapter has been making is that policy response to bureaucratic practices could aim at removing undue privacy, and all forms of restrictions and access to public data either financial, political, educational, legal, technological etc. In particular the chapter has attempted to create linkages between bureaucracy in Africa and what is expedient to foster efficiency in the implementation of organizational policies and programmes .

Among others there is urgent need for institutionalization of bureaucratic transparency through the establishment of OG portals which could serve as a data bank for accessible information. At the same time, restraints should equally be exercised against state detractors who may hack into official data for extraneous uses.

Increased data transparency provides the basis for delineation of sectoral performance and boundaries. This suggests the assessment and understanding of the performance of various sectors of government in line with stipulated key performance indicators. OG could facilitate public participation and collaboration in the creation of innovative, value-added services.

For African scholars and policy makers, OG may require the increasing need to develop a new kind of praxis one that avoids the fixation of a model based solely on government data rather a model of inclusive bottom top government in which the people themselves are part of the apparatus for generating the information . There is need for the emergence and spread of the open data movement where voluntary disclosures could be institutionalized by the government. This includes issues of budgetary allocation, economic reform agenda, urban planning, informed citizen decisions and choices. OG could provide a platform for resource allocation including revenue and fiscal formula directions.

FURTHER RESEARCH DIRECTIONS

There are potentials for fruitful future research agenda. It is evident that a little is known about OG initiatives in developing democracies, however its robust strides in recent scholarship points to the saliency of research in this direction. The proliferation of OG initiative makes it an interesting tool of economic and political advancement of the developing democracies .More so, a strategy of re-tooling North –South dichotomy both in the context of governance and economic advancement .

Further research should focus on themes such as "making OG initiative sustainable in an asymmetrical capitalist order, this should be grounded in debates linking OG to the World System perspectives and dominant themes in structural inequality and dependency. One which seeks to radically interrogate the development import and purport of the OG initiative, such neo Marxist paradigm remains a useful framework in studies on critical evaluation of the structure of the international capitalist system.

In particular, centre/periphery dichotomy. Again, research agenda on strategic and radical institutional overhaul of bureaucracy in Africa is necessary for inclusive growth and development.

CONCLUSION

The chapter attempts to re-engage with the ongoing debate on OG initiatives among the developing societies. In a distinct manner linking bureaucratic secrecy in Africa to OG initiatives. The aim is to re-articulate the dominant bureaucratic practices in Africa largely shrouded in secrecy. This increasingly constricts accountability and transparency which are ideals of democracy. It demonstrates that against the dominant notion on proliferation of OG initiatives since the mid-2000s,much of its impacts have rarely been felt in most developing societies particularly in sub Saharan African(SSA) societies. This is identified with salient conceptual and theoretical issues raised in some African societies which provided useful insights and evidence on barriers and challenges towards the institutionalization of OG initiatives. These as the chapter suggests include bureaucratic corruption, red tape, depersonalization etc which tend to suggest bureaucratic inefficiency.

The chapter argued for policy engagement with the question of OG to foster the much needed bureaucratic efficiency particularly within the context of access to public information and related data which are indispensable for inclusive government. These salient issues associated with OG were explored including insights that could bolster the understanding of the relevance of OG particularly in relation to policy makers and reinvigoration of the public sector.

The chapter suggests that despite democracy across Africa since the 1990s, informal institutional structures notably patrimonial sentiments remain strong, and forms the nucleus of the resilience to open government. This is important as policy transparency and collective engagement with democracy transformation seems blurred. It provided apt analysis of this complex matrix and explored the interaction between e-governance which underscores the logic of openness and goes beyond this to suggest that reliance on technological dynamics of OG alone may not chart inclusive initiatives.

It argued that, despite the political space provided by democracy, inclusive governance and accountability have been minimal. Thus, openness has rarely penetrated into the core bureaucratic culture of developing democracies of Africa. The chapter opened the debate to further studies and recommends data transparency on the grounds that policy response in this regard since the return to democracy has been less clear. It provided the basis for public participation and collaboration in the creation of innovative, value-added and inclusive governance and demonstrates that, data openness will improve the decision making of both governments and individuals and in particular, advance the course for participatory governance in the developing democracies such as Africa.

REFERENCES

Acemoglu, D., Johnson, S., & Robbinson, J. (2002). Reversal of fortunes: Geography, and institutions in the making of the modern world income distribution. *The Quarterly Journal of Economics, 118*(4), 1231–1294. doi:10.1162/003355302320935025

Acemoglu, D., & Robinson, J. (2010). Why is Africa poor? *Economic History of Developing Regions, 25*(1), 21–20. doi:10.1080/20780389.2010.505010

Adam, C., & Dercon, S. (2009). The political economy of development: An assessment. *Oxford Review of Economic Policy, 25*(2), 173–189. doi:10.1093/oxrep/grp020

Africa, S. (2009). *Well-kept Secrets: The right of access to information and the South African intelligence services.* South Africa Institute for Global Dialogue and Friedrich-Ebert-Stiftung.

Amadi L., and Ekekwe, E. (2014). Corruption and development Administration in Africa: Institutional Approach. *African Journal of Political Science and International Relations, 8*(6), 163–177. doi:10.5897/AJPSIR2013.0634

Amadi, L., & Imoh-Ita, I. (2017) Intellectual capital and environmental sustainability measurement nexus: a review of the literature. *Int. J. Learning and Intellectual Capital, 14*(2).

Andrain, C., & Apter, D. (1995). *Political Protest and Social Change.* New York University Press.

Appadurai, A. (1996). *Modernity at large: Cultural dimensions of globalization.* Minneapolis, MN: University of Minnesota Press.

Bhabba, H. (1994). *The location of culture.* New York: Routledge.

Birdsal, N. (2005). Why Inequality Matters in a Globalizing World. In *WIDER Annual Lecture.* Washington, DC: Center for Global Development.

Bratton, M., & Van de Walle, N. (1994). Neopatrimonial regimes and political. *Transitions in Africa World Politics, 46*(4), 453-489.

Chiara-Ubaldi, B. (2015). *Open Data: A Roadmap to Delivering Impact!* OECD.

Chong, A., & Calderon, C. (2000). Causality and Feedback between Institutional Measures and Economic Growth. *Economics and Politics, 12*(1), 69–81. doi:10.1111/1468-0343.00069

Collier, P., & Garg, A. (1999). Collier, Paul and Ashish Garg. (1999)."On Kin Groups and Wages in the Ghanaian Labour Market. *Oxford Bulletin of Economics and Statistics, 61*(2), 131–151. doi:10.1111/1468-0084.00122

Collier, P., & Gunning, J. (1999, Summer). Why Has Africa Grown Slowly? *The Journal of Economic Perspectives, 13*(3), 3–22. doi:10.1257/jep.13.3.3

Collier, P., & Gunning, J. (1999a). Explaining African Economic Performance. *Journal of Economic Literature, 37*(1).

De Cock, C., & Bohm, S. (2007). Liberalist fantasies: Zizek and the impossibility of the open society. *Organization, 14*(6), 815–836. doi:10.1177/1350508407082264

Development Portfolio Management Group. (2017). *Open Government Partnership: Mid-Term Review*. University of Southern Carolina.

Diallo, F., & Calland, R. (Eds.). (2013). *Access to Information in Africa: Law, Culture and Practice.* Brill Publishers.

Evans, J., & Rauch, J. (2000). Bureaucratic Structure and Bureaucratic Performance in Less Developed Countries. *Journal of Public Economics, 75*(1), 49–71. doi:10.1016/S0047-2727(99)00044-4

Fafchamps, M., Gunning, J. W., & Oostendorp, R. (1998). *Inventories, Liquidity and Contractual Risk in African Manufacturing Journal of Economic Perspectives*. Department of Economics, Stanford University.

Ferguson, J. (2006). Decomposing Modernity: History and Hierarchy after Development. Department of Anthropology University of California, Irvine.

Garside, J., Harding, L., Watt, H., Pegg, D., Bengtsson, H., & Bowers, S. ... Hopkins, N. (2016). What are the Panama Papers? A guide to history's biggest data leak. *The Guardian*. Available at https://www.theguardian.com/news/2016/apr/03/what-you-need-to-know-about-the-panamapapers

Giddens, A. (1999). *Runaway World: How Globalization is Reshaping our Lives*. London: Profile.

Gómez-Peña, G. (1996). *The new world border: Prophecies, poems and loqueras for the end of the century*. San Francisco, CA: City Lights.

Gould, D., & Mukendi, T. (1989). Bureaucratic Corruption in Africa: Causes. *Consequences and Remedies International Journal of Public Administration, 12*(3), 427–457. doi:10.1080/01900698908524633

Holsti, O. (1969). *Content Analysis for the Social Sciences and Humanities*. Reading, MA: Addison-Wesley.

Huijboom, N., & Van der Broek, T. (2011). Open data: an international comparison of strategies. *European Journal of ePractice, 12*. Retrieved from http://www.epractice.eu/files/European%20Journal%20epractice%20Volume%2012_1.df

Hyden, G., Court, J., & Mease, K. (2003). *The Bureaucracy and Governance in 16 Developing Countries*. Overseas Development Institute (ODI) World Governance Survey Discussion Paper 7.

Janssen, K. (2012). *Open government data: right to information 2.0 or its rollback version?* ICRI Working Paper.

Joseph, R. (1991). *Democracy and Prebendal Politics the Rise and Fall of Nigeria's Second Republic*. Spectrum Books Limited.

Kendall, W. (1960). The "open society" and its fallacies. *The American Political Science Review, 54*(4), 972–979.

King, J. (2006). Openness and its discontents. In J. Dean, J. W. Anderson, & G. Lovink (Eds.), *Reformatting politics: Information technology and global civil society*. New York: Routledge.

Kitchin, R. (2013). *Four critiques of open data initiatives | Open Data Research Network*. Available at www.opendataresearch.org/tumblr/2013/four-critiques-open-data-initiatives

Klaas, B. (2016). *The Despot's Accomplice: How the West Is Aiding and Abetting the Decline of Democracy*. Oxford University Press.

Lasswell, H. (1948). Power and Personality. New York, NY: Academic Press.

Lathrop, D., & Ruma, L. (Eds.). (2010). Open government: Collaboration, transparency, and participation in practice. O'Reilly Media.

Lee, I., & Anas, A. (1991). *Manufacturers' Responses to Infrastructure Deficiencies in Nigeria: Private Alternatives and Policy Options*. Washington, DC: World Bank.

Lessig, L. (2005). Open code and open societies. In J. Feller, B. Fitzgerald, S. A. Hissam, & K. R. Lakhani (Eds.), *Perspectives on free and open source software*. London: The MIT Press.

Linz, J., & Stepan, A. (1996). Toward Consolidated Democracies Journal of Democracy 7.2 (14-33

Luhrmann, T. (1989). The Magic of Secrecy. *Ethos (Berkeley, Calif.)*, *17*(2), 131–165. doi:10.1525/eth.1989.17.2.02a00010

Mbakun, J. (1996). Bureaucratic corruption in Africa: The Futility of Cleanups. *Cato J, 16*(1).

Mduduzi, K. (2015). *The West Stole Africa's Wealth. Xilibris Press.*

Moynihan, D. (1999). *The Science of Secrecy.* Retrieved from http://www.aaas.org/spp/secrecy/Presents/Moynihan.htm

Muller, J. (2013, March). Capitalism and Inequality, What the Right and Left Get Wrong. *Foreign Affairs.*

Narayan, D., Patel, R., Schafft, K., Rademacher, A., & Koch-Schulte, S. (2000). *Voices of the Poor: Can Anyone Hear Us?* Washington, DC: The World Bank. doi:10.1596/0-1952-1601-6

North, D. (1993). The New Institutional Economics and Development. *Economic History, 9*(8), 1-10.

Obama, B. (2010). *President Obama's Address to the United Nations General Assembly.* Available at http.//www.whitehouse.gov/the-press-office2010/09/23

Pieterse, J. N. (1994). Globalisation as hybridisation. *International Sociology*, *9*(2), 161–184. doi:10.1177/026858094009002003

Pieterse, J. N. (2010). *Development theory: Deconstructions / reconstructions* (2nd ed.). London: Sage Publications Ltd. doi:10.4135/9781446279083

Pikettey, T. (2014). *Capital in the Twenty First Century*. London: The Belknap Press of Harvard University Press Cambridge. doi:10.4159/9780674369542

Pollock, R. (2006). The value of the public domain. *IPPR*. Retrieved from http://www.ippr.org/publication/55/1526/thevalue-of-the-public-domain

Popper, K. (1962). *The open society and its enemies*. London: Routledge and Kegan Paul.

Posner, D., & Young, D. (2007). *The Institutionalization of Political Power in Africa. Journal of Democracy*, *18*(3), 127–140.

Pradhan, S. (1996). *Evaluating Public Spending*. World Bank Discussion Paper 323, Washington, DC.

Relyea, H., & Kolakowsk, M. (2007). *Cong. Research SERV., 97-71 GOV, Access TO Government Information in the United States, at CRS-2.* Retrieved from http://www.dtic.mil/dtic/tr/fulltext/u2/a470219.pdf

Rosenau, J. (1997). Complexities and Contradictions of Globalization. *Current History (New York, N.Y.), 96*(613).

Scott, R. (2004). Institutional Theory: Contributing to a Theoretical Research Program. In *Great Minds in Management: The Process of Theory Development.* Oxford, UK: Oxford University Press.

Simmel, G. (1950). The Secret and the Secret Society. In K. H. Wolff (Ed.), *The Sociology of Georg Simmel* (pp. 330–344). Glencoe, IL: The Free Press.

Stiglitz, J. (1999). *On Liberty, the Right to Know, and Public Discourse: The Role of Transparency in Public Life.* Oxford Amnesty Lecture, Oxford, UK. Retrieved from http://derechoasaber.org.mx/documentos/pdf0116.pdf

Stiglitz, J. (2004). *The Post Washington Consensus.* The Initiative for Policy Dialogue.

Stiglitz, J. (2016). Globalization and its New Discontents. *Project Syndicate.* Available at https://www.projectsyndicate.org/default/library/c198d0035bc7db1aa409717cf4020935.square.pgitemprop=thumbnail

Straubhaar, J. (1991). Beyond media imperialism: Asymmetrical interdependence and cultural proximity. *Critical Studies in Mass Communication, 8*(1), 29–38. doi:10.1080/15295039109366779

Thelen, K. (1999). Historical Institutionalism in Comparative Politics. *The American Political Science Review, 2*(1), 369–404. doi:10.1146/annurev.polisci.2.1.369

Tomlinson, J. (1999). *Globalization and Culture. University of Chicago Press.*

Vernon, R. (1976). The "great society" and the "open society": Liberalism in Hayek and Popper. *Canadian Journal of Political Science, 9*(2), 261–276. doi:10.1017/S0008423900043717

Weber, M. (1968). Economy and Society: An Outline of Interpretive Sociology. Berkeley, CA: University of California Press.

Wedel, J. (2009). *Shadow Elite: How the World's New Power Brokers Undermine Democracy, Government, and the Free Market.* New York: Basic Books.

Werbner, P., & Moddod, T. (Eds.). (1997). *Debating cultural hybridity: Multi-cultural identities and the politics of anti-racism.* London: Zed Books.

Williams, S. (2002). Free as in freedom: Richard Stallman's crusade for free software. Sebastopol, CA: O'Reilly & Associates, Inc.

Yiu, C. (2012). A right to data: Fulfilling the promise of open public data in the UK. *Policy Exchange Research*. Available at http://www.policyexchange.org.uk/publications/category/item/a-right-todata-fulfilling-the-promise-of-open-public-data-in-the-uk

Young, C. (2000). Africa: Democratization, Cultural Pluralism, and the Challenge of Political Order. *Macalester International, 9*. Retrieved from http://digitalcommons.macalester.edu/macintl/vol9/iss1/7

Yu, H & Robinson, D. (2012). The New Ambiguity of "Open Government". *UCLA Law. Rev., 59.*

Chapter 2
A Privacy Perspective of Open Government:
Sex, Wealth, and Transparency in China

Bo Zhao
University of Tilburg, The Netherlands

ABSTRACT

Open government and freedom of information are key values in today's democracy, rule of law, and public governance. Their further development may have to be equally taken into consideration with other important public interests, such as state secret, public security, and other individual rights including reputation and privacy. In particular, there is the need to consider how individual privacy can be protected in the digital era in which both the concept and practice of open government may claim more territory. Taking China as an example, this chapter tries to reveal the complex, dynamic relationship between open government (transparency) and privacy protection, in particular by studying two specific privacy-related issues: the disclosure of official's public interest-related private life and the disclosure of family asset. In the sense that they can be regarded as the benchmarks to measure the level of open government and FOI development in a community, both can reflect the cultural and political complexities that affect such developments.

DOI: 10.4018/978-1-5225-4987-1.ch002

INTRODUCTION

In recent decades, digital technology advancement has increasingly facilitated the development of open government across the world. This has improved many public goods by means of citizen's increasing access to more open information/data, including transparency, efficiency, decision making quality, e-governance, freedom of information, etc. Personal data collection and processing nowadays become an indispensable, fundamental element of open government information (OGI). This is especially the case in view of: firstly, the wide spreading data set platform sharing among different government bodies, and secondly, the procurement of data processing to the private sector that usually acts on behalf of public bodies. Also new categories of personal data are available for abuse or misuse in government's possession, including biometric data such as IRIS and finger print, and the increasing connectivity crossing data platform also makes data profiling possible which might be against data subjects' interest.

In general, the ever growing large data set that serves open government meanwhile can lead to other problems of increasing public concern, for instance, data quality, data security, data integrity, data reach and abuse, and potential biased decision making. Especially privacy concern has been on the rise in the context of the global movement of open government and freedom of information (FOI) in recent years. When citizens demand accessing more information held by government for transparency and exercising their FOI right, they might be asking for personal data/information, whose disclosure is an intrusion of other's privacy. Disclosure of sensitive personal information may affect a person's reputation in some communities as well; for instance, disclosure of the extramarital affairs of a government official. This is the reason why debate over the dynamics between privacy, freedom of expression and transparency has been on the rise, not only at national level, but also at international level.

What personal information in possession of government bodies can, or cannot, be disclosed *to the public* becomes a critical issue, and the relationship between privacy and open government (transparency) shall be reconsidered an increasingly digitized, connected world. Privacy protection can be used to justify non-disclosure of personal information and thus may hinder the development of open government and transparency on the one hand. On the other hand, however, good privacy protection can indeed enhance open government and transparency. Having faith in good privacy protection, individuals are willing to provide more personal information to improve open government, public governance and economic efficiency. Privacy and open government are thus both competitive with and complementary to each other. In reality, they unfold much complicated relationships which are dispensable on concrete political, social and economic contexts. Scholars have studied open governance from many aspects already. However, how privacy protection may hinder or improve the development of open government lacks further reflection, despite some initiative work in recent years (Cannataci, Zhao, Bonnici, & etc., 2016).

This chapter, *by taking China as an example,* explores some dimensions of the much complicated relationship between privacy and open government against the backdrops of the digitalization of public governance. In order to do that, it will address two important aspects of privacy in China's open government context, namely the disclosure of asset and extramarital life of Chinese officials. By analyzing the selected Chinese cases, which are not necessarily legal ones, this chapter describes how privacy protection can facilitate, or hinder open government development, and what are the implications of China's open government practices, especially in view of China's trapped political-societal transition from an authoritarian state to a democracy(Pei, 2006).

OPEN GOVERNMENT AND PRIVACY PROTECTION IN CHINA

The concept of open government has been popular in the recent decade. With fast development and deployment of Information and Communication Technology (ICT) in the public sector, the concept of open government now refers not only to transparency of government information and data to the public, or open access, but also encompasses public participation and interaction in public affairs. Transparency and information sharing at different levels within government, between government and the public, and in the public sphere, mean that information shall be accessible by default to promote the understanding of accountability, and that information is interoperable and open for reuse both by different government agencies and the private sector (Hansson, Belkacem, & Ekenberg, 2015, p. 1).

Since late 1980s, China's political and economic reform has, in a much larger scenario, included the development of open government with a key goal to improve transparency and public-government interaction, although that was not originally meant for democracy development. In late 1990s, China's strong economic and market growth had increasingly demanded a transparent government for economic efficiency, and this demand has been taken into consideration by Chinese government. In addition, Chinese Communist Party (CCP) understood well that its legitimacy in transferring from a revolutionary party to a governing party partly relied on open government and more transparency that can improve public trust and confidence (Batke, Breuer, & Matthias, 2016). Also it was well believed that a strong sunshine law in China that forces Chinese officials to disclose their asset, would effectively curb the widespread corruption and graft (Parker, 2013).

In addition to previous efforts (Zhou, 2003), the 2008 Open Government Information Regulations (OGIR) is the landmark legislation that establishes the first top-down legal framework of government transparency. This single piece legislation, as China's sunshine law, generally prescribes the supervisory authority, scope of disclosure, methods and procedures for disclosure, supervision and safeguards, although still far from an ideal law with apparent deficiencies (Wenjing, 2011, pp. 992–998). A simple review of the relevant policy making and the implementation efforts from Beijing since then reveals that the Chinese government has taken the promise seriously in many aspects, (Batke et al., 2016). Like in other Chinese law enforcement circumstances, many follow-up executive orders have been issued by the Council of State in order to enhance transparency, in particular to improve public participation and input. Till 2016, in eight years' time, Chinese citizens have submitted a large number of information requests to various government bodies, and it is estimated 60 percent of them resulted in government disclosure (Batke et al., 2016).

However, the open government promise seems to have not been fully kept, at least according to some recent empirical research on Open Government Data (OGD) (H. Liu, 2016). There exist many red lines that can not be crossed in China's open government development due to the political nature of a Party Sate. To take a top-down approach, not a FOI right-based one, certainly will leave the matter in the Part State's hands and compromise the full potential of open government commitment. From the very beginning, the half-hearted commitment is partially to obviate public discontent and improve political legitimacy. When the Party State senses real danger against its authority and ruling, open government development can be suspended or stopped for legally proved reasons.

Article 8 of the 2008 OGIR prescribes that information disclosure shall not endanger state security, public safety, economic safety and social stability. Under Article 14, state secrecy, business secrecy and protection of privacy are the legitimate justification to exempt information disclosure, *unless* their non-disclosure may lead to great impacts on public interest. China's national secret law and business secrete law actually cover a large scope that is vague in compliance(Susan, 2014). Previously, state secrecy and business secrecy have been quoted to reject public disclosure but not in a successful way, since the manipulation is blunt and can be easily detected by the public. In previous years, a series of privacy cases involving Chinese officials were brought up for various reasons, whether demanding exposure of their general incomes, or of information of family members, especially information concerning extramarital offspring. Extramarital affair is not in violation of Chinese law, and could only be disciplined by CCP's internal rules. The disclosure of such affairs with negative public impression usually leads to non-promotion or dismissal from key public positions.

With respect to fighting corruption and power abuse, disclose of public official's personal information is of crucial value, but can be rejected for the sake of privacy protection. Asset disclosure can help with monitoring the Politically Exposed Persons (PEPs). The term PEPs refers to persons "who are or have been entrusted with prominent public functions, such as heads of state or government, and their family members and close associates". They may "abuse their position and influence to carry out corrupt acts, including accepting and extorting bribes, misappropriating state assets, and using the domestic and international financial systems to launder the proceeds(Rossi, Pop, Clementucci, & Sawaqed, 2012, p. 7). This is especially the case when Chinese official's personal interest is so closely affiliated and overlapped with family interest in the present Chinese community that is structured on the notion of "family". The concept of family includes not only spouses and children, but also relatives with direct blood tie, such as parents, brothers and sisters even their families. Another issue is the direct, close connection in China between extramarital affairs and official's misconducts

In a sense, whether open government includes assets and information disclosure of PEPs *could be a genuine test* of the real development of open government and Freedom Of Information (FOI). One cannot imagine a well-developed open government and FOI mechanism without decent asset and family information disclosure. Personal information concerning asset and family circumstances falls within the concept of privacy. Chinese law provides a vague definition of privacy on paper, and privacy protection in the open government context covers an extremely wide scope in practice (Chen, 2015, p. 275). This has in reality created a big loophole in China's OGI and FOI law development. Chinese courts have confronted numerous cases consequent to escalating conflicts between the growing demand for disclosure of officials' personal information, and the privacy protection claim from Chinese officials.

On the whole, there has been fast, substantial legal development in China's OGD, including open access to government policies, archives and budget plan. However, has been very little formal legal progress that prescribes Chinese officials the legal obligation of asset and family status disclosure. In China's political-societal context, their disclosure is closely affiliated with public interest, and the most difficult part of China's open government development. With corruption being the default among Chinese officials, disclosure of extramarital status and asset might mean political suicide before the public.

There have been a few studies exploring the conflict between privacy protection and open government development in China. For instance, Chen's recent study covers several cases concerning the disclosure of general incomes of officials, among other issues(Chen, 2015). From the perspective of accountability, it reveals the drawbacks of the vague definition of privacy under Chinese law and its conflict with the right to FOI, and points out how privacy has been used to cover mal-administration and malfeasance. The research discusses some privacy cases with respect to social welfare distribution, housing demolition compensation, outstanding historical issues, general incomes of officials, and general exercise of administrative power. Its discussion of asset disclosure in privacy context is insufficient, and does not cover disclosure of private life and family circumstances, which will be further discussed in the following.

PRIVACY AND TRANSPARENCY: SEX, WEALTH AND POWER

In the following, this chapter will focus on analyzing multiple cases that involve controversies over Chinese official's extramarital life and asset disclosure. Both categories of case have attracted rising public concern, since both have been found in close connection to corruption and power abuse among Chinese officials. Analyzing the two special categories of cases, although some of them are not typically legal, can best demonstrate the growing conflicts between privacy protection and open government. It can show especially how their conflicts have been made possible and even amplified by ubiquitous use of digital devices in present China. Also the growing privacy-transparency conflict will help us understand the gradual power shift between Chinese citizens and the Party State in the digital era.

Disclosure of Private Life: Extramarital Affairs and Power for Sex

China might not be the country in which people have strong privacy protection consciences as found in western democracies. Despite a vague, slippery privacy concept defined under Chinese law, details of private life, in particular of extramarital affairs, are always a "private" issue that falls within the core meaning of privacy, attracting wide public interest. The rising interest in Chinese public official's extramarital affairs comes partially from public curiosity or voyeurism, but mostly from the strong will to combat popular corruption. Because extramarital/sex life, or "love affairs", are rather expensive with rising spends to meet lovers' needs, which can only come from corruption and abuse of power(Minter, 2012).

In Nov. 2016, Mr. Gang Huang, the ex-director of China Railway Corporate (CRC)'s safety and supervision management bureau, was disciplined by the CCP. Huang is a top official in charge of the CRC which is a state-owned enterprise. The disciplinary watchdog of CRC published an official report online that documented the lurid details of his inappropriate relationship with an inferior female colleague, and possibly with her daughter too. It was reported that Huang has abused his power to benefit both ladies in multiple ways. This document was circulated soon on China's social media and within hours shared by thousands of internet users many of which questioned the necessity of a detailed story of sexual activity in an official report((Yimin, 2016).

In this case one may argue that Huang also has the right to privacy protection under Chinese law. CCP's disciplinary measure, as an internal penalty over the extramarital affair, is somehow illegal in nature *per se*. It is very common in Chinese court judgements and party disciplinary documents that only very general descriptions of similar misbehaviors were provided to introduce the conclusion that a person at stake led a corrupt life, or traded power for sex services, but never depicted in such specific details. Many may argue that the open disclosure of public officials' private life in a party document on the Internet itself can be breaching the Chinese law, and so did the online distribution of that document. However, this point is arguable since the official's ex-marriage affair is closely affiliated with his abuse of power in repositioning the mother to a new job near his work location to facilitate their meetings, as well as offering a traineeship to her daughter. It would be in the public's interest to know the associated abuse of power, so that the extramarital issue should be exposed and disclosed. The key issue at this point is only a matter of *proportionality*. As a public officer, Huang may face the charge of abuse of power, a crime that is punishable under Chinese law; but the private information of the two ladies shall not be made known publically, even with surname, which is very identifiable in their life circle. Because they still deserve dignity and decency that is protected under the right to privacy. In this case, the Party's disciplinary body certainly took a wrong step, which may lead to law suit for privacy breach in western jurisdictions.

Having his privacy invaded maybe, but Huang was not prosecuted for abuse of power after accepting CCP's internal punishment. He was very lucky if compared to others who are imprisoned for corruption that was found incident to similar online exposure of sex affairs. Zhengfu Lei, a former CCP secretary at a local Chongqing municipality, became notorious for his ugly appearance in an online sex video clip. The video was known national wide and quite damaging to CCP's reputation. Lei was sentenced to 13 years imprisonment for corruption with a fine of $49,000 for taking bribes. The lady involved was paid by unnamed property developers to hunt down local key officials for business interest by recording having sex with and blackmailing them (Chin, 2013). The lady was accused for blackmailing after her confession of taking the role and payment afterward. Also more than 10 local officials were sacked and punished over the same exposure. In this case, the explicit, sex video has been circulated widely and there was no privacy concern brought up by any scholar. Nevertheless the majority Chinese still share a popular conscience that criminals especially corrupted officials, do not deserve privacy protection according to China's cultural tradition. This public view may compromise the already weak privacy protection in Chinese law.

Serious corruptions usually go hand in hand with penchant of mistress or young lovers, in forms of abuse of power, bribes and embezzlement. Sometimes mistresses or secret lovers may serve as power brokers or officials' White Gloves to arrange power-for-money trade. This is because officials' direct involvement may lead to direct public suspicion. There has been a mistress culture coming into being in China not very long ago in that if rich businessmen and high-rolling government officials do not have mistresses, they don't receive due respect, as seen in the mafia culture portrayed by the movie *Goodfellas* (NPR, 2014). The distinction between official's public role and private life becomes largely blurred, when many business deals and political decisions would be made at off-office hours privately with mistresses involved. This reality makes the disclosure of private life extremely important to protect public interest. The anti-corruption campaigns in China in a sense become campaigns that investigation of extramarital affairs or mistress secrecy of officials will end up with prosecution of power abuse and corruption. In this case, protection of the privacy of officials becomes an issue less justified in light of the growing public frenzy for more exposure.

This does not meant that there is no privacy protection for Chinese officials at all. For instance, Mr. Xin Feng, ex-vice director of a local national treasury bureau, became an Internet celebrity after a video clip covering his hotel date with a female, inferior staff, which attracted public attention on the Internet. Unlike in other cases, he was not punished by the Party. Instead, the vice deputy of the local police bureau was arrested and sentenced to two year and a half imprisonment for abusing of police power and taking bribe. Because he "helped" others to illegally acquire the video from the hotel concerned for about $ 800 dollars. Although the revealed immoral extramarital affair may denote abuse of power by Feng, it is not significant for the public. This time, their focus is more on the out-of-track law enforcement power abuse that they believe is more danger and harmful than Feng's private affair.

What we observed in the above cases is the shifting boundaries of privacy protection in different contexts. When sex, power and money are mixed together in China's special political-legal context, a fine line between the right to privacy protection and open government (transparency) is rather hard to be drawn by Chinese rule makers either in law or in party policy. When the public demand for transparency to combat corruption and improve public governance to protect public interest is on the rise, to increase exposure of official's private life is nonetheless unavoidable. This public momentum may provide a strong support for the tradeoff of privacy protection for transparency, since only a number of public officials are at stake. Furthermore, party disciplinary measures taken against corrupted officials in the Party's internal investigation procedures are really a blunt violation of their right to privacy (or private life) against Chinese law. For instance, many Chinese officials have been detained by the Party's disciplinary bodies in hotels for months and interrogated of their personal issues without the presence of designated lawyers. Some even committed suicide under high physiological pressure, in order to avoid personal humiliation and indecency, or to protect family members or others involved(Huang, 2014).

However, too much exposure of power-for-sex trade-off is in the end negative to CCP's moral authority and its legitimacy in that such exposure clearly tells how corrupted Chinese officials are in a systematic way. In this sense, to protect the privacy or private life of Chinese officials is certainly to serve the Party State's best interest. Proper cove up will prevent negative, explosive revelation that generally leads to public unrest. Thus privacy protection can be used by Chinese officials to block the public's monitoring, which is a justification supported by both Chinese law and the state authority. The involvement of state reputation, privacy, sex, freedom of information and speech, and the value of open government (transparency) has set out a much complicated landscape in China's development of open government. This area is still very muddy, since there has not been a refined fine lines developed either under Chinese statutory law or Chinese case law, with regard to the privacy protection of Chinese officials(Chen, 2015, pp. 275–276).

If extramarital (sex) life is an important aspect of private life (privacy) that is closely connected to transparency and open government, as well as the exercise of public power in China, a discussion of asset disclosure can further help clarify the underlying, real obstacles to China's open government development.

Detecting Corruption: Difficult Asset Disclosure

To disclose senior officers' finances is a popular practice in mature democracies for which a good balance between privacy and transparency is needed. As an important part of open government, disclosure of assets and sources of income can be a deterrent against graft, corruption, collusion and patronage in the public sector(Opengovguide, 2017). Asset disclosure is a very sensitive issue in China, since its strict implementation will directly reveal the illegal wealth that many top Chinese leaders hide from the public by taking bribes, embezzlement and operating business via family ties. This is well proved in China's difficult, slow progress of assert disclosure legislation. This law was drafted earlier in 1988 by the Chinese National People's Congress (CNPC) and listed on its official agenda, but soon disappeared from public view without a trace and sound explanation.

Despite the fact that the legislation on asset disclosure is nearly on the brink of death, the CCP has nevertheless maintained an internal assert disclosure mechanism that collects similar information from partisans above the deputy county level. The CCP requires its members who take the prescribed positions to report all asset of their family, including both direct family members such as spouses and children, and their natural children who are born outside marriage. The required disclosure covers personal salary, subsidies and other incomes, as well as real properties, stocks, funds, investment insurances, savings, and the holdings and operations of any businesses. The internal party policies in particular demand the disclosure of a family's overseas savings and investments. As a policy implementation measure, about 10% of the filed reports will be audited by the CCP(W. Liu, 2016). Since most Chinese key government positions are in the hands of CCP members, the majority of high profile public officials can be monitored and controlled by the Party from within. One has to remember, however, the disclosure obligation remains an internal code of CCP, but without any legal binding force.

The drawbacks of this party policy are apparent. As many criticized, firstly, the disclosure is only kept within the CCP itself in the form of self-filing and self-reporting. In specific such reports and data are filed to and kept by CCP's HR agents only. They are not open to public access and therefore cannot reach their full potential in open government development. Further, CCP's HR departments are not independent bodies that can supervise and monitor the filing systems in a very hierarchical political organization within which orders from the superior matter only. The development of CCP's asset disclosure mechanism is a direct response to the increasing public demand for transparency and open government, half satisfying the public need, and half keeping the issue with CCP's own hands.

In reality, open call for asset disclosure of Chinese officials' has been on the rise especially after the promulgation of the 2008 Government Information Regulation. University students had made, in a number of cases, open soliciting for disclosing salary of Chinese officials. But they mostly received negative replies from responsible bodies on the ground that such information did not fall within the scope of the 2008 OGIR(You, 2012). Many pro-democracy activists were even jailed for their open call for an asset disclosure legislation, which drew wide international criticism(Wee, 2014). In recent years, representatives from NPC had publically initiated a legislative draft for four times, but all got turned down. Some Chinese local governments conducted sporadically asset disclosure experiments following the open government policy, but ended up nowhere with no further follow-up. For instance, the most famous one is Alatay(阿乐泰) municipality's experiment in family asset disclosure among low ranking officials in Xin Jiang Province in 2009, which was called off soon by the superior (Qian, 2012). Nowadays it seems that the public open call for asset disclosure has apparently faded away and attracts no close public attention in the context of an enhanced open government campaign pushed by the CCP.

One reason is that many recent reported corruption cases, ironically, indicate clearly the large amount of wealth that Chinese officials can amass according to their ranking in China's bureaucratic system. This is especially the case when some of the state-level leaders, for instance Yongkang Zhou, the ex-Security Chief of China, was caught in a new round of power struggle in 2014. That $ 14 billion of illegal family wealth was accumulated via different means, as well as that of his partners, lays out the scale of family wealth that China's state-level leaders may have equally accumulated(Forsythe, 2015). The publicized information has provided the public with a rough assumption of how large and serious the widespread corruption is at the top level, so that no further enquiry (or disclosure) is really needed. Another reason might be the state authority's continuous firm rejection of the public demand for asset disclosure and especially for a formal national legislation. This has made it rather clear that there will be no new legislation on asset disclosure in the seeable future, unless a fundamental political-legal change may come.

Asset disclosure encounters blockage at China's top level politics. This point can be further observed in two recent cases that reveal how CCP's internal asset disclosure mechanism could not work to fight corruption and power abuse. They prove how important an external monitoring system is for building up open government and for China's anti-corruption project, either in forms of assuring citizen's FOI right, or in form of a formal legal obligation of asset disclosure. The self-disciplining may work at lower and local level in China's robust officialdom, but certainly will not work when top leaders are at stake.

In 2012, the world might have been stunned by the disclosure of the billions of hidden riches of China's ex-Prime Minister Jiabao Wen's family in a New York Time report(Barboza, 2012a). Wen's mother Zhiyun Yang, a 90 years old widow then, was outright rich at least on paper. Just one investment in her name according to corporate and regulatory records, in a large Chinese financial services company, had a value of $ 120 million in 2007. Many relatives of Wen, including his son, wife, daughter, younger brother and brother in law, were all extraordinarily wealthy during his leadership following the report. They had controlled assets worth at least $ 2.7 billion and the accumulation of their wealth has endless connections to Wen's power as the first man governing China's economy, making important policy or regulatory decisions. As The New York Time reported, in China's senior leadership, there is no family that does not have these problems as one of Wen's former colleague claimed. At that period, the CCP regulations called for top officials to disclose their wealth and that of their immediate family members, but no law or regulation prohibited relatives of even the most senior officials from becoming deal makers or major investors. It is a big loophole allowing them to trade on their family name. This New York Time's report had been totally banned and not accessible from mainland China.

However, five years later in May 2017, the New York Times published a special report telling a big story of the year about an unusual Chinese billionaire. Wengui Guo, a tycoon in self-implicated exile in the U.S., has made the Chinese state stand down before an individual for the first time (Forsythe & Stevenson, 2017). From his $68 million apartment overlooking Central Park in Manhattan, Guo, still on Interpol's red hunting list, has sent highly explosive bombs to the CCP for months by Twitting and live broadcasting on YouTube. His unproved, big revelations directly point to Mr. Qishan Wang, who is the second man in China, Czar of China's recent anti-corruption campaign, and also head of CCP's Central Discipline Inspection Commission, as well as a few other high profile Chinese officials. One of the strong features of his allegation is their astonishing oversea family wealth, worthy of billions of dollars, and the radical private/sex lives of these top Chinese officials, including multiple extramarital kids living abroad. It is not that the Chinese public does not believe anything about the serious corruption of top Chinese officials. But this time the plain, direct exposure from an insider, even if hard to be proved, does indicate that their previous presumption of their oversea wealth could be true, *at an unbelievable scale*. It certainly shadows the political reputation of Mr. Wang who has openly claimed himself a clean, anti-corruption fighter, times and again.

The two stories indeed reveal three things. First, if one compares NYT's report on Wen's family wealth with what Guo claims at present, if he is right, it is clear that the present situation with respect to family asset disclosure has not changed that much and family wealth of top CCP leaders has not stopped growing. Second, it is rather apparent that CCP's internal asset reporting mechanism to improve transparence and public governance does not work, although that is a key issue to restrict and detect corruption and power-for-money tradeoff within the top elite circle. Third, it may show that the top CCP leaders have no one to monitor themselves. It shows who are the real opponents of the asset disclosure legislation, and who might have blocked its way into legislation in previous years.

However, neither is CCP's internal asset disclosure mechanism successful at the local level. As Chen revealed, China's law approach actually offers free rein to the manipulation of the privacy exemption to withstand public pressure from inquiring into prima facie illicit enrichments among officials, even if such issues were brought to court(Chen, 2015, pp. 273–274). For instance, a case from Shanxi Province concerned the income of a middle level official who became a symbol of alleged official extravagance on Chinese social media in 2012. Dacai Yang, the head of the provincial work safety supervision, was caught grinning at the scene of a fatal bus crash that killed 36 people. Chinese Netizens were outraged by his contempt of the dead, and a university student sued the two provincial bodies that rejected his request to disclose Yang's annual income. The local court, not even reviewing the case details at all, simply dismissed the two litigations together without any formal explanation. Yang was later convicted for his possessing property of unclear origin (about $ 817,000) and taking bribes, and sentenced to 14 years imprisonment. However, the whole prosecution was initiated and largely processed by the local CCP internal disciplinary body(Chen, 2015, pp. 273–274).

THE DRIVING FORCES OF CHINA'S OGI: LEGITIMACY, ECONOMIC DEVELOPMENT AND TECHNOLOGY DEVELOPMENT

On the official side, the strongest, legal justification for non-disclosure of family asset is to protect official's privacy including their private life and family members'. Many officials take the public disclosure of family assets as against their personality, dignity and family interest. This excuse is understandable and even acceptable to many Chinese, if one understands China's long tradition of having a broadly defined concept of "family". Xiao (孝) which means full respect for parents and forefathers in Chinese society is still a very strong mental and ethical tie among the majority Chinese, so that parents still have a last say in determining family issues. "Family", unlike in most western communities, is a concept to include one's spouse, children and even brother's or sister's families, in many occasions covering family members of three generations.

Chinese families have more commonly shared interests while living together, and there does not exist a clear-cut line of their financial interests and responsibilities. Thus it is hard to separate official's personal finances from their children's, parents' and brother's; sometimes even parents in law's. To draw an artificial/legal line might not be acceptable and difficult to implement in China, even if the majority of Chinese support assert disclosure. This societal consent or consciences among the Chinese public is problematic for the Chinese law to operate on a clear-cut definition of privacy protection, in particular between family life and individual life, between family interest and individual interest, and between legal and illegal interest. It is impossible to rebut the privacy protection argument from Chinese officials in an abstract sense. This may explain partly the vagueness of the concept of privacy under Chinese law, and the judicial approach of Chinese courts(Chen, 2015, pp. 266–268). Chinese courts protect privacy in the OGI context with an extremely wide approach, which almost equals privacy with personal information. This is against the mainstream civil law doctrine that excludes the personal information relating to the public interest(Chen, 2015, p. 275).

Furthermore, it may not be in the Chinese State's best interest to have a full asset disclosure law up to the standard of many western democracies. Since China's corruption is so popular, penetrating each corner of the political system, that blunt disclosure may destruct the legitimacy of the Party State, leading to national political insurgence. This will explain why CCP's internal asset disclosure mechanism is not openly accessible to the public, and why the Party pronounced that it can manage corruption and power abuse within itself. The Party State is halfhearted in promulgating a formal asset disclosure law, which is crucial to open government development.

If this assumption is true, then the key issue is: in which direction will China's open government develop in the near future in such a difficult political-societal context? There is no simple answer yet. But all in all, there will be slow, but firm development in China's open government, for the sake of the following reasons.

Firstly, as the CCP has clearly realized itself, to gain political and legal legitimacy among the Chinese public in order to survive any future political insurgence, it must promote open government and transparency, both on Partisan issues and on public governance issues. Secondly, to enhance China's economic development, which has been one of the key cornerstones of the Party's legitimacy, it must take effective measures to improve public governance, reduce corruption and prevent power abuse. This needs open government development to improve transparency, so that the private sector can be more productive by reducing market transaction costs with publically accessible information of all market players. This is the reason why we have seen in the New York Time's reports that a lot of information concerning Chinese leader's family wealth can be analyzed by merely accessing open corporate data base with a fee. This is the core issue for a health economic order and economic growth.

Thirdly, Chinese citizens have become more aware of their FOI right and taken it to action by filing numerous law suits against both local and central government, though they may have not won all battles. The public active use of OGI regulations has expanded the boundaries of public information and narrowed down the scope of stat secrecy(Horsley, 2016). Even ordinary citizens can hire lawyers or consulting firms to request corporate and finacial documents for a fee from $ 100 to 200. However, after the Time's revelation of Wen Jiabao, China tightened access to corporate information; for instance, in Beijing, it became difficult to obtain corporate records from the local bureau of the State Administration for Industry and Commerce(Barboza, 2012b). Now the corporate and financial information is still open for public access, but to find out the complex relationship of the family members as corporate and stock holders of Chinese officials behind the scene is not an easy job for ordinary citizens, but one for professional reporters or investigators. However, whether such news report could be successfully published in traditional Chinese media and on the Internet for public knowledge is really a problem in China's tightening censorship under Xi's presidency(Schlesinger, Henochowicz, & Wang, 2016).

Last, but most importantly, the rapid, overwhelming deployment of social media and social network services in China has been a strong driving force of China's OGI development. Due to fast technology developments, Chinese people now have alternative channels of information dissemination and importing, in addition to traditional official sources. In many cases, official information cannot get the upper hands over the information shared on new social media and social networking services that have become extremely popular among ordinary Chinese to conduct daily communications and even e-banking. In the 2015 Tianjing Explosion that left 70 death and more than 700 injured, alternative versions of the explosion on China's social media Sina Weibo (the Chinese version of Facebook) were told by those directly involved, and got top attention among Chinese internet users, leading to their questioning of the official report(Tiezzi, 2015). The fast development of new social media and self-made media compete with official news channels and forced the latter to be more open and nearer to reporting facts, in particular regarding misconducts of Chinese officials. That the Internet assists the public to have an easier access to information and to monitor officials, has been endorsed by the official media(Yang, 2015).

The Way Forward: Privacy Protection, Public Interest Test and Proportionality

China's OG development is irresistible and irreversible because of the reasons aforementioned. However, it remains a crucial matter how can the privacy of both ordinary Chinese and of officials can be better protected in China's particular political-legal context, on the one hand. And, on the other hand, how a strong privacy protection will not hinder the OG development with respect to private information disclosure of Chinese officials. Therefore the two must be well balanced in OG context. For this purpose, there is the need to assess the gravity of transparency and privacy protection in each specific case. As in western jurisdictions, one of the key criterions is the Public Interest Test(PIT). If public interest is undermined, then individual privacy might be compromised; and if individual privacy may be infringed, then transparency would not be required unless this is in pubic interest; The public interest test or public interest override allows us to address power asymmetries (Abraham, 2015).

The PIT should be the criterion to evaluate if any private information of Chinese officials shall be disclosed for public scrutiny. When less public interest involved, but more privacy is of concern, the balance shall tip for privacy protection, and *vice versa*. The key is to define the gravity of pubic interest at stake. In the Chinese open government context, for instance, top officials at state level shall enjoy less privacy protection because of their critical roles in Chinese politics in which critical public interests are always involved, if compared to officials at local level. Similarly, official's privacy should be less protected than ordinary citizens', because of their public roles and authority in which public interest can be involved. But at local level, the exemption from privacy protection for PIT should be specific and without reasonable doubt. For instance, when a public official's extramarital life involves clear evidence of abuse of power in policy decision making or government procurement, privacy protection shall not be an excuse for non-disclosure.

Furthermore, there is the need to seek a level of proportionality in privacy protection. Even when there is public interest involved in specific case, information disclosure shall be proportional according to the gravity of public interest involved, not going beyond what is necessary. As seen the CCP's internal disciplinary report, the much detailed sexual depiction should not be presented on a public document, but a general, short sketch is more preferred. Also personal information of the involved females shall be protected, especially in the context of crime investigation. Proportionality is a legal principle that has been well recognized in many western jurisdictions, for instance, under the EU law(De Wite, 1999, p. 861). When politicians are not willing to design a delicate mechanism to balancing privacy and transparency in the OG context, Chinese court shall play an active role in this regard, since legislators and politicians may lack the legal skills and determination in doing so.

Chinese courts are still reluctant to make decisions over issues that carry stronger implications for government accountability(Chen, 2015, p. 271). Thus for promoting open government in future, Chinese court, especially the Supreme People's Court (SPC), shall offer more active judicial support under the present Chinese legal framework. We will see the difficulties in pushing forward a formal legal arrangement for full asset and private life disclosure regarding top Chinese leaders, especially those state level leaders, because of the dependence of Chinese judicial system on the Party State. However, judicial dedication might have in-depth and long run influence on the Chinese society, considering the support from ordinary citizens in asserting their FOI right and the legitimacy need of the CCP in promoting China's OG development.

CONCLUSION

This chapter has reviewed briefly the developments of OG in China and its growing conflict with privacy protection in China's OG context. Two specific aspects of OG progress have been discussed in detail, namely, the disclosure of private extramarital life and family asset of Chinese officials. This is because both are the difficult parts in China's OG development with privacy protection involved. It is clear that privacy protection has been used as a legalized ground to justify non-disclosure of personal information in the two fields. This chapter shows first that disclosure of private life, especially extramarital life, is a complicate issue and can be justified by proportionated privacy protection even when public interest is involved. It also reveals that disclosure of asset (family asset) of public officials in China is a more tricky issue for which privacy protection offers less justification, especially when there is the growing public interest in monitoring the tradeoff of power for money and political patronage. In contrast to the fast development of OGI in the economic field, asset disclosure, which is critical to identify and monitor PEPs, is very much underdeveloped and remains a backyard garden of the CCP itself. Without the establishment of a formal legal obligation and external monitoring via enforcing citizen's FOI right, CCP's internal asset reporting mechanism does not work as efficiently as it has claimed. In this case, an independent judicial system is a crucial player in the OG context. Without that, good balancing and proportional protection of privacy, which is not conflicting with, but complementary to open government, cannot be realized.

The implications of the complex Chinese story in OG development might be the following. Firstly, the progress in public official's asset disclosure and private life disclosure, especially those holding top positions, can be used to assess the level of OG development in a community. The more of such information is obliged to disclosure, the higher the level of the OG development of that community. Secondly, another useful benchmark to assess OG development is how delicate privacy protection that community can provide. It is the case that the more refined, proportional privacy protection is provided, the better developed an open government mechanism. Vague or broader privacy protection may in many occasions mean that it can be misused or abused by those in power, and that an OG system is less open than it seems to be.

REFERENCES

Abraham, S. (2015, January 1). *Privacy vs transparency*. Retrieved July 19, 2017, from https://newint.org/features/2015/01/01/privacy-transparency

Barboza, D. (2012a, October 25). *Family of Wen Jiabao Holds a Hidden Fortune in China*. Retrieved from http://www.nytimes.com/2012/10/26/business/global/family-of-wen-jiabao-holds-a-hidden-fortune-in-china.html

Barboza, D. (2012b, October 26). Obtaining Financial Records in China. *The New York Times*. Retrieved from https://www.nytimes.com/2012/10/27/business/global/obtaining-financial-records-in-china.html

Batke, J., Breuer, J., & Matthias, S. (2016, November 22). *Open government in China: bound to improve, within bounds - MERICS China Blog*. Retrieved June 2, 2017, from http://blog.merics.org/en/blog-post/2016/11/22/open-government-in-china-bound-to-improve-within-bounds/

Cannataci, J., Zhao, B., & Bonnici, J. P. M. (2016). *Privacy, free expression and transparency: redefining their new boundaries in the digital age*. UNESCO. Retrieved from http://unesdoc.unesco.org/images/0024/002466/246610E.pdf

Chen, Y. (2015). Privacy and Freedom of Information in China: Review through the Lens of Government Accountability. *European Data Protection Law Review*, *1*(4), 265–276. doi:10.21552/EDPL/2015/4/5

Chin, J. (2013, June 28). *China Crows as Sex Tape Official Gets 13 Years*. Retrieved June 19, 2017, from https://blogs.wsj.com/chinarealtime/2013/06/28/china-crows-as-sex-tape-official-gets-13-years/

De Wite, B. (1999). The Past and Future Role of the European Court of Justice in the Protection of Human Rights. In *The EU and Human Rights* (pp. 859–898). Oxford, UK: Oxford University Press.

Forsythe, M. (2015, June 11). Zhou Yongkang, Ex-Security Chief in China, Gets Life Sentence for Graft. *The New York Times*. Retrieved from https://www.nytimes.com/2015/06/12/world/asia/zhou-yongkang-former-security-chief-in-china-gets-life-sentence-for-corruption.html

Forsythe, M., & Stevenson, A. (2017, May 30). The Billionaire Gadfly in Exile Who Stared Down Beijing. *The New York Times*. Retrieved from https://www.nytimes.com/2017/05/30/world/asia/china-guo-wengui.html

Hansson, K., Belkacem, K., & Ekenberg, L. (2015). Open Government and Democracy: A Research Review. *Social Science Computer Review*, *33*(5), 540–555. doi:10.1177/0894439314560847

Horsley, J. P. (2016, April 28). *China's FOIA Turns Eight.* Retrieved June 22, 2017, from http://www.freedominfo.org/2016/04/chinas-foia-turns-eight/

Huang, Y. (2014, December 1). *The Anticorruption Campaign And Rising Suicides In China's Officialdom.* Retrieved July 13, 2017, from http://www.forbes.com/sites/yanzhonghuang/2014/12/01/the-anticorruption-campaign-and-rising-suicides-in-chinas-officialdom/

Liu, H. (2016). Comparison Research on Open Government Data Websites in China——Base on the Investigation of Nine OGD Websites. In *Proceedings of the Doctoral Consortium at the 18th International Conference on Asia-Pacific Digital Libraries (ICADL 2016), and Asia-Pacific Forum of Information Schools (APIS 2016).* Retrieved from http://icadl2016.org/apis/19_Liu.pdf

Liu, W. (2016, January 27). *Family Asset Audit Forces Chinese officials to File Genuine Report* (in Chinese). Retrieved July 20, 2017, from http://epaper.ynet.com/html/2016-01/27/content_180488.htm?div=0

Minter, A. (2012, October 2). *In China, Mistresses and Corruption Go Hand in Hand.* Retrieved from https://www.bloomberg.com/view/articles/2012-10-02/in-china-mistresses-and-corruption-go-hand-in-hand

NPR. (2014, March 2). *Corruption Blurs The Lines Of China's Mistress Culture.* Retrieved June 20, 2017, from http://www.npr.org/2014/03/02/284905579/corruption-blurs-the-lines-of-chinas-mistress-culture

Opengovguide. (2017). *Establish a law requiring public disclosure of income and assets by elected and senior public officials - Open Government Guide.* Retrieved July 18, 2017, from http://www.opengovguide.com/commitments/asset-disclosure/

Parker, J. (2013, September 4). *The Privacy vs. Transparency Debate in China.* Retrieved June 13, 2017, from http://thediplomat.com/2013/09/the-privacy-vs-transparency-debate-in-china/

Pei, M. (2006). *China's trapped transition : the limits of developmental autocracy.* Cambridge, MA: Harvard University Press. doi:10.4159/9780674041981

Qian, Z. (2012, April 9). Calls growing for national law to force officials to disclose full assets. *Global Times.* Retrieved July 18, 2017, from http://www.globaltimes.cn/content/703857.shtml

Rossi, I., Pop, L., Clementucci, F., & Sawaqed, L. (2012). *Using Asset Disclosure for Identifying Politically Exposed Persons*. Retrieved June 6, 2017, from https://openknowledge.worldbank.org/handle/10986/26790

Schlesinger, D., Henochowicz, A., & Wang, Y. (2016, March 17). *Why Xi Jinping's Media Controls Are 'Absolutely Unyielding'*. Retrieved July 16, 2017, from https://foreignpolicy.com/2016/03/17/why-xi-jinpings-media-controls-absolutely-unyielding-censorship-china-economy-speech/

Susan, F. (2014, December 23). *How China Classifies State Secrets*. Retrieved July 18, 2017, from http://thediplomat.com/2014/12/how-china-classifies-state-secrets/

Tiezzi, S. (2015, August 14). *The Tianjin Explosion, As Chronicled on Chinese Social Media*. Retrieved July 17, 2017, from http://thediplomat.com/2015/08/the-tianjin-explosion-as-chronicled-on-chinese-social-media/

Wee, S.-L. (2014, April 18). China sentences activists for urging asset disclosure: Lawyer. *Reuters*. Retrieved from http://www.reuters.com/article/us-china-activists-idUSBREA3H04H20140418

Wenjing, L. (2011). Approaching Democracy Through Transparency: A Comparative Law Study on Chinese Open Government Information. *American University International Law Review, 26*(4). Retrieved from http://digitalcommons.wcl.american.edu/auilr/vol26/iss4/4

Yang, G. (2015, February 4). *Calls grow for top down asset disclosures*. Retrieved June 12, 2017, from http://www.chinadaily.com.cn/opinion/2015-02/04/content_19490935.htm

Yimin, R. (2016, November 16). *The Story of Gang Huang and His Mistress* (in Chinese). Retrieved July 18, 2017, from http://eurcb.com/html/xinwen/zixuan/201611162330.html

You, P. (2012, October 28). *Those secrets that cannot be told (说的秘密(组图))*. Retrieved June 12, 2017, from http://www.aboluowang.com/2012/1028/265889.html

Zhou, H. (2003). *Open Government in China: Practice and Problems*. Retrieved July 18, 2017, from https://academiccommons.columbia.edu/catalog/ac:126700

Section 2
Technical Barriers to OGI

Chapter 3
Open Mexico Network in the Implementation of National Open Data Policy

Rafael Valenzuela
Autonomous University at Juarez City, Mexico

Alberto Ochoa
Autonomous University at Juarez City, Mexico

ABSTRACT

The objective of the chapter is to identify some barriers to accessing public data through the study of one of the pillars of Mexico's national open data policy, the Open Mexico Network. Based on the exploratory analysis of the "Mexico Abierto network" and the description of a case study in northern Mexico, an attempt is made to answer the following question: Does Mexico's national open data policy generate timely data and have efficient access to data? and the final question, Is it easy for citizens to obtain? The study identifies major problems from the design of the national policy of open data, such as not having foreseen the creation of positive incentives for local governments to update the databases in the "México Abierto network."

DOI: 10.4018/978-1-5225-4987-1.ch003

INTRODUCTION

Through the review and use of the Mexico Abierto platform, we identified the absence of updated data and a low number of useful data sets. A network by nature is horizontal and requires dialogue between equals, but it is inferred that local governments are conceived as a subordinate order to the central government and as public organizations without the ability to establish their own platforms and generate useful data. The federal government of Mexico applies a policy that imposes its conditions and parameters of information to local governments, without taking into account the local reality. This, plus the difficulty of having local governments whose administrations exceed three years, add a cocktail that prevents detonating an organizational culture to release data and information, timely and useful for citizens. Between January and March 2017, the update, number of accesses and number of open data that the network of strategic actors has been feeding in the México México Open Network were reviewed. The network groups 14 municipalities of the country and is hosted on a platform generated by the Mexican federal government. The changes that are necessary and sufficient to establish an open data culture are far from materializing, as can be seen from the review of the open Mexico Network portal and interviews with public officials, who requested anonymity in the conversation. Additionally, a case is described in the north of Mexico, in which it was identified that from the national policy of open data, is not being achieved promptly in the release of the data, there are no methodologies to evaluate its usefulness and the level of Institutionalization to build open data, is very low.

The national open data policy was conceived from top to bottom (top-down implementation model), shaping a unicentric network, poorly interconnected and distributed. The mentioned network in Mexico, only groups to the 0.58 percent of the municipalities of the country, indicative of the small size of the network. Mexico Abierto receives inputs from the municipal governments, at the request of the federal government. Without a greater culture of transparency, the creation of useful data for society and the lack of roots in a conversational practice with civil society, local governments will continue to be little active nodes of the network. The registration of information update shows that it takes 2 to 9 months to update the data and information presented on the micro site. During the implementation of the policy, the municipalities renewed their mandates and in several cases, the colors of the party in the municipal government changed. This led to the need to establish again, agreements to keep the node that connects it to the national network in force. In reviewing the case of the local government of Ciudad Juárez,

Mexico, no evidence was found of common and aligned objectives between the municipal digital policies of that municipality, with the national policy of open data implemented by the Office of National Digital Strategy of the Presidency of the Republic. This is one of the barriers that hinder the proper implementation of the national open data policy. This chapter is organized into four sections. The first establishes brief theoretical references in the perspective of open government and open data. The second part indicates characteristics of the policy of open data in Mexico and provides analysis on that policy and its Open Mexico strategy. The third part, addresses the experience of Ciudad Juárez, Chihuahua, Mexico and, finally, it is up to the conclusions.

USEFUL AND USELESS OPEN DATA

It is sometimes thought that open government and open data are synonymous concepts. Open data is required to achieve open government, but not vice versa. Open data are quantities of information, reduced to their minimum expression. Gathering the data, they can provide reliable information and create knowledge once they are subjected to a data mining process or check the existence of data that are useless (data smog). Gathering the data, they can provide reliable information and create knowledge once they are subjected to a data mining process or check the existence of data that are useless (data smog). The meaning and interpretation of the data correspond to who uses the data. Hence the necessary capacity and importance in the development of citizen competencies associated with civil rights, but also the ability of governments to process and construct the data. (Goëta & Davies, 2016) demonstrate that data liberation puts less and less attention on citizens' access through softwares that allow their reading and download with ease for the citizen. The proliferation of data is not accompanied by the infrastructure that makes it possible to read, use and allow adding value. The benefits of having open data are greater than the costs, having technology and digital platforms, which implies "Making public sector data open helps citizens to better understand what a government does and the level of performance achieved" (Olayiwola et al, 2016). (Yu and Robinson, 2012) highlight the ambiguity of the concept of open government and open data. They are not synonymous, but both have a different origin, and diverse practical use. Following the authors cited, the term open data shows great potential as an instrument of political, social and economic opening; Spheres where the benefits and scope of open government are debated (Yu and Robinson, 2012: 182). If open government is a model for managing public policies, based on the co-production, use and access to public information, through collaboration of citizens to improve their quality of life, open data plays a central role to activate the technical dimension of Public policies, and thus detonate a set of decisions based on evidence, for the solution of public problems. When referring to open government policy, we will be talking about the components of transparency and participation, both with a collaborative approach. These are two interdependent components. Although Welch (2012) suggests that participation is positively associated with transparency, but not vice versa, several studies find that transparency promotes participation (Cejudo, 2017). The link promoting participation from transparency could be the route of open data. Transparency is collaborative and instrumental in an open government, and in addition to complying with the standards set forth in the law, should contribute to making public information more affordable, strategic and useful. Achieving government openness will require the use of interoperable platforms that communicate decisions, encourage citizen participation, and define an organizational model where data-based management can add value to government decisions through multiple actors (Valenzuela, 2015).

(Grimmelikhuijsen and Welch, 2012), quoted by (Bearfield and Bowman, 2016: 563) define transparency in terms of "disclosure of information by an organization that allows external agents to assess their internal functioning and performance", is insufficient. Transparency of open government is collaborative and characterized by public information in the form of open data, and it allows improving the quality of public decision, but also the private decisions of citizens (Valenzuela, 2015). Open is dependent on collaborative transparency, and this in turn, on open data. From the above it is inferred that it is not the same to refer to the policy of government, as to the policy of open data. The latter is a precondition for governmental opening. The new era of transparency requires open data. The production (generation) of the data, is a complex matter, given the technological backwardness of a certain sector of government, the lack of interest of the public servant in sharing data and information, and having sufficient organizational capacities to interoperate information, are among the Causes that hinder an open data policy (Höchtl et al, 2016: 150). The aspiration in an open government is to go beyond transparency and refer in the direction of collaboration for the creation, use and transmission of the data, on multiple digital bases, fed between government and society. Open data is presented to the discussion of open government, through technological innovation and to expand the bases of knowledge, in order to make them available to the public, through the internet. It is also necessary to be present in the way of transparency and citizen participation.

According to the Sunlight Foundation, a data is open when it fulfills the following characteristics:

1. **Completeness:** That they reflect all the information that is possible.
2. **Primary:** That the data privilege the original basis of the information and the methodology that allowed its collection.
3. **Timely:** That the data is released when they are in the moment of generating useful information and if they are released in real time, it is better.
4. **Digital Access:** That new technologies be used to make the constructed data more accessible and understandable.
5. **Contents in Reusable Format:** Public information and even data, are made in formats that do not facilitate their reuse. For example in PDF.
6. **Access Without Discrimination:** That there are no records or other requirements to access the database, much less requirements related to religion, sex, color or age to access data.
7. **Use With Software Available for the Majority:** That the data can be read in common software and without difficulties to obtain them. Even the data could be offered along with the software required for reading.
8. **Free Access:** That there is no requirement to access the payment of fees for licenses or other restrictions.
9. **Permanent:** That data is available indefinitely.
10. **Reduced Usage Costs:** That open data must have minimum access costs, but also as far as its use is concerned (Wonderlich, 2010).

The data is a means to achieve openness, and the calculation, interpretation and dissemination action, as well as the use of specialized software, platforms and algorithms, will necessarily imply training and acquisition of specific knowledge. At present, it is unthinkable to conceive the activity of government, business and civil society organizations, without the use of resources, tools and technological innovations, which does not cancel the political content of the open government, but rather strengthens it. Technological evolution in the twenty-first century accelerated the transition from the analogue to the digital world, and today the digital age is assumed to be inherent in associated life. In order to generate conditions of production, use and access to public information, digital platforms are required, if one starts from the fact that the first citizen contact is not given in direct contact with the public servant, but with a digital platform as an intermediary. Notwithstanding the above, not all the information and data in the hands of the government, is public. As in the company, the protection of private data is an inherent obligation in the legal framework. Understanding openness as an institutionalized rule or principle that promotes public ethics and the responsible use of information marginalizes the idea of governmental openness, in terms of dogma or doctrine, which supposes publicity at all costs, without the slightest analysis. The nature of the open data requires publicity, while the nature of the private data requires the reservation. This dichotomy reflects a line of research, similar to that of open versus traditional government. Data open on its own does not mean more transparency, and perhaps in certain cases does not aim at transparency. But when you have the government data open, certainly pays in favor of transparency, if it is accompanied by instruments that facilitate the use and dissemination of the data. The analysis of large data will involve the use of social intelligence, new technologies and innovative capabilities to discover relationships, phenomena and facts that generate public policies of greater political, social and economic value.

THE NATIONAL OPEN DATA POLICY

The Open Data Policy of the Government of Mexico is in charge of the National Digital Strategy Office of the Presidency of the Republic, which launched the Open Mexico Network between 2015 and 2016, a program whose purpose is to innovate in the Public sector on the use and re-use of information in the hands of the government. However, it is not the only program that shapes national open data policy, this chapter focuses on the study of the network. The premise for forming a network is the assumption that liberating data and putting it in open format will produce more favorable economic conditions for citizens by having reusable data for the purpose of generating economic value, especially through innovation. Mexico Open is aimed at promoting the culture of open data in the Internet portal, data.gob.mx, where the bases and records of public information are housed, which are being released and made available to all interested parties. In Latin America, Mexico is not the only country to have an open data portal of the government. It is enough to activate a simple search in google, to realize that Chile, Colombia, Ecuador, Peru, Dominican Republic, Argentina, as well as the subnational and local governments of each one of the countries enunciated, develop actions and implement strategies and policies to Release data. From a study published by the Organization for Economic Cooperation and Development (OECD), 17 municipalities and 12 federative entities are reported to be incorporated into the Open Mexico Network (OECD, 2016: 156). The information presented in the report probably reflects up-to-date information, which is not provided by the Network's website (http://mxabierto.org/) which was last consulted in the preparation of this chapter, on March 24, 2017. The Portal indicates that 14 municipalities and 9 federal entities are on the Net. Reports on progress or studies from the government do not exist in the web portal of the Network that provides some results obtained or describe goals to be achieved. The 14 municipalities that identify the map of the open data portal, identified from north to south, are the following: Mexicali, Ahome, Ciudad Juárez, Torreón, San Pedro Garza Garcia, Reynosa, Victoria, Minatitlan, Jiutepec, Xalapa, Veracruz, Puebla, and Merida Solidarity. The first contact of the citizen in governments, is no longer with the public servant, the bureaucrat or the politician, but with a portal programmed to respond to a registration, provide a service or link the public administration with the citizen. In this way, new technologies are essential, both in the language of programming and creation of exchanges and communication between government and citizens, as in the delivery of services from government to citizens. From the review of the open data portal of the Mexico Abierto Network, it was observed that the network formed from the municipalities corresponds to a uni-centric type network, in which each local government responds to the federal government to comply with this policy. From the analysis of the information published in the portal, the review of documents and references to the Open Mexico Network, we can identify some strengths and weaknesses. Among the first of these is that a policy of these dimensions is launched for the first time in Mexico, whose effort deserves great national and international recognition. In 2016, the OECD published text in which it gives account of the importance for the economic development of this type of policies. Strength is the formation of an organizational culture to create data and release them. Although incipient, there is no way to deny the influence that such a policy will have on creating a new public servant profile. If this strategy of the Mexico Abierto Network continues, in a sustained manner and evaluated for its improvement, it will have benefits in relation to data that could be reused to create public value. Among the weaknesses is that it is not a distributed and interconnected network in its nodes. It is a network that reports the release of data to the federal government and not an initiative built between the various orders of government, although it is implemented between the three levels. This is relevant, since it dictates tradition in the design of public policies in Mexico: from the center to the periphery. In fact, when selecting the option "all data" located in combo on the top right, in the level of government category, only "Autonomous", "Federal" and "State" appear. The municipalities grouped them under the label of "Organizations". Another weakness of the national open data policy is its failure to update the information provided. While the OECD indicates that there are 17 municipalities adhering to this strategy, the portal shows only 14. Likewise, for the updating of information, months pass, losing continuity and immediacy of information. A third weakness is to consider only the perspective of the public servant. In the design phase, there is no diagnosis that suggests what information is useful to the public. Because it is a national policy, it is understandable that the government's view of open data prevails, but this is meaningless if there is an audience for which they are destined, or a citizen voice that indicates the urgency of releasing data. A fourth weakness is the lack of correspondence between the national open data policy and the municipal programs that consider releasing data or promoting the development of technologies. It seems to be a federal initiative, which must be maintained at that level. As we will see in the case study below, there are municipalities that have made interesting efforts in the development and deployment of new information and communication technologies. The strengths and weaknesses of the national open data policy described in this chapter allow contextualizing the information presented in the form of open data. The portal displays the information shown in Table 1.

Ahome, does not provide the software with which to read the information and data provided. Access to resources is not available from the website of the Network. It should be noted that some of the resources of the municipality of Ahome, were located via the search engine www.datos.gob.mx and not from the interactive map. The number of 393 resources was revised and not 23, organized under the labels "municipal (11)", "implode ahome (9)", "opening plan (1)", "inventory (1) "And" ahome (1). " In the municipal section presents a mobility survey in xls format (Excel), but only the results and not the data to co-create value. Ciudad Juárez, presents 7 available resources and all updated two months ago. You can access the list of resources, but when you try to access, the page marks an error. It was tried from the search engine and is the same result. It is noteworthy that we have as an open data the list of the operating agencies of drinking water of Cd. Juarez, being more information available, than an open data. As described above, it is observed that information is not available and consequently, there are no conditions for the creation of public value. As for Torreon, they are available but some that could create value are not updated since 2015, such as the Excel file containing road accident data. It does not present the software available, and some databases are in spss, which costs its acquisition. It was identified that 2 of the 11 resources are not available. Unfortunately most of what they are if they are available contain only information from 2015. Under these conditions, value creation is minimal. In the case of San Pedro Garza Garcia, it is reported that there are two resources available, but in fact there are 8. The data set that is indicated as most popular by the number of downloads, is not even mentioned within the 8 resources listed by the town. Victoria presents 5 sets of data. Only one is readable in excel and the rest is available

Table 1. Municipalities in the Open Mexico network

	Municipality	Resources Published According to the Website of the Open Mexico Network	Number of Updates in 12 Months	Access to Open Data From Map of the Open Mexico Network	More Downloaded According to the Website of the Open Mexico Network
1	Mexicali, Baja California	0	0	No	None
2	Ahome, Sinaloa	393	2	No	Route of trucks of Los Mochis
3	Ciudad Juárez, Chihuahua	7	2	Yes	Atlas of risk of Juárez
4	Torreón, Coahuila	11	2	Yes	Road accidents due to inebriation
5	San Pedro Garza García, Nuevo León	8	2	Yes	Traffic Accidents
6	Reynosa, Tamaulipas	16	0	Yes	Institutional inventory of City Hall data
7	Victoria, Tamaulipas	5	0	Yes	Statistical Directory of Economic Units
8	Minatitlan, Veracruz	16	2	Yes	Land use type catalog
9	Jiutepec, Morelos	0	0	No	None
10	Xalapa, Veracruz	106	5	Yes	Medical center of Xalapa
11	Veracruz, Veracruz	23	5	Yes	Property identification data
12	Puebla, Puebla	82	2	Yes	Directory of Neighborhood Policy Boards in Barrios
13	Mérida, Yucatán	0	0	No	None
14	Solidaridad, Quintana Roo	0	0	No	None

Source: (Author's Own elaboration with data from Recursos, 2017)

in compressed zip files, but without the software that facilitates its reading. This municipality created two months ago each of the resources shown. The presentation in the form of text, makes them informative documents that are of some importance and not just databases in an open format. The creation of value is potentially limited and the regularity with which the information will be updated is still unknown. In

Reynosa, 9 of the 16 resources available are listed on different subjects. Among them is a list of hotels, which would be very useful if not because the private sector has information seekers and specialized platforms in that area. Other listings such as the list of works, is updated to 2016 and is interesting, but more information is required of those works. The creation of value is potentially limited and the regularity with which the information will be updated is still unknown. Minatitlan presents a resource with only two data. It is the resource "catalog of conditions of use", which refers to both types of land use. The resource "cadastral region" contains a list of cadastral regions and is a file with 28 data. Your description does not match the content of the resource. The possibility of creating value from what is shown is null. Everything shown or "released" is merely informative and limited. Xalapa announces 106 available resources in the Network, but in reality it has 49. All are available to users and it presents databases, downloadable in excel. This council represents a relevant effort for the number of times they have been concerned with updating the information. It is a potentially relevant case to explore in the process of creating value.The case of Puebla seems to be in better condition, together with the municipalities of the State of Veracruz. Although it reports that there are 82 resources, 86 are actually shown. It is also the only municipality that, because the resource is not available on the Red Mexico Open platform, re-addresses you to its own open data portal. Mérida, Solidaridad and Mexicali, were the municipalities that did not present available resources of the platform Red Mexico Open. However they are on the map as active municipalities and counted in the strategy analyzed in this chapter.

Unicentric Network Policy With Low Interconnectivity

All the municipalities have in common that they do not present a methodology to construct the data, which leads to a limitation to use data with greater confidence. There is a range of municipalities without data, others without useful data, and exceptionally municipalities with the intention of improving the quality and presentation of their data. Despite emptying the information on a platform like the Open Mexico Network, it became a straitjacket that limits innovation. In the search for local governments with databases, we identified that Ciudad Juárez had a program focused on the use of technologies based on data provided by citizens in terms of public safety, public services and improvement of roads to the functionality of the city. It is an unprecedented effort to generate a local public policy, based on private and public data, that the citizens shared with that local government. Projects based on open data favor the creation of smart cities. Therefore, the national policy of open data, should define strategies that encourage the generation of value, not only economic, but social and human capital. Incentives in strategies for creating open data are a key factor missing from the national open data policy. Correspondence with local context, programs and local interests, as well as facilitating national communication and interoperability of municipal data, will promote the creation of a less unicentric network, thus moving towards a more distributed, interconnected network. Open. From the case of Ciudad Juárez, we realize the importance of the local context in national policies.

Open data will have the ability to create value, if citizens have the capabilities to use them. And for this it is necessary to create relations of power, better distributed, interconnected and generator of conditions space and adequate time where the data have sense and utility. It is worth remembering Manuel Castells, when he affirms Communication is the space in which relationships of power are constructed. This does not mean that the media has the power. This is empirically false: they do not have the power. They are much more important than that, because they are the space where power is built (Castells, 2012).

DESCRIBING THE EXPERIENCE OF A LOCAL GOVERNMENT IN MEXICO

During 2016 the Interactive Municipality Program was reviewed, implemented by the local government of Ciudad Juárez, Mexico. It was identified that there is no link with the national policy of open data, except for the obligation to submit data to the Open Mexico Network. Ciudad Juárez, developed during the 2013 and 2016 administration, the interactive municipality program in Cd Juárez (known as MI Juárez). However the change of municipal administration, rendered ineffective that program. MI Juarez could be monitored by the authors during 2016 and interviews were conducted with public servants, who asked to omit their names to avoid any risk situations in their jobs. With the re-election of city councils from 2018, it could preserve innovative public programs. Although this does not guarantee that local governments are successful in their policies, programs and actions, programs such as MI Juarez could survive the change of municipal administration, if re-election produces incentives for sustained planning in this kind of continuity Of programs and capacity building to improve coordination among the three orders of government.

Ciudad Juárez is a border town in northern Mexico, which had a period of significant economic prosperity, but more recently it is a social crisis that resulted from a wave of violence and insecurity, which led to its being known in the world in that complicated stage. Due to its geographical advantages, it accounts for 18% of the maquiladora industry, the highest in Mexico. Historically, economically and politically it is a city of enormous importance, both in the region and in the country, of enormous contrasts in the social, diverse in its traditions and a cultural mosaic. The modernization of the State, public administration, public services and models for managing public affairs require the exploration of new approaches. Today the debate about the conditions to move towards a more open and intelligent government, allows to identify attributes of the governments under a new lens, and to observe variables that once were underestimated in the studies of public affairs. The debate about open government, is no longer under construction and is in clear evolution. Transparency and citizen participation, their initial components, have ceased to be ends to be conceptualized as means in the governmental opening. This implies the transformation of government action into tangible results. Sensitive issues such as public safety are relevant in the light of new approaches such as open government.

Interactive Municipality

At the moment the City of Ciudad Juárez develops a modernizing process of the administration, through a strategy denominated "MI Juárez. Interactive Municipality ". This innovative program is part of a municipal modernization policy to address security challenges. Five strategies develop the Government of Ciudad Juárez to achieve public policy objectives:

The first is to make the website of the municipality more functional through its permanent updating; Second, to incorporate more public services online; Third, to offer applications to civil society to provide useful information; Fourth, to coordinate efforts of the three orders of government, enterprises and civil society organizations; Fifth, to expand the municipality's digital network to achieve interoperability among local government agencies.

These strategies are framed in new trends of implementation in public management. The open government as a political and technological platform, indicates that traditional public management models must be modified, to others more flexible and innovative in political, social and economic. In the open government debate, there is a shift towards society and we have forgotten the actor government, limiting it only to a relational context and neglecting the organizational one. Huge challenge is presented for when it is raised in the public service, transparency as a mere legal requirement. Assuming it as an essential component of the new paradigm of open government, translates the concept of transparency into the border of the open. This requires a new organizational culture, as a daily practice that produces useful information, focused and based on attributes of quality and immediacy. In this sense, transparency as the opening of the government implies sharing useful information, which can be applied to public services, in the form of open data, which represent key input in the development of software, digital applications, all for the improvement of services Municipalities. Governments must rely on citizenship as allies to generate reliable public information. This leads to the assumption that governments co-produce information to improve public services where citizens had a veto to participate, in times of authoritarian governments and passive societies. Specifically, public security was recognized as a prohibited subject for citizenship. Governments are now modernizing and societies are more open, suggesting that some information is being coproduced by government and citizens to improve in particular that function that is reserved for the Mexican State, such as public security. By system of competencies, in the governments of proximity security has been restricted to the surveillance, the transit and the prevention of the crime. The issues of justice, prosecution of violence and crimes are the responsibility of another instance, state or federal. This effort is unprecedented in municipalities of this population density. The applications that have been generated so far are three:

1. **The Alert Application:** The Alert app allows to send several types of emergency alerts or that endanger the integrity of the citizen:
    a. Public safety corporations,
    b. Transit,
    c. Civil Protection, and
    d. Red Cross.

    As indicated by the municipal authorities, "This tool, although it is very useful for a rapid attention to emergencies, requires a responsible use of the citizen, because when pressing the buttons, causes the deployment of elements of the forces of Security and rescue, as well as vehicles for their care "(municipal government, 2015).

    Accessing this online application requires a process of registration and validation of data provided by the citizen electronically through the Portal of the Municipality of Juárez. In this last portal, the citizen can download the application and install it on his cell phone. The information provided in the registry, will allow the dependency that corresponds to attend the emergency, to be able to assist with the minimum elements essential to provide a timely and efficient service. In this sense, the citizen shares personal data, as is done with any web application.

The cell phone that is used for this digital tool, must have access to the Internet, as it is applications for mobile devices. It is essential to activate the GPS function of the cell phone, to locate the place of the emergency and generate the quickest route of care and help. Once the application is installed, it will be possible to access a screen that contains 5 buttons, each one offers an alert service:

a. Sending alerts to the Municipal Police,
b. Health,
c. Firefighters, and
d. Transit that puts in contact with the emergency telephone number 066.

To activate the alert, it is necessary to hold down the required button for 5 seconds, according to the type of emergency, it will activate the sending of the telephone number, time and date of the emergency, as well as the closest geographical position of the place. This information, in addition to that provided by the citizen in the registration process, is sent to the Emergency and Immediate Response Center dispatch area, activating the protocol previously defined by each of the corporations that attend the emergencies.

2. **Protege Application:** The Protege app, aims to keep citizens informed of different situations such as road closures, climatic or health contingencies, and possible risks that are manifested in the city. This app intends to provide inputs to the citizen to decide in their daily life, such as taking the best route to their destination on the morning that goes to work, avoiding flooded areas in case of rains, taking alternate routes in cases of risks to their Integrity, among others. The digital tool defines information flows that seek to create social value of information, seeking to be a support tool for the citizen.
3. **The Watch App:** This app seeks to have a more focused government according to the information provided by the citizen and, at the same time, to be responsible for the current situation in the City in relation to the current state of streets and avenues. It is sought that through the app, the citizen is a coproducer of solutions by means of the denunciation and generation of evidence, through photos and denunciation, that indicates if the public servant is fulfilling its function of serving. The idea of the app is that the citizen denounces if the public services are failing and if there are repairs that must be done to the urban infrastructure, either through a photograph and description of the fact, or through a voice message where Explain the situation to be reported (Municipal Government, 2015). In this way the citizen has the opportunity to assess whether his or her municipal government is more proactive or if it is just another way of citizen complaint similar to the traditional telephone call, which was inefficient.

The guidance provided by the municipal government indicates that citizens can denounce situations such as deteriorating infrastructure, risky places such as abandoned homes, among others.

All the applications described, were elaborated with public and private data for the benefit of the citizenship. The impact of the MI Juárez program is unknown, but it was innovative and should continue until the results are proven.

CONCLUSION

The national open data policy in Mexico is not generating timely data and efficient access for citizens. When exploring the Red Mexico Open strategy, one of the most important pillars of the national open data policy is design flaws in policy, but also technological flaws. On the one hand, local governments do not have appropriate incentives to publish data and information for long periods of time and not just occasionally. The data are not useful, when they are not provided in a short time. Among barriers to accessing public data in the open format is the lack of constant updating of sites and the lack of active links that provide timely information. The goal of creating data and releasing ourselves is not being met. If the Open Mexico Network is maintained, as an undistributed network, the possibility of institutionalizing the generation of data in open format from local governments will be lost. If the first contact of the citizen to obtain data is precisely the portal of the Open Mexico Network, the creation of a methodology in the creation of the data and establishment of periodicity in the update of the portals should be reviewed. This could explain why the OECD study on the Mexico Abierto network does not coincide with what is shown on the portal. The logic of collaboration between governments must prevail if more open governments are to be achieved. Governments persist in making policies on their own, when a nineteenth-century government recognizes that its capabilities are limited to address data-creation processes. For the creation of open government data, linkage between national open data policy and local policies will be required. The municipalities are the order of government closest to the citizenship, but also the most vulnerable before the electoral political swing. As long as a culture of openness and open data generation, shielding the mandates of elected politicians every three years, cannot be consolidated, open governance and open data practices in the local area will hardly become entrenched. The case study presented in the chapter suggests that there was a modernizing policy in the local government of Ciudad Juárez, but without the evaluation of its results when it was canceled by the new local government that assumed its mandate in 2016. This implies reestablishing

A policy of open data and new institutional arrangements. The complex reality that local governments face in Mexico, allows to emphasize that the open data are seeds that germinate if they manage to be used to co-produce (government and citizens) solutions to eternal problems of corruption, inefficiency in public management, opacity in the Budgetary exercise and capture of regulatory bodies, among others. A public service proposal based on open government policies and open data is essential to move towards an organizational culture where government decisions are made on the basis of evidence and information on public affairs. Open data allows to add collective intelligence to the decision processes and to define a more open, interactive and modern public management, as corresponds to the governments of the nineteenth century.

REFERENCES

Bearfield, D., & Bowman, A. (2016). Can You Find It on the Web? An Assessment of Municipal E-Government Transparency. American Review of Public Administration, 1-17.

Castells, M. (2012). *"El poder en la era de las redes sociales" en revista*. Nexos.

Cejudo, G. (2017). *Métrica del gobierno abierto*. CIDE- INAI.

Gobierno municipal. (2016). *Micrositio del Ayuntamiento de Ciudad Juárez*. Retrieved from http://mi.juarez.gob.mx/mijuarez/tech

Goëta, S., & Davies, T. (2016). The Daily Shaping of State Transparency: Standards, Machine-Readability and the Configuration of Open Government Data Policies. *Science & Technology Studies*, *29*(4), 10–30.

Höchtl, J., Parycek, P., & Schöllhammer, R. (2015). Big data in the policy cycle: Policy decision making in the digital era. *Journal of Organizational Computing and Electronic Commerce*, *26*, 1–2, 147–169.

INEGI. (2015). *Censo de población 2010*. INEGI.

Meijer, A., Curtin, D., & Hillebrandt, M. (2012). Open government: connecting vision and voice. In *International Review of Administrative Sciences* (pp. 10–29). London: SAGE.

OCDE. (2016). *Open Government Data Review of Mexico: Data Reuse for Public Sector Impact and Innovation*, OECD Digital Government Studies, OECD Publishing. Retrieved from http://www.keepeek.com/Digital-Asset-Management/oecd/governance/open-government-data-review-of-mexico_9789264259270-en#page158

Olayiwola, Akinwandc, Oluwatoyosi, & Ahmed. (2016). Open Data Portals in Africa: An Analysis of Open Government Data Initiatives. *African Journal of Library Archives and Information Science*, *26*(2), 97–106.

Recursos. (2017, March 14). Retrieved from http://mxabierto.org/

Red Mexico Abierto. (2017). *Micositio de la oficina de Estrategia digital nacional del gobierno federal*. Retrieved from http://mxabierto.org/

Valenzuela, R. (2015). La transparencia colaborativa: una herramienta para gobierno abierto. Buen Gobierno para que la democracia funcione, (18), 2-18.

Welch, E. (2012). The relationship between transparent and participative government: A study of local goverments. In *International Review of Administrative Sciences* (pp. 78–93). SAGE.

Wonderlich, J. (2010). *Ten Principles for Opening Up Government Information.* Washington, DC: Sunlight Foundation.

Yu, H., & Robinson, D. (2012). *The New Ambiguity of Open Government. In Law review Discourse, no. 59* (pp. 178–208). UCLA.

Chapter 4
Open Government Data (OGD) Initiative in India:
An Empirical Analysis

Rupak Chakravarty
Panjab University, India

ABSTRACT

Open Government Data (OGD) is a relevant discussion concerning transparency in governmental procedures. The chapter examines how India has followed up on the open data policy and constituted the Open Government Data (OGD) Platform and National Data Sharing and Accessibility Policy (NDSAP) to ensure that citizens can access data generated from public-funded governmental activities. The author has conducted an empirical examination of the status of the Open Government Data initiative in India, its scope, how the programme ranks against other countries, and has evaluated the same against the parameters of Democracy Index (33 out of 165), Open Data Barometer (43 out of 100) of Open Government Data and webometric analysis. India has taken proactive steps towards releasing government data to public domain. This can be seen in the rising growth in contribution of datasets and increase in OGD literature. The NDSAP and OGD Platform can be applauded as a healthy step on the part of the Government of India towards transparency and encouraging public participation in governance.

DOI: 10.4018/978-1-5225-4987-1.ch004

INTRODUCTION

Structured data available in open format and open license for public access and use is usually termed as "Open Data," and is of prime importance in the contemporary world. Data is also one of the most valuable resources for modern governance, sharing of which enables various and non-exclusive usage for both commercial and non-commercial purposes. Licenses, however, are crucial to ensure that such data is not misused or misinterpreted (for example, by insisting on proper attribution), and that all users have the same and permanent right to use the data.

National Data Sharing and Accessibility Policy (NDSAP)

The open government data initiative was started in India with the notification in the Gazette, of the NDSAP, and was submitted to the Union Cabinet by the Department of Science and Technology, on 17th March 2012. While the appropriate open formats and related aspects for implementation of the Policy has been defined in the "NDSAP Implementation Guidelines", which was created by an inter-ministerial Task Force constituted by the National Informatics Centre, the open license for data sets published under NDSAP and through the OGD Platform remained undefined till now.

Aims and Objectives

The NDSAP intends to "provide an enabling provision and platform for proactive and open access to the data generated by various Government of India (GoI) entities. The objective of this policy is to facilitate access to GoI owned shareable data (along with its usage information) in machine readable form through wide area network all over the country in a periodically updatable manner, within the framework of various related policies, acts and rules of Government of India, thereby permitting a wider accessibility and usage by public." (Government of India, n.d.)

Scope

The NDSAP states that it "covers all data and information created, generated, collected and archived using public funds provided by Government of India directly or through authorized agencies under the various Ministries/Departments/ Organizations/Agencies and Autonomous bodies. Data sharing and access are to be based on the principles which include but are not limited to: Openness, Flexibility,

Transparency, Quality, Security and Machine-readable." (Open Data Government Platform India, n.d.)

Identification of Datasets

According to the NDSAP mandate, every Department should identify datasets as per either of the two defined categories which are the Negative List and the Open List. Datasets which are of confidential nature and could compromise security of nation if made public, come under the Negative List. Personal information comprising datasets are also placed under the Negative List. Open List consists of datasets which do not fall in the negative list. Open List datasets are further categorized by priority into high value and non high value datasets.

Formats

NDSAP recommendation on the format for datasets is that is should be in machine readable open format. To ensure uniformity and standardization, it has been advised that government data be published in any of the given formats as follows:

- CSV (Comma Separated Values)
- XLS (Spread sheet - Excel)
- ODS/OTS (Open Document Formats for Spreadsheets)
- XML (Extensive Markup Language)
- RDF (Resources Description Framework)
- KML (Keyhole Markup Language used for Maps)
- GML (Geography Markup Language)
- RSS/ATOM (Fast changing data e.g. hourly/daily)

Permissible Use of Data

According to the mandate of the NDSAP; that applies to all shareable, non-sensitive data, available either in digital or analog forms, generated using public funds by agencies under the Government of India, and subject to the conditions listed under section 4 (Terms and Conditions of Use of Data) and 7 (Termination) of the NDSAP policy document; all *users* are provided an international, royalty-free, non-exclusive license to *use, adapt, publish* (either in original, or in adapted and/or derivative forms), translate, display, add value, and create derivative works (including products and services), for all lawful commercial and non-commercial purposes, and for the duration of existence of such rights over the data or information.

Open Government Data (OGD) Platform India

The policy visualizes the proactive distribution of governmental resources which include but are not limited to datasets, apps, and tools, through the OGD Platform to foster innovation; improve delivery of government information & services besides promoting transparency, accountability and public participation in governance.

The datasets released on the Data Portal India receive the advantage of visualization, enhanced discover-ability, and usage. By making data available in machine-readable formats, the OGD Platform also facilitates collaboration and cooperation between the government and the public.

Content Moderation and Approval Policy (CMAP)

India's Open Government Data Platform is a repository for a large number of datasets meticulously divided into catalogues. All the datasets are made available in adherence with the principles of Open Data Movement, which mandate easy access for further reuse in machine readable format. The datasets on the platform are primarily sourced from the huge amounts of data which are amassed by various government institutions for administrative purposes, and put together in machine readable format.

In accordance with the NDSAP, the various governmental departments and ministries are to appoint Chief Data Officers and contributors from their respective departments to become the point person for data sourcing, following which the data provided by the Chief Data Officer and the contributor, is published on the platform after due moderation.

The Content management here goes through three tier process which includes:

1. Data moderation i.e. Data Management System,
2. Content moderation i.e. Content Management System and
3. Engagement with the larger user base or public taking into account their feedback and requirements i.e. Visitor Relations Manager.

This particular platform in essence provides its user with important datasets of the various government departments without comprising its original value. The moderation process is confined to formatting and ensuring that the datasets are made available in concurrence with the principles of Open Government Data, where no compromise or change is made to the original values of the datasets which are provided by the data owners. The process of releasing the datasets into Open format creates the base for standardization in this particular platform.

Content Review Policy (CRP)

Open Government Data Platform has a very robust policy of review. This is carried through routine testing of web pages and the content. Since this is a platform which boasts of datasets and catalogues, the Project Management Unit (PMU) is frequently in the process of updating and reviewing the same, in order to provide updated datasets to its users. The feedback and engagement policy with the users presents itself as an effective measure of review-and-check towards the content on the platform. Monitoring of the Platform is done on a regular basis.

OGD DATASETS

This section will focus on the GoI initiated mobile apps status in various sectors like agriculture, government, health, marketing, environment, etc. It will also present the statistical analyses of central publication metrics and data visualizations.

The OGD India datasets have been viewed approximately 11 million times, and have been downloaded 4.5 million times. 110 Chief Data Officers (CDO) are contributing significantly towards maintaining and sustaining the OGD platform. The main role and responsibility of a Chief Data Officer is to "lead the open data initiative of Department/Organization, nominate Data Contributors, to ensure that the datasets being published are in compliance with NDSAP, periodically monitor the release of datasets as per predefined schedule, take action upon suggestions about new datasets made public through the OGD Platform" (Government of India, n.d.). There are 444 APIs and 1084 visualization available at OGD platform.

Figure 1 shows the growth of datasets from 2012 to 2017 which shows a steady upward growth. Figure 2 shows the number of datasets contributed in the year 2017 from January to May. Total number of datasets submitted by 105 contributing departments (state - 0.18%; central - 9.82%) is 100092. These datasets are organized into 4133 catalogues. Figure 1 depicts an increasing trend in terms of new datasets added to the OGD portal during 2012 to 2017. While contribution from central department has continued in 2017, no datasets have been submitted by the State governments till May 2017. Total datasets downloads is 4.5 million, while total views of the same is 10.94 million. The dominating file format is CSV (60538 files) followed by Excel (20009 files), and XML (3220 files). Total number of registered users of the OGD platform are 124039, while the portal has received 1590 suggestions for new datasets inclusion. Total APIs on the platform are 444, and OGD has launched 23 mobile apps. The OGD portal offers 1084 highly informative visualizations apart from 12 infographics.

Figure 1. OGD dataset resources 2012-2017

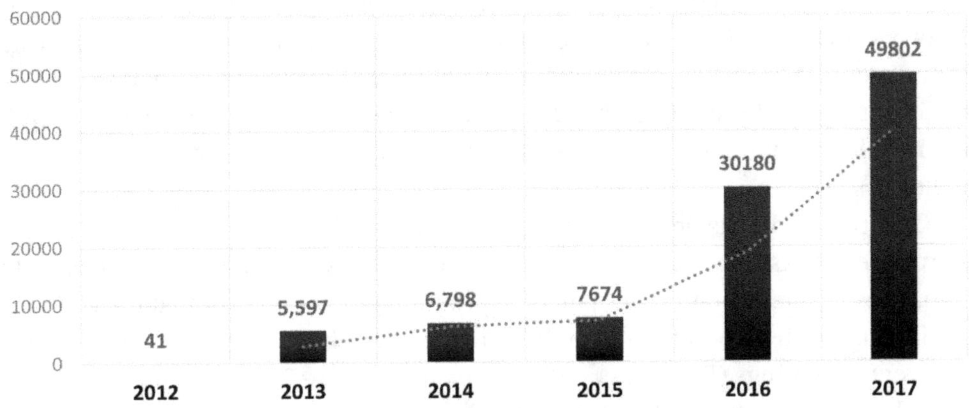

Figure 2. Datasets Statistics 2017

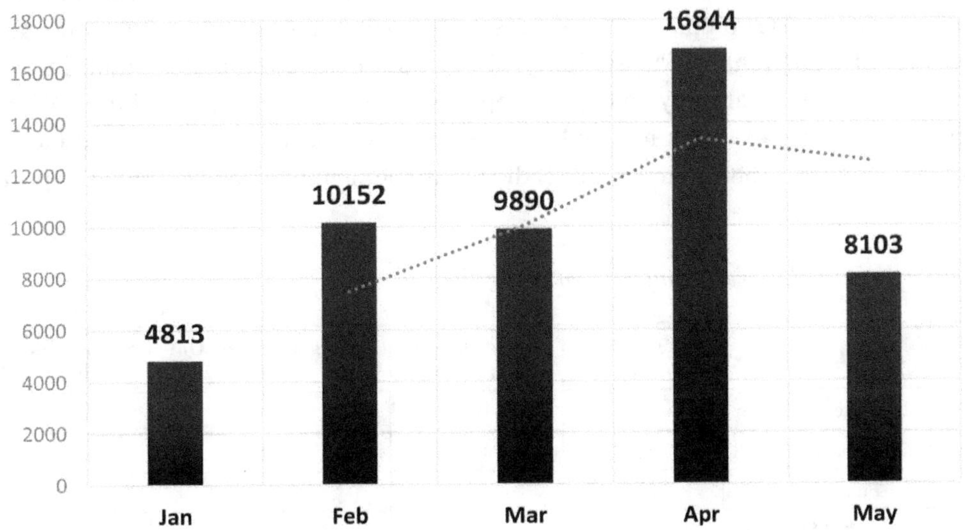

OPEN GOVERNMENT DATA (OGD) STATUS OF INDIA

The status of India and other countries pertaining to Open Government Data (OGD) has been studied by the Open Data Barometer (ODB) -2016. The relative position of these countries has been analyzed from the Democracy Index. OGD status was also compared with Corruption Perceptions Index (CPI) published by the Transparency International (TI).

Produced by the World Wide Web Foundation as a collaborative work of the Open Data for Development (OD4D) network and with the support of the Omidyar Network, the Open Data Barometer (ODB) (4th edition) aims to uncover the true prevalence and impact of open data initiatives around the world. It analyses global trends, and provides comparative data on countries and regions using an in-depth methodology that combines contextual data, technical assessments and secondary indicators.

Covering 115 jurisdictions in the fourth edition (July 2015 to June 2016), the Barometer ranks governments on three components: Readiness for open data initiatives, Implementation of open data programmes and impact that open data is having on business, politics and civil society with each of these components given different weightings (Readiness - 35%, Implementation - 35% and Impacts - 30%).

Table 1 clearly depicts that as per the Open Data Barometer (ODB) values, UK is currently positioned at the top (score = 100) in the ODB rankings followed by Canada, France & USA. Both South Korea and Australia are placed at rank 5 (score = 81) followed by New Zealand, Japan, Netherlands and Norway. It is interesting to note that under the component Readiness, France has got the highest score although its overall ODB rank is 3rd. Similarly, Korea has secured the highest rank in the Emerging Impact category among the top 10 countries of the ODB rankings. With overall score of 43, India has ranked 33 with 81 countries below it in the OGD status. It obtained 68, 32 and 35 in readiness, implementation and emerging impact

Table 1. Open Data Barometer world ranking

ODB Rank	Country	Readiness Out of 100	Implementation Out of 100	Emerging Impact Out of 100	Score Out of 100
1	United Kingdom	**99**	**100**	94	100
2	Canada	**96**	87	82	90
3	France	**100**	71	88	85
4	United States of America	96	71	80	82
5	South Korea	95	59	**100**	81
5	Australia	85	78	78	81
7	New Zealand	92	58	**99**	79
8	Japan	84	60	89	75
8	Netherlands	94	64	68	75
10	Norway	77	71	73	74
33	INDIA	68	32	35	**43**

respectively. Figure 3 depicts the Implementation parameters with respect to status of Indian OGD. It can be noted that India has scored highest (80) in the Openness of primary/secondary education performance data followed by data related to Budget (65) and Census data (60).

Figure 3 describes the implementation scores of India are provided in detail. India scored most in the Primary or Secondary Education Performance data (80). In figure 4 as can be seen, under the category Readiness, OGD regarding government policies has scored the highest (77) closely followed by Government action, citizens & civil rights and entrepreneur & business.

Figure 5 explains the OGD impact, and the impact on the economy has been found to be the highest on the Indian economy followed by social and political impact.

DEMOCRACY INDEX

The Democracy Index is an index compiled by the UK-based Economist Intelligence Unit that measures the state of democracy in 167 countries, of which 166 are sovereign states (Democracy Index, n.d.). 165 are UN member states. The index is based on 60 indicators grouped in five different categories. Based on their scores on a range

Figure 3. OGD status India: implementation

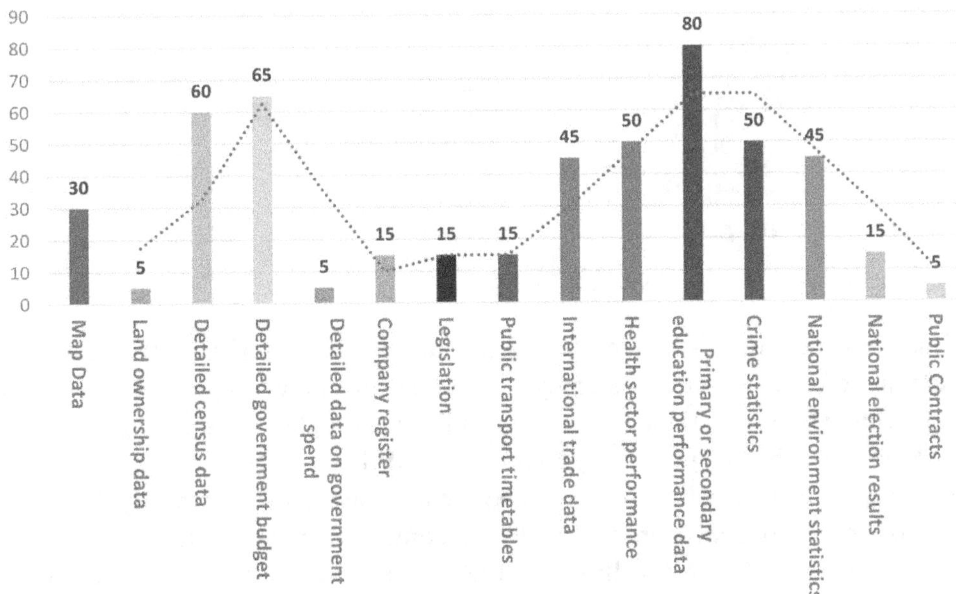

Figure 4. OGD status India: readiness

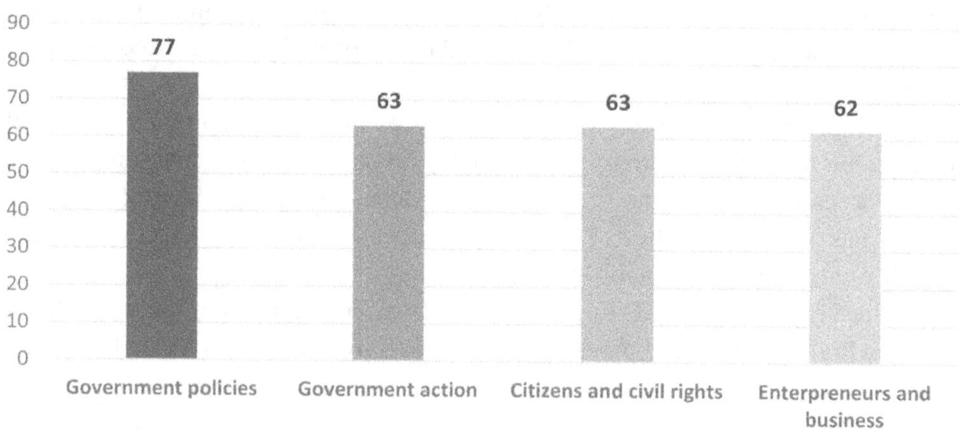

Figure 5. OGD status India: Impact

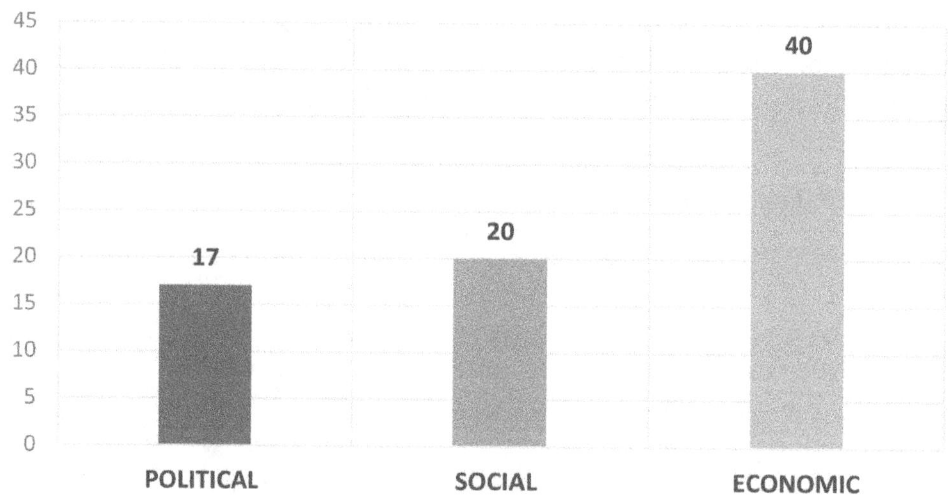

of indicators within these categories, each country is then itself classified as one of four types of regime: "full democracy"; "flawed democracy"; "hybrid regime"; and "authoritarian regime". Table 2 reveals that India scored highest in the electoral process (9.58) followed by and pluralism; civil liberties (9.12), functioning of government (7.5), political participation (7.22) and political culture (5.63). It ranked 33 out 165 nations with the overall score of 7.81 which comes under flawed democracies (6≤ score < 8). Table 3 however illustrates the interesting fact that, India's OGD rank is 33 - very close to the democracy index rank of 32.

Table 2. Democracy Index scores

Country	Rank	Overall Score	Electoral Process	Functioning of Government	Political Participation	Political Culture	Civil Liberties
Norway	1	9.93	10	9.64	10	10	10
Iceland	2	9.5	10	8.93	8.89	10	9.71
Sweden	3	9.39	9.58	9.64	8.33	10	9.41
USA	21	7.98	9.17	7.14	7.22	8.13	8.24
India	**32**	**7.81**	**9.58**	**7.5**	**7.22**	**5.63**	**9.12**
Sierra Leone	108	4.55	6.58	1.86	2.78	6.25	5.29
Pakistan	111	4.33	6	5.36	2.78	2.5	5
China	136	3.14	0	4.64	3.33	6.25	1.47

Table 3. Comparison of OGD rank, Democracy Index rank, and CPI rank

OGD Countries	OGD Rank	Democracy Index Rank	CPI Rank
UK	1	16	10
Canada	2	6	09
France	3	24	23
USA	4	21	18
Korea	5	24	52
Australia	6	10	13
New Zealand	7	4	01
Japan	8	20	20
Netherlands	9	12	08
Norway	10	1	06
INDIA	33	32	79

Correlation Matrix

Table 4 shows the correlation matrix.

Correlation Plot

Note: There is a negative relationship between the variables.

Table 4. Correlation matrix

Correlation Table			
Ranks	**Tests**	**OGD Rank**	**Democracy Index Rank**
Open Government Data (OGD) Rank	Pearson's r	—	-0.387
	p-value	—	0.269*
	Spearman's rho	—	-0.407
	p-value	—	0.243*
	Kendall's tau B	—	-0.315
	p-value	—	0.209*
Democracy Index Rank	Pearson's r		—
	p-value		—
	Spearman's rho		—
	p-value		—
	Kendall's tau B		—
	p-value		—
*p < .05 (α)			

Figure 6. Correlation plot

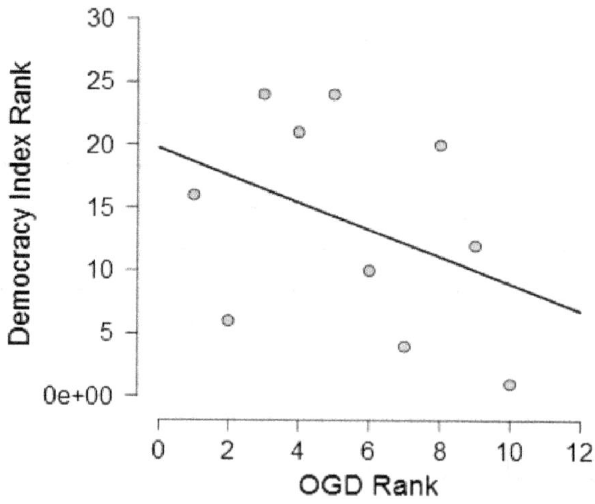

Figure 7. Correlation plot (supplement)

$r = -0.387$

$\rho = -0.407$

$\tau = -0.315$

In most sciences, results yielding a p-value of .05 are considered on the threshold (cut-off) of statistical significance. If the p-value is under .01, results are considered statistically significant and if it's below .005 they are considered highly statistically significant. In the present case, the table 4, and figures 6 explains that P-value > α ($\alpha = .05$), indicating that the correlation is not statistically significant. Figure 7 is supplement to the data analyzed. Further correlation (Pearson, Kendall, Spearman) found to be negative indicating a weak association between the variables. Thus, there is no evidence for relationship between Open Government Data (OGD) Rank and Democracy Index Rank.

WEBOMETRIC ANALYSIS

Webometrics is the study of web based content with primarily quantitative methods for social science research goals using techniques which are not specific to one field of the study (Thelwall, 2009). It is concerned with measuring units of the web such as web sites, web pages, words in web pages, hyperlinks and web search engine results. Webometrics is a quantitative study of web-related phenomena and webometric studies can be applied to the web with commercial search engines creating raw data and the discipline appears to be widely accepted by the academia along with the term Cybermetrics (Shukla & Tripathi, 2015). One of the efficient methods to conduct webometric analysis is through the application of web analysers. Some of the prominently known web analyzers are Sitebeam, Site Analyzer, GT Matrix, Ahrefs and Woorank.

In this section of the chapter, the Open Government Data (OGD) India Website was tested by using the web analyzer Nibbler.

Results and Findings

Figure 8 highlights Accessibility, Experience, Marketing, Technology and Overall score distribution of Open Government Data. The website scored 9(20%) out of 10 in Accessibility. The Accessibility test helps to access the website through Mobile and disabled users. It scored 9.6 (22%) out of 10 in Experience Test which depicts that users of this website are satisfied with the website and its Content. The Marketing Test scored 9.5 (21%) out of 10 which focusing the popularity of the website. Table 5 gives details on the examination.

Nibbler has been tested on 18 tests where the highest score i.e. 10 out of 10 were scored by 11 tests comprising of Printability, Metatags, URL format, Facebook page, Mobile, Twitter, Incoming Links, Analytics, Headings, Page Titles, Freshness. This indicates that OGD website is excellent for Printability, its URL is easy to remember.

Table 5. Webometric analysis

	Category	Description	Score
i. I	Accessibility	How accessible the website is to mobile and disabled users	9.0
ii. II	Experience	How satisfying the website is likely to be for users	9.6
iii. III	Marketing	How well marketed and popular the website is	9.5
iv. IV	Technology	How well designed and built the website is	7.5
Overall		The overall score for this website.	**8.9**

Figure 8. OGD website score distribution

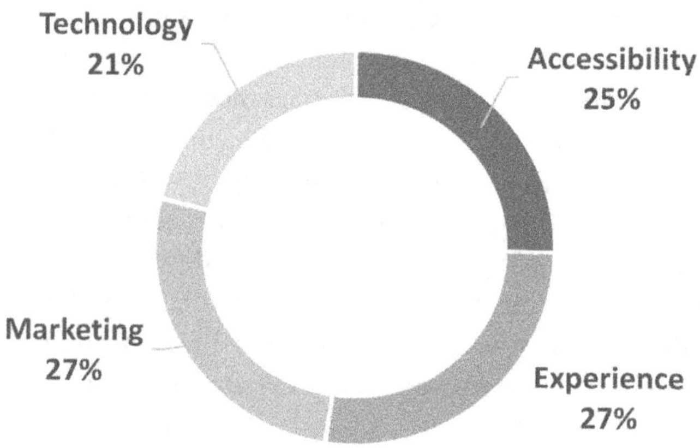

Figure 9 explains the webometric analysis conducted on the website. All the elements i.e. page description, keywords, author the document, etc. of the OGD website are adequately placed. The website is fully equipped and accessible through Mobile. It has an account in Facebook as well as Twitter. It has also scored highest in Analytics test which means that the website has access of the visitors counts. The website has proper headings and page titles. It has also scored highest in Freshness Test which means it is updated frequently. The website scored slightly low i.e 9 out of 10 in Internal Links and Amount of Content. In Popularity Test OGD Website secured only 4 out of 10 whereas in Images test it scored 3 out of 10 that means the heavy images of the website are difficult to download. The website scored least in Code Quality i.e. it scored only 1 out of 10 this means the website has poor quality code which is a big hindrance in rapid speed of the website.

Figure 9. Website score components

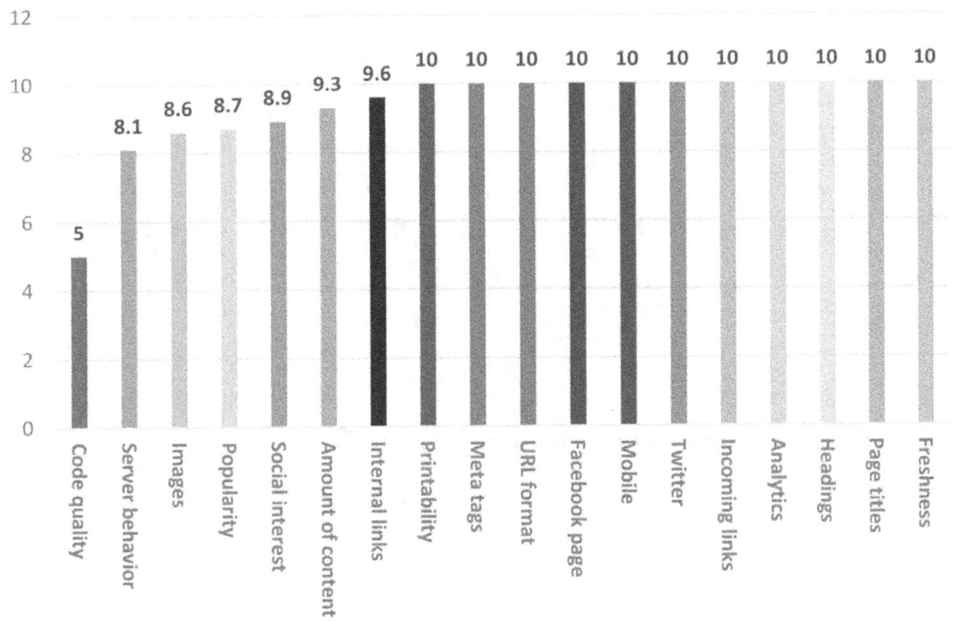

OGD LITERATURE TRENDS

To trace the growth of literature pertaining to ODG globally, the database Scopus was search with the query string TITLE-ABS-KEY (*"open government"*). 1035 document results were retrieved which were analyzed with various parameters. The period covered includes 1967-2017.

The figure 10 reveals that there was very little growth in Open Government Data generation from 1967 to 1997. The growth of Open Government Data started picking up in the time period 1997-1999 which was again followed by stagnation phase till 2005. Open Government Data literature growth gained momentum after 2005. Then again we could see the fall on OGD literature from 2007 till 2009. There was a remarkable growth in OGD literature from 2009 to 2016. First five months of 2017 have also witnessed an increase in OGD growth.

The figure 11 indicates the literature growth pattern of Open Government Data from 2005-2017. The figure reveals that there were only 8 publications in 2005 which rose to 13 in the year 2006. Between the year 2006 to 2009 there was an erratic growth in the number of publications. There was a substantial growth from 2009 to 2010 with 43 publications contributed to OGD. Remarkable rise in OGD can be

Figure 10. OGD literature growth pattern

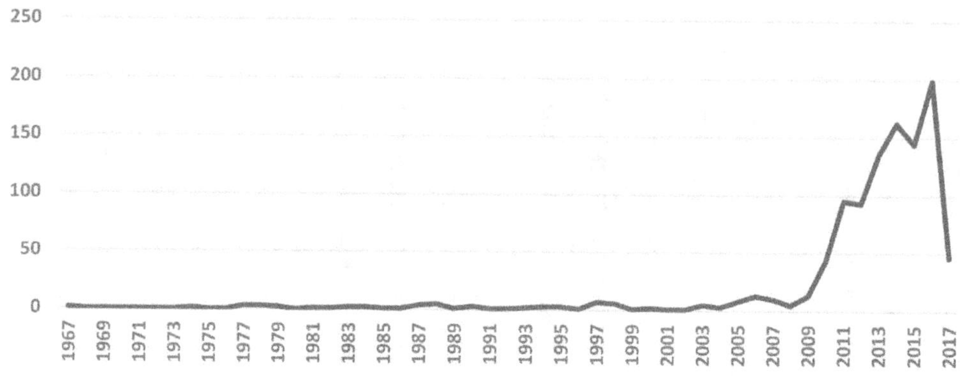

Figure 11. OGD literature growth pattern 2005-2017

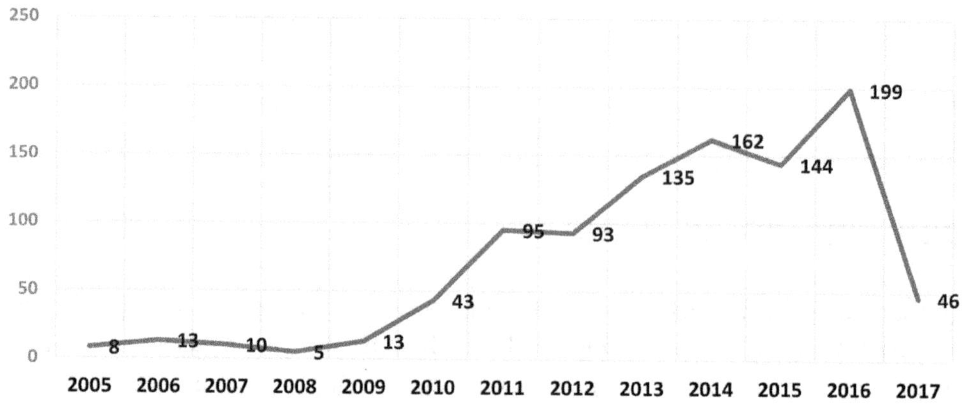

seen in the year 2011 with more than a twofold increase in publications which were uploaded in OGD portal for public use. The year 2012 witnessed a slight decline in the number of publications as compared to 2011. In the year 2013 the number of publications fairly increased to 135 followed by 162 in the year 2014. There was again a decline in the year 2015 as the uploaded publications fell to 144. The year 2016 saw a steep rise in the number of publications as it rose from 144 to 199. 46 publications can be seen in the first 5 months of the year 2017.

Top Five Journals per Year

Figure 12 shows the top 5 journals which contributed documents in OGD. Government Information Quarterly as shown by the figure is oldest Journal which contributed

Figure 12. Top five journals per year

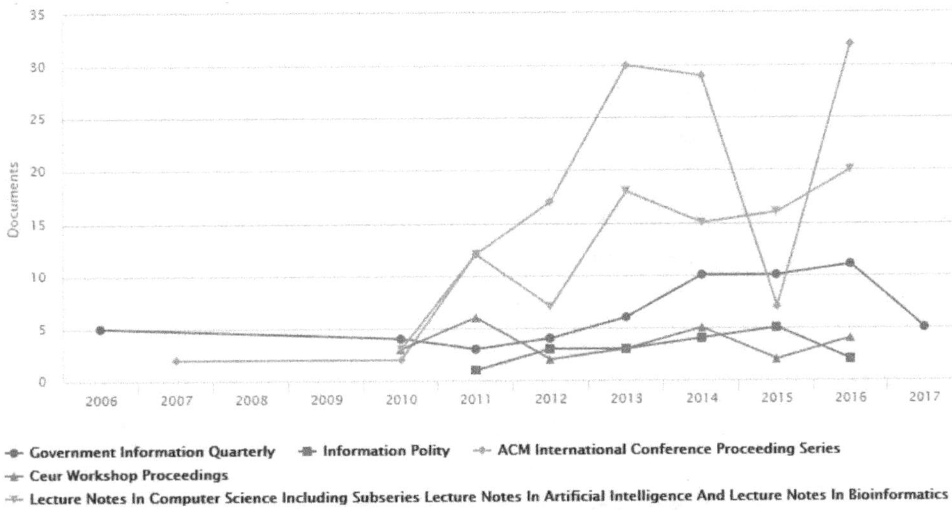

**For a more accurate representation see the electronic version.*

5 documents in OGD portal in the year 2006. There was a decline in the number of documents from 2006 to 2011. The period between 2012 to 2014 saw a growth in the literature in OGD which again fell minutely in 2015. Again the year 2016 witnessed a minor rose in the number of publications. Information Polity started its contributions in the year 2011 which gained slight momentum from 2012 to 2015 followed by the fall in 2016. ACM International Conference Proceeding Series started its contribution in the year 2007, remained stagnant till 2010. Steep rise in the number of publications can be seen in the year 2011 which shows remarkable growth till 2013. There was a slight downfall in the number of publications in 2014 which led to steep fall in 2015. The number of publications rose tremendously in 2016. Ceur Workshop Proceedings and Lecture Notes in Computer Science Including Subseries Lecture Notes in Artificial Intelligence and Lecture Notes in Bioinformatics started their contributions in 2010. Both the journals showed an erratic growth with lesser number of documents contributed by Ceur workshop proceedings as compared to Lecture Notes in Computer Science.

Top Authors in the Area of OGD

Figure 13 depicts the contributions of top 10 authors towards Open Government Data. Janssen, M. has contributed the most with 24 publications to his credit followed by Zuiderwijk with 19 publications. The least number of publications amounting to 7 were contributed by Wimmer and Sayogo as shown by the figure.

Figure 13. Top authors in the area of OGD

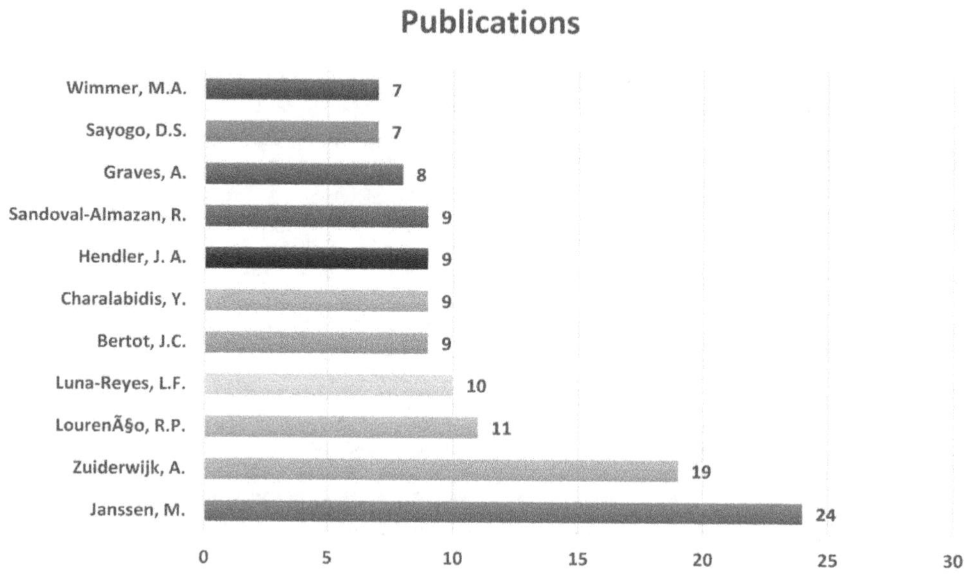

The figure 14 explains about the institutions and their publication output towards open government data. Delft University of Technology tops the list of Institutions with 31 publications contributed in Open Government Data. University at Albany occupied second slot with 27 publications. Universidade de Sao Paulo contributed 19 documents and holds the third position. University of Maryland and Researcher Polytechnic Institute contributed 15 and 12 publications respectively. There are 9 contributions made by three universities, 5 Universities made 8 contributions, 10 Universities made 7 contributions and 6 Universities contributed 6 documents.

Figure 15 indicates the contributions made in Open Government Data by top 10 contributing nations. United States has emerged as the top contributor with 232 publications coming forth from its authors. It is followed by United Kingdom with 88 publications. Spain (66), Netherlands (59), Brazil (58), Germany (57), Italy (44), Austria (32), Mexico (30) and Greece (27) were among the top ten nations in terms of contributions to OGD.

Figure 16 throws light on the contributions made by India in comparison with other Nations. United States leads the list of nations in terms of contributions of publications while India hold 20th position with only 14 publications in terms of its contributions to Open Government Data.

Figure 14. Institution wise publication output to OGD

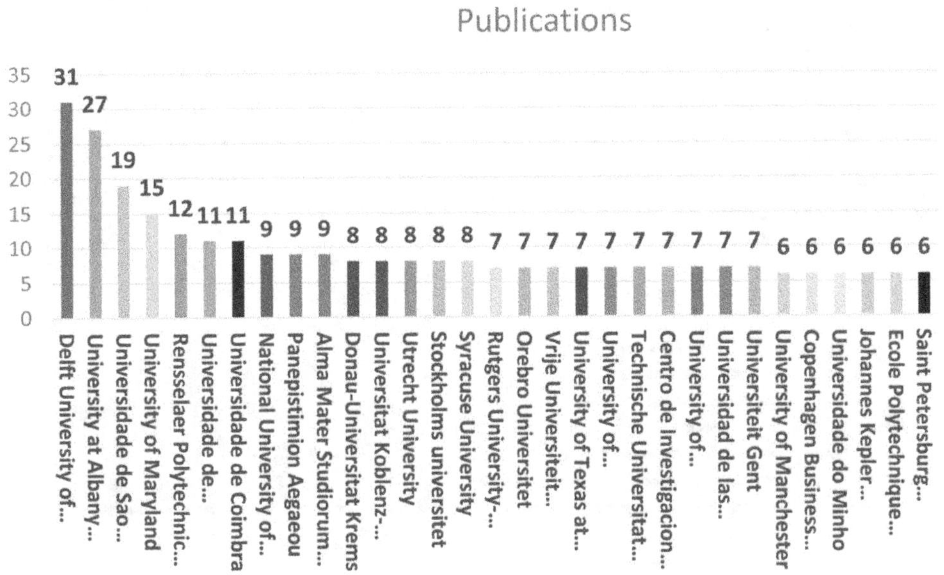

Figure 15. Country wise publication output to OGD

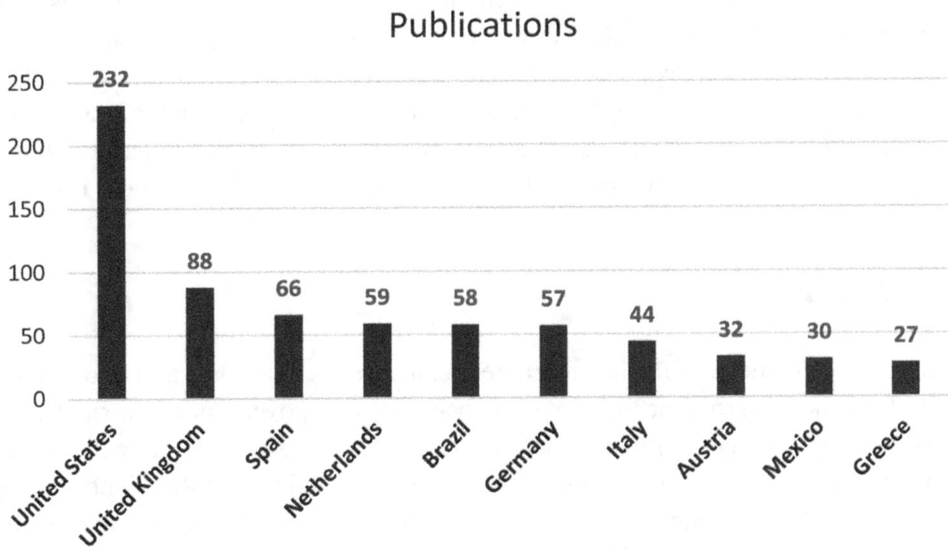

Figure 16. Top contributing countries

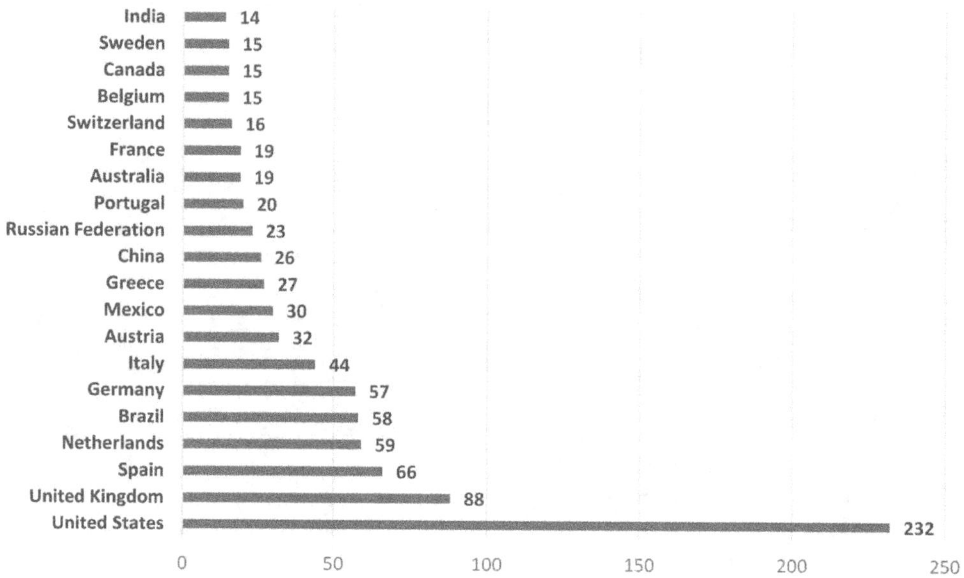

Publication Types

The figure 17 explains the preferred document type in which the contributions have been made. The figure reveals that Conference Proceedings have been the most sought after document type i.e., maximum publications have come in the form of conference papers followed by the article publications in the journals. Other forms of document types like book chapter, article in press, review, editorial, letters, notes were also among preferred modes which made way to Open Government Data.

CONCLUSION

A democracy is successful when its citizens can have access to data and information as to how the government functions. Transparency in governance is a right unto citizens that every government should provide. Corrupt governments will seek to hide the data and information, though it may be generated from public funds. Thus, for successful governance to occur, making governmental data open is part of the mandate. The Government of India has set up Open Government Data Platform and the National Data Sharing and Accessibility Policy towards this same objective. The author examined how much has been achieved under the OGD mission.

Figure 17. Preferred document type for contributions made

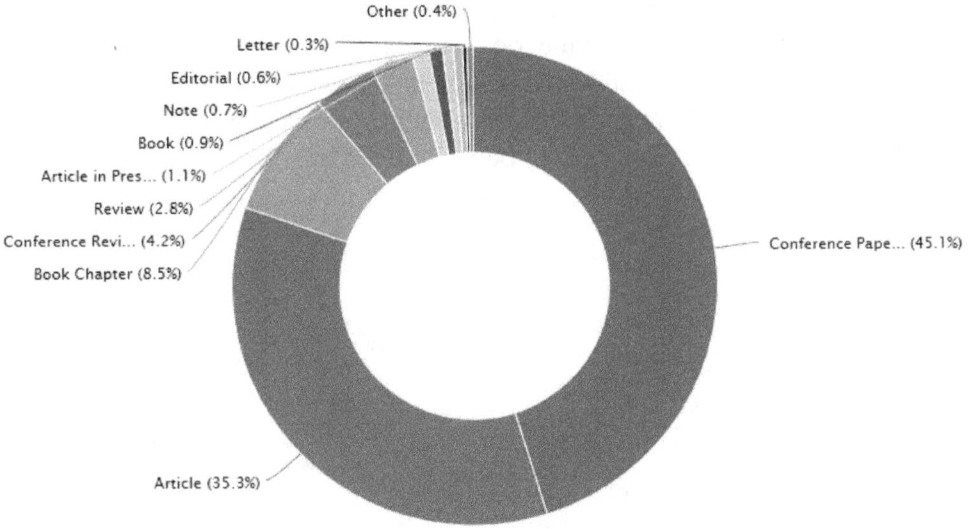

It was found that Indians were actively visiting the Platform and downloading the open datasets. There are presently 124039 registered users on the platform, and 1590 suggestions have been made for new dataset inclusions. The author found a steady upward growth of datasets contribution in the period from 2012-2017. the OGD has launched 23 mobile apps, 1084 informative data visualizations, and 12 infographics. The status of OGD in India has been examined for the study.

India scored 43 out of 100 in the Open Data Barometer. It was found that India scored highest (80) in the openness of primary/secondary education performance data followed by data related to Budget (65) and Census data (60). Under the category readiness, OGD regarding government policies has scored the highest (77) closely followed by government action, citizens and civil rights, and entrepreneur and business. The OGD impact on the economy was the highest on Indian economy followed by social and political impact. India ranked 33 out of the 165 nations which comes under flawed democracies category as per the Democracy Index. But India scored highest in the electoral process, followed by pluralism; civil liberties, functioning of government, political participation and political culture. The author examined the OGD India Platform using web analyzer Nibbler, which revealed the website's score to be a respectable 8.9 out of 10. The study examined the growth of literature in the subject and the journals, authors, countries contributing towards it. India does not have a substantial amount of contributions when compared to countries like UK and US. This needs to be rectified.

To conclude, it can be agreed upon that there is active interest for the development of OGD in government sector itself, and this is showing itself in the growth in numbers of contributions and number of citizens who are actively using the open data. Overall, this shows a healthy sign of a democracy where steps are being taken for transparency, and where citizens are remaining informed of governmental data. But along with this, there is a need to boost for literature on OGD in India.

REFERENCES

Democracy Index. (n.d.) Retrieved from http://www.eiu.com/topic/democracy-index

Government of India. (2012, March 17). National Data Sharing and Accessibility Policy (NDSAP) 2012. *Gazette of India.*

Government of India. (n.d.a). *Open Data Government Platform India*. Retrieved from https://data.gov.in/

Government of India. (n.d.b). *National Data Sharing and Accessibility Policy (NDSAP)*. Retrieved from https://india.gov.in/national-data-sharing-and-accessibility-policy-ndsap

Janssen, K. (2012). Open government data and the right to information: Opportunities and obstacles. *The Journal of Community Informatics*, *8*(2).

Janssen, M., Charalabidis, Y., & Zuiderwijk, A. (2012). Benefits, adoption barriers and myths of open data and open government. *Information Systems Management*, *29*(4), 258–268. doi:10.1080/10580530.2012.716740

Manish, S. (2017, January 27). India improves rank in democracy index; civil liberties curtailed: EIU. *Business Standard.* Retrieved from http://mybs.in/2USj08G

Papińska-Kacperek, J., & Polańska, K. (2015). Open Government Data initiatives. *Collegium of Economic Analysis Annals*, (38), 191-202.

Shim, D. C., & Eom, T. H. (2008). E-government and anti-corruption: Empirical analysis of international data. *International Journal of Public Administration*, *31*(3), 298–316. doi:10.1080/01900690701590553

Thelwall, M. (2009). Introduction to webometrics: Quantitative web research for the social sciences. *Synthesis Lectures on Information Concepts, Retrieval, and Services, 1*(1), 1-116.

Transparency International. (n.d.). *Corruption Perceptions Index*. Retrieved from https://www.transparency.org/research/cpi/overview

Ubaldi, B. (2013). Open government data: Towards empirical analysis of open government data initiatives. *OECD Working Papers on Public Governance*, (22), 0-1.

KEY TERMS AND DEFINITIONS

Democracy Index: It is the index compiled by UK based Economist Intelligence Unit (EIU) body that categorizes and ranks countries according to how democratic their governance is.

National Data Sharing and Accessibility Policy (NDSAP): This is a Government of India policy to enable constitution, enactment, and conduct of open government data dissemination to public in a standard and uniform format.

Open Data: Open Data is data that can publicly available for use without any restrictions of copyright or license.

Open Government Data: Open Government Data is datasets generated by governmental ministries, departments, agencies from public funds, which are made available to all for access, use, and adaptation without restriction.

OGD Platform: Government of India started the open government data initiative according to the NDSAP mandate on the publicly accessible platform of OGD Platform India.

Web Analyzer: Web analyzer is a tool used for assessing websites on a set range of parameters.

Webometrics: Webometrics is the research area concerned with measurements of the World Wide Web in terms of number of links, webpages, structure of web, and usage patterns.

Section 3
Financial Barriers to OGI

Chapter 5
Openness of Public Financial Management:
Assessing an Emerging Economy

Salah Uddin Rajib
Jahangirnagar University, Bangladesh

Mahfuzul Hoque
University of Dhaka, Bangladesh

ABSTRACT

This chapter reviews the open government model and assesses the position of public financial management (PFM) of an emerging economy, Bangladesh. Open government (OG) is an emerging issue that is identified as the prerequisite of ensuring the accountability and transparency. From different research platforms, OG is suggested to pertain to the development goals of the country as well. Therefore, it has an importance to the emerging economy. This chapter investigates the openness of public financial management (PFM) through the theory of accountability, transparency, and open government model in Bangladesh. It seems that though the ease of accessibility of government data is demanded in the developing economy for accountability, transparency, and development, the situation of public financial management is far reaching from the demand in Bangladesh. The open government data platform and different PFM agencies are disclosing very little information regarding the public finance. The chapter argues to strengthen the basic structure of opening up the PFM.

DOI: 10.4018/978-1-5225-4987-1.ch005

INTRODUCTION

In market economy, the public administration is becoming complex regarding the scope and multi-factorial tasks. Public administration is accused of poor performance since long ago as well (e.g. Bevan & Hood, 2006). Therefore, the stockholders always demand the accountability and transparency of public sector. The situation is acute in developing nations who are striving for economic development, corruption reduction and poverty alleviation. Various development partners and donor agencies are demanding the accountability and transparency of public sector. Therefore, accountability and transparency of public sector have received the concentration in many research platforms (e.g. Romzek & Dubnick, 1998; Bertot et al. 2007; Bovens et al. 2014; World Bank, 2015). The concept of New Public Management (NPM) contributes to this issue which aims to modernize and increase the efficiency of public sector (Adhikari et al. 2012; Vries & Nemec, 2013). In these issues, Open Government (OG) is recognized as a prerequisite of accountability and transparency (Bovens et al. 2014; Lurenco et al. 2017).

It is agreed that the term public accountability is involved with at least two features (Bovens et al. 2014; Rajib et al. 2017). First, the term public relates to the openness, i.e., it is accessible to the citizens (Bovens et al. 2014). Second, public refers to the public sector. Traditionally, the term 'accountability' is originated from the term 'bookkeeping' or 'accounting'. Therefore, public financial management (PFM) of a country is assumed to face the demand of accountability and transparency. Consequently, it is expected to open the PFM to the citizen to ensure the accountability and transparency.

The researches on open government are seen extensively during the last few decades (e.g., Chandler, 1998; Baum & Di Maio, 2000; Layne & Lee, 2001; Evans & Campos, 2013; Hellberg & Hedstrom, 2015; Adu et al. 2016; Maseh & Katuu, 2017; Lurenco et al. 2017). Where developed countries are taking initiatives to open the government data by self, developing nations are doing it with the association of donor agencies and development partners very often. With the aim of digitization, the Bangladesh government has taken various initiatives to develop the open government data (OGD) practice. The development partners and the donor agencies are contributing to these efforts of Bangladesh.

In different research platforms the benefit of open government data has been noticed. It is mentioned that open government allows citizens to monitor data stream which improves the accountability and transparency of government (DPADM, 2017). Citizen accessibility in public finance/accounting is investigated in previous research as well (e.g., Perez et al. 2005). However, to capitalize the benefits of open government, government require huge investment like new skill, train employees, advanced technologies and upgrade network infrastructure and others (Lee & Kwak,

2012). Therefore, failure of open government initiatives can cause huge financial loss as well as goodwill of the government (see Kim & Kim, 2003; Dada, 2006). Hence, the public financial management of Bangladesh which is under the pressure of different stakeholders to ensure accountability demands investigation to explore the current scenario and identify the area of development.

The aim of this chapter is fourfold. First, methodology of the study has been disclosed. Second, origin of the research and literature is reviewed. Third, the current status of Bangladesh regarding the open public financial management has been explored. Forth, a constructive discussion has been presented.

RESEARCH METHODOLOGY

The aim of this chapter is to assess the position of PFM of Bangladesh regarding the openness and to draw attention on the area of development. To assess the position of Bangladesh previous proposed model on the open government has been considered (e.g., Lee & Kwak, 2012; Kalampokis et al. 2011).To conduct the study various documents and websites related to public financial management of Bangladesh have been used. We have investigated the strategic plans related to the PFM, reports, white papers, websites, blogs, pages of social media run by the concerned authorities, memorandums of the related authorities, Acts/Laws of the country, reports of international organizations (e.g., United Nations) and others. Analyses of the evidences and conclusions have been drawn by ensuring the ethical standard of the research (e.g., Rajib & Mou, 2014).

A number of open government (OG) models have been developed and proposed by the scholars (e.g., Layne & Lee, 2001; Siau & Long, 2005; Andersen & Henriksen, 2006; Gottschalk, 2009; Klievink & Janssen, 2009; Di Maio, 2010; Kalampokis et al. 2011; Valdes et al. 2011; Lee & Kwak, 2012; Evans & Campos, 2012). But, it is mentioned that there is no dominant model to assess open government (Sandoval-Almazan & Gil-Garcia, 2016). Although there are models, all the models are accused of some limitations. Among all the models of open government, maturity perspective open models have received more concentration along with their limitations. Therefore, considering the scenario PFM scenario, a maturity model developed by Lee and Kwak (2012) is used in this study to assess the position of PFM of Bangladesh.

It seems logical to notice that Bangladesh just has launched the open government data portal (http://data.gov.bd/) to disclose all the information of the government. However, investigation finds that the portal disclose very few information regarding the PFM. Therefore, all the PFM related agencies of Bangladesh along with the open government data portal of Bangladesh has been investigated.

ORIGIN OF RESEARCH

Public accountability and the open government are the premise of this study. Therefore, theory of accountability (Bovens, 2007) and the open government maturity model (Lee & Kwak, 2012) has been integrated to attain the objective of this study.

Theory of Accountability

Bovens (2007) defines accountability from the perspective of actor and forum. It is defined as a relationship between the actor and a forum. In the relationship, the actor has an obligation to explain or to justify his or her conduct to a forum. The forum can raise questions and can pass judgment as well. Consequently, the actor can face consequences on his/her activities. This relationship can be traced to the relationship between the government and the citizen. Government has an obligation like an actor to his/her citizens.

Bovens (2007) search the answer of four questions to set the framework of accountability regarding various components contained within the concept of accountability. They are –

- The first question pertain to accountability is *to whom* the account to be rendered?
- The second question is *who should* render the account?
- The third question is about *what is* account to be rendered?
- The forth question regards that of *why* the actor feels compelled to render account?

In this chapter, it has been tried to identify the position of Bangladesh, and identify the area of development regarding the above questions and open government maturity model. In previous researches, it is found that a number of researches have used the Bovens (2007) theory of accountability in the research of public accountability and openness (e.g., Linders & Wilson, 2011; Wasike, 2016; Lourenco et al. 2017).

Open Government Model

To assess the openness of government, a number of models have been developed and a number of investigations have been conducted accordingly (e.g., e.g., Lee & Kwak, 2012; Kalampokis et al. 2011; Evans and Campos, 2012; Valdes et al. 2011; Layne & Lee, 2001; Andersen & Henriksen, 2006; Gottschalk, 2009; Klievink & Janssen, 2009; Di Maio 2010; Siau & Long, 2005). As it has been mentioned earlier, though a number of models have been developed, there is no dominant model to assess the openness of government as well as PFM. However, it is seen that maturity perspective models have received more concentration along their limitations (Sandoval-Almazan & Gil-Garcia, 2016).

Considering the situation of Bangladesh, fair practice of PFM in the world (e.g., Ministry of Finance of Macedonia) and open government models, model offered by Lee & Kwak (2012) is selected for this study. Lee & Kwak (2012) have developed the Open government model based on the U.S. federal health sector. They offered 5 stages in the models that are suggested to achieve gradually. Model of Lee & Kwak (2012) is presented in figure 1.

Model of Lee & Kwak (2012) is interchangeable with the other models to an extent as well (e.g., Layne & Lee, 2001; Klievink & Janssen, 2009; Gottschalk 2009). Level 1 of Lee and Kwak (2012) model assert on the basic structure of government agency to broadcast the information to the public. Minimal online visibilities of information of the government agencies, limited catalogue data to the public, one-way and static communications are the characteristics of government agency lying in level 1. Level 1 does not provide any means for the public engagement in the agency's activities as well. It is assumed that an agency lying in this level has a website. The agency is assumed to disclose information through the website. By counting the number of visitors, number of pages viewed and others, the government agency can assess the performance of the website. The website is rarely updated in this level.

Transparency of the data is the main concern in level 2 of the model offered by Lee and Kwak (2012). Lee and Kwak (2012) have addressed this level as the basic step to open the government to the citizen. Social media can be used in this level to increase the interaction between the government agencies and the citizens. However, its use may be limited (Lee & Kwak, 2012). Agencies are responsible to perform two main task at this level – 1) identifying hig-value, high-impact data for the public

Figure 1. Open Government Maturity Model (OGMM)
(Source: Lee & Kwak, 2012)

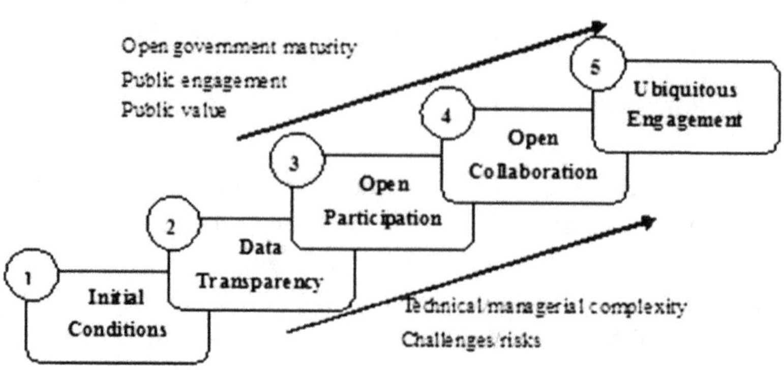

and 2) Improving and assuring the data quality in terms of accuracy, consistency, and timeliness. This level is process centric as well. The government agencies try to increase the transparency and make the data easily accessible to the citizen.

Open participation of the citizens is the concern in level 3 in the model of Lee and Kwak (2012). Social media and other methods can play a role in this stage. The government agency encourages the use of public ideas and knowledge. The anecdotes, stories, conversation, ideas and comments through the social media, web dialogue, blogs, micro-blogging, social networking, photo/video sharing, social bookmarking/tagging of citizens are appreciated to enrich the performance of the agencies. The true use of crowd sourcing of knowledge can be seen in this level. However, the agencies should review the benefit of open government in this level. Innovation, agencies' capability to understand the citizens, community interactions, citizen perceptions and agencies feedback should monitor in this level.

The government agency should promote the open collaboration (level 4) after ensuring the open participation (level 3). Other government agencies, public and/or private organizations might be found as partner to collaborate in this level. Co-creation of specific through the public engagement in the complex tasks is the aim of open collaboration (Lee & Kwak, 2012; Bovaird, 2007). The agency can develop the policy, application, can get idea in the crucial moment of the nation and can innovate the product/service through the open collaboration. Wiki, Google Docs and Yammer are the example of open collaboration. It is expected that in this level data analytics capabilities of agency will be build up and will be used for the decision making in large volume of data.

Public engagement is the final level of the model offered by Lee and Kwak (2012). This level is outcome centric rather than process centric. Government should go for the public engagement (Level 5) after ensuring the transparency (Level 2), participation (Level 3), and collaboration (Level 4). Lee and Kwak (2012) have addressed two prominent characteristics of this level. First, advanced technologies have made the tasks of public engagement easier nowadays. Therefore, the government agencies should grab this opportunities. Second, platform of interaction between the government and citizens are user friendly i.e., platforms will contain all the links of relevant web pages. The information is expected to be accessible to the citizens without login or without other requirements. An effective government structure and strive for innovation by the government agencies are expected in this level. Both the financial and non-financial performance is expected to monitor and measure in this level as well.

Level 1 in the model of Lee and Kwak (2012) has been recognized as a basic step. Lee and Kwak (2012) have mentioned that the true activities of opening up the government start from the Level 2. It have been mentioned the government agencies should not try to achieve all the levels (from Level 2 to 5) simultaneously. Consider the high-value and high impact criteria, the government agencies should prioritize the component of the level and should try to achieve gradually.

PROFILE AND STATE OF BANGLADESH

Public Financial Management (PFM) in Bangladesh

Public financial Management (PFM) of a country deals with the public revenue and the expenditure. The public expenditure deals with the budget cycle, including budget preparation, internal controls, accounting, audit, procurement, and monitoring and reporting arrangements. The public revenue deals with the taxing, vat and others. The PFM of Bangladesh can be depicted by figure 2.

As Bangladesh is a parliamentary democratic country, the activity of PFM is started in the parliament through the budget presentation by the Ministry of Finance (MoF). Money is allocated among the ministries in the budget. After the budget being passed in the parliament, it started to implement in the ministries. The Office of the Controller general of Accounts (CGA) takes the charge of compiling and consolidating the government accounts. The Office of the Comptroller and Auditor General of Bangladesh (C&AG) which is the Supreme Audit Institution (SAI) in the PFM audit the accounts prepared by CGA. The C&AG submit the audit reports to the

Figure 2. Public Financial Management of Bangladesh (Stages and functions)
(Source: Hoque et al. 2016)

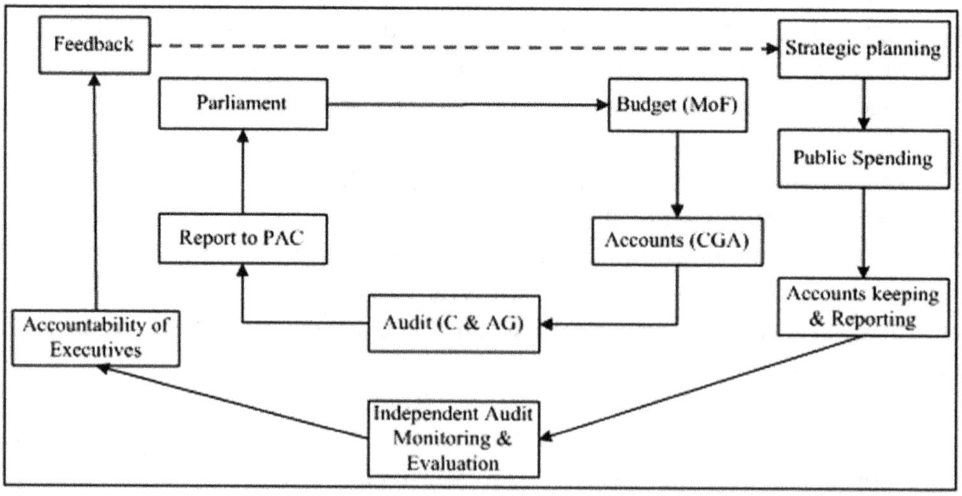

Public Accounts Committee (PAC). PAC observes the audit reports and comments on it as suggestions. Suggestions of PAC are expected to take into consideration of the next year budget preparation.

Bangladesh Open Information and PFM

Bangladesh has passed the Right to Information (RTI) Act in 2009. The bill on RTI passed in the parliament on March 29, 2009. The law becomes effective on July 1, 2009. An Information Commission was established on July 2 in 2009 to ensure the implementation of RTI properly. It is expected that RTI will change the culture of government officials in Bangladesh, will increase the transparency and will enhance the interactions between the government agencies and the citizens (WB, 2013). The prime minister of Bangladesh along with her government is working for the digitization of government service form the very beginning of empowerment (DPADM, 2014).

The Division for Public Administration and Development Management (DPADM) of United Nations Department of Economic and Social Affairs (UNDESA) is supporting the initiatives of open government data in Bangladesh under a project. The project title is "Strengthening of Capacities of Developing Countries to Provide Access to Information for Sustainable Development through Open Government Data (OGD)". The aim of the project is to create awareness among the citizens, government officials and other stakeholders regarding open government data.

The initiative to disclose the government data is taken in 2016. As a process, an open government portal (http://data.gov.bd/) was launched in 2016. The portal broadcast data from various ministries. At present, the portal is broadcasting data from more than 35 ministries and related agencies. After investigating the website in 2017, it seems that the portal is not disclosing the information in detail, especially the data related to PFM. It is found that GDP, GNP, amount of foreign trade and investment is disclosed in gross numerical figure without any explanation. Moreover, data for only one is disclosed till now and the data is broadcasting from the Bangladesh Bureau of Statistics (BBS).

The websites and the related pages of the relevant government agencies has been investigated. The details are given below –

Parliament

In a democratic parliamentary country, the parliament plays an important role. Discussion on budget in the parliament contributes to the PFM. Finance minister takes opinion of the member of the parliaments who are the representative of citizen on the budget before finalizing.

An investigation of the website of the parliament of Bangladesh (http://www.parliament.gov.bd) finds that various information are disclosed in the website. The website has referred the RTI act and has mentioned that it adheres to the act. Information is disclosed in the format of audio, image and in text format in the website. The website is updating the information regularly. Although there is no specific section for public financial management in the website, discussion on the budget are disclosed regularly and disclosed in time.

A section entitled 'blog' is visible in the website. But, the section is not working. The webpage is showing the number of visitors. The website presenting links the social networking platform of parliament as well (facebook, twitter, linkedin, Myspace, Youtube). Investigation of the relevant social networking pages find that the citizens are allowed to comments on the news or information provided in pages. But the authorities are not responding to any comment. Both the website of parliament and social networking pages are not providing any scope for citizen participation and engagement.

Budget (Ministry of Finance (MoF))

The Ministry of Finance (MoF) plays the key role in PFM of the country. It's responsible for the state finance including the state budget, taxation and economic policy in Bangladesh. Under the MoF, there are four division, namely – a) Finance Division (http://mof.gov.bd/en/), b) Economic Relations Division (http://www.erd.gov.bd/), c) Internal Resources Division (http://www.ird.gov.bd/) and d) Bank and Financial Institutions Division (http://www.bfid.gov.bd/). Considering the objective of the chapter, the finance division of the MoF has been investigated deeply.

The *finance division* of MoF is one of the main actors in PFM. In the website of the MoF, RTI act and the Information Release Guidelines (IRG) 2015 have been referred. It has been mentioned that the MoF abides by the RTI act and the IRG 2015. The website is disclosing the budget related information regularly and timely. The website is providing most of the information in .pdf form. The webpages are visible in two languages (Bangla[1] and English). But, most of the accessible information are provided in one language (Bangla) only. The website never compares the information in terms of the years. It is not using graph to present the information to the citizens. The investigation of the website has not found any links in the social networking platforms. It is found that there are 47 downloadable articles. The investigation of the website has not found any scope for the citizens to participate and engage in the activities of ministry of finance as well.

Accounts (CGA)

After allocating the resources as per the budget among the ministries and subsequent offices, The Office of the Controller General of Accounts (CGA) records the accounting data when it takes place The CGA works for the compilation and consolidation of government accounts. The CGA is disclosing information through the website (http://www.cga.gov.bd). In the website of CGA, it has been mentioned that they abide the RTI act and the IRG.

The CGA is mainly preparing the monthly accounts, finance and appropriation accounts for the government. It supervises the subordinate offices like the Divisional Controller of Accounts (DCAs), the District Accounts Officers (DAOs) and the Upazilla Accounts Officers (UAOs). It reconciles the claim and payment of these subordinates as well. Recently, CGA has developed a computer based network with the association of donor agencies named Integrated Budget and Accounting Systems (iBAS) (Hoque et al. 2016; Rajib et al. 2017).

The iBAS helps the CGA to interact with the subordinates directly and instantaneously the transaction takes place. Through the use of the iBAS, the CGA can monitor the financial activities of subordinates as well.

An investigation of the website of CGA finds that the CGA is not disclosing the Finance Accounts and the Appropriation Accounts in details. Only the summarized/ gross amount is disclosed. Moreover, it has been mentioned that the information is restricted to disclose by state law. It has been found that the information of this website is not updated. Most of the files uploaded in the website are available in scanned image format. Up to the investigation, there are 24 downloadable files. The website never compares the financial data in terms of the years. Information is not presented in the graph format as well. The investigation of the website indicates that it is not using the social networking platforms. There is no scope for the citizen participation and citizen engagement as well.

Audits (C&AG)

The Office of the Comptroller and Auditor General of Bangladesh (C&AG) plays an important role in PFM. Its responsibility is to audit the government receipts and expenditure and to assess whether the expenditure is worthy or not.

The website of C&AG mentioned that they abide the RTI act and the IRG like the other financial agencies of the government. An investigation of the website of C&AG finds that the website is disclosing various types of information. The downloadable information are provided under two headings – 1) Publication and 2) Audit Reports. Under the heading of *publication,* information like a) Annual reports, b) Quarterly

Newsletter of the Office of the CAG, c) Review Archive (Quarterly Journal of the Office of the CAG) and d) Strategic plan and others are disclosed. However, it is found that Review Archive (c) is not working, i.e., there is no information.

Under the heading of *Audit Reports*, the information like a) Compliance/Financial audit report, b) Special/Issue based audit report, c) Performance audit report and d) Summary of audit report are disclosed. But, the investigation finds that neither the *Publications* nor the *Audit Reports* is disclosing the updated information. There is no sequence (chronological order) or category of information as well. There are 56 downloadable files. Most of the files are uploaded in scanned image format and available in only one language (Bangla). The auditors opinion or the report are not presenting in the form of comparison. For presenting the information graph has not been used as well. It seems that there is no scope for citizen participation and engagement in the website.

Public Accounts Committee (PAC)

The C&AG submits the audit reports to the Public Accounts Committee (PAC) in the PFM systems in Bangladesh. The duty of PAC is to observe and comments on the audit reports and suggesting the principal accounting officers (Secretaries of different ministries) and concerned officials (C&GA, PAC).

In Bangladesh, it is found that PAC is not disclosing any information to the citizens. There is no website of PAC. However, some information related to PAC is disclosed through the website of C&AG (http://www.cagbd.org/in.php?cp=pacmeet). But, no information is disclosed except the meeting date of PAC, meeting agenda and audit directorate. But, the researchers have mentioned that PAC can play an important role to ensue the accountability of the country (Hoque, 2015). In previous research it has been mentioned that the success of PAC depends on the behavior of committee member, media's interest in government accounts, and the sufficient independent sources of information. But, there is no environment to understand these phenomena.

DISCUSSION

In table 1, the state of different PFM government agencies has been presented. It shows that most of the agencies are staying in level 1 and still surviving for a strong ground to ensure the transparency, participation, collaboration and public engagement. Among the 5 agencies, 4 agencies have website and only 2 agencies are using the social networking platforms.

Table 1. Characteristics of different public financial management (PFM) related Agencies in Bangladesh

Level/Govt. Agencies	Parliament	Budget (MoF)	Account (CGA)	Audits (C&AG)	PAC
Information Platform/ Initial Condition					
Website	http://www.parliament.gov.bd/	http://mof.gov.bd/en/	http://www.cga.gov.bd/	https://www.cagbd.org/	https://www.cagbd.org/ *
Full general and Relevant information (PFM) are accessible	Accessible. But, there is no specific classification of data in the website	Yes	No	No	No
Timeliness	Information disclosed in time	In time	Not in time	Not in time	No
Comparability of information	No	Possible. But, It's Difficult	Difficult	Difficult	N/A
Graphic presentation	No	No	No	No	N/A
Website has specific hyperlink regarding the information	Yes	No	Yes	No	N/A
Electronic format of the information (Html, Pdf or doc, Xls)	Html, Pdf	Html, Pdf	Some valuable documents are available in Scan image	Some valuable documents are available in Scan image	N/A
Email address or mail list for contact person	Yes	No	No	No	No
Visitors count	Yes	No	No	No	No
Languages	Two (Bangla & English)	Webpages are in English, but most of the documents are in Bangla	Webpages are in English, but most of the documents are in Bangla	Webpages are in English, but most of the documents are in Bangla	Webpages are in English. There is no downloadable documents
Flow of information	One way	One way	One way	One way	One way
Appearance in Social Networks					
Visibility	Official page in Facebook, Twitter, MySpace, Linkedin	Official page in Facebook	No	No	No
Updated	Up to date	Up to date	N/A	N/A	N/A
Interaction	Citizen can comment. But, there is no sign responds against citizen comments	Citizen can comment. But, there is no sign responds against citizen comments	N/A	N/A	N/A
Scope for Public Participation	No	No	No	No	No
Scope for Collaboration	No	No	No	No	No
Scope for Public Engagement	No	No	No	No	No

* Information is partially disclosed through the website of C&AG. There is no website for PAC
**Bangladesh Open Data website http://data.gov.bd/ . The website contains little information regarding the PFM. Therefore, it has not been inserted in the table.

The situation of Bangladesh is not unexpected considering the overall rank of open government. Assessment of The Division for Public Administration and Development Management (DPADM) of United Nations Department of Economic and Social Affairs (UNDESA) finds that the rank of Bangladesh is 124 among 190 countries regarding the openness of the country (DPADM, 2016). In the report of DPADM, the health and education sector of Bangladesh has received positive points. But, PFM has failed to get any notice. In contrary, it has been found that the PFM of some countries are doing excellent job regarding the openness. For example, website of Macedonian Ministry of Finance (http://www.finance.gov.mk) (DPADM, 2003). The website is providing the scope for the public participation and engagement (see MoFM, 2017).

In most of the website of PFM agencies of Bangladesh, it has been mentioned that they abide the RTI act 2009. In general, the RTI act of different countries is appraised by scholars and different research platforms. But, it is mentioned that the open government data and the RTI will remain elusive if a digital preservation infrastructure is not pursued (Adu et al. 2016). It is obvious that the right to information act will ensure the citizen the right to access the information. However, to exercise the right it must be ensure that the information are created, received, maintained and preserved in a usable way for a long time. But, the investigation of the websites and the relevant documents of PFM agencies of Bangladesh government finds exceptional.

The investigation finds that the poor structure or base (level 1) to open the PFM. Most of the information and the format (no xls files) of the information are not usable. Information is not disclosed timely (Specially CGA and C&AG) and there is no specific classification of information. All the agencies are adhered to one way communication also. All these factors are bottlenecking the proliferation of openness and indicating the weak position of Bangladesh regarding the openness of PFM.

CONCLUSION

To ensure the accountability and transparency of public financial management of a country, openness is required. Open PFM can increase communication between the government and citizens or other stakeholders to expose the transparency of government expenditure and revenue income. Open government data allows citizens and other stakeholders to monitor the data which ultimately can enhance the transparency and efficiency of public expenditure. Consequently, poverty can be alleviated through the OG. Therefore, both the government and various stakeholders can be benefited from the open government data.

In this paper it has been found that although different initiative has been taken, Bangladesh is still in the primary stage of open government regarding the public financial management. Without ensuring the basic step and infrastructure, it is not possible to ensure the transparency, citizen participation, collaboration and engagement. Therefore, it is suggested to deal with these factors gradually. The right to information act will fail without ensuring the strength of openness structure through recording the information properly and retrieving the information efficiently. In future research, the challenges of open PFM can be identified through the survey, interviews and in details investigations in Bangladesh and in other developing countries.

REFERENCES

Adhikari, P., Timoshenko, K., & Garseth-Nesbakk, L. (2012). Reforming central government accounting in diverse contexts: A three-country comparison. *International Journal of Public Sector Performance Management*, *2*(1), 44–60. doi:10.1504/IJPSPM.2012.048743

Adu, K. K., Dube, L., & Adjei, E. (2016). Digital preservation: The conduit through which open data, electronic government and the right to information are implemented. *Library Hi Tech*, *34*(4), 733–747. doi:10.1108/LHT-07-2016-0078

Andersen, K. V., & Henriksen, H. Z. (2006). E-government maturity models: Extension of the Layne and Lee model. *Government Information Quarterly*, *23*(2), 236–248. doi:10.1016/j.giq.2005.11.008

Baum, C., & Di Maio, A. (2000). *Gartner's four phases of E-government model.* Gartner Group. Retrieved on 2 April, 2017 from https://www.gartner.com/doc/317292/gartners-phases-egovernment-model

Bertot, J. C., Jaeger, P. T., & Grimes, J. M. (2007). Promoting transparency and accountability through ICTs, social media, and collaborative e-government. *Transforming Government: People. Process and Policy*, *6*(1), 78–91.

Bevan, G., & Hood, C. (2006). What's measured is what matters: Targets and gaming in the English public health care system. *Public Administration*, *84*(3), 517–538. doi:10.1111/j.1467-9299.2006.00600.x

Bovaird, T. (2007). Beyond engagement and participation: User and community coproduction in public services. *Public Administration Review*, *67*(5), 846–860. doi:10.1111/j.1540-6210.2007.00773.x

Bovens, M. (2007). Analysing and assessing accountability: A conceptual framework. *European Law Journal*, *13*(4), 447–468. doi:10.1111/j.1468-0386.2007.00378.x

Bovens, M., Goodin, R. E., & Schillemans, T. (2014). *The Oxford handbook of public accountability.* Oxford University Press.

Chandler, H. E. (1998). Towards open government: Official information on the web. *New Library World*, *99*(1144), 230–237. doi:10.1108/03074809810236784

Dada, D. (2006). The failure of e-government in developing countries: A literature review. *The Electronic Journal on Information Systems in Developing Countries*, 26.

Di Maio, A. (2010). *Gartner group government maturity model.* Gartner Group.

Division for Public Administration and Development Management (DPADM). (2003). *UN Global E-government survey 2003*. United Nations and American Society for Public Administration. Retrieved on 5th January 2017 from https://publicadministration.un.org/egovkb/en-us/Reports/UN-E-Government-Survey-2003

Division for Public Administration and Development Management (DPADM). (2014). *United Nations E-government survey 2014: E-government for the future we want*. United Nations and American Society for Public Administration. Retrieved on 15th January from https://publicadministration.un.org/egovkb/en-us/Reports/UN-E-Government-Survey-2014

Division for Public Administration and Development Management (DPADM). (2016). *United Nations E-government survey 2016: E-governance in support for sustainable development*. United Nations and American Society for Public Administration. Retrieved on 4th April from https://publicadministration.un.org/egovkb/en-us/Reports/UN-E-Government-Survey-2016

Division for Public Administration and Development Management (DPADM). (2017). *Open Government data and services*. Retrieved on 1st January 2017 from https://publicadministration.un.org/en/ogd#popup

Evans, A. M., & Campos, A. (2013). Open government initiatives: Challenges of citizen participation. *Journal of Policy Analysis and Management*, *32*(1), 172–185. doi:10.1002/pam.21651

Gottschalk, P. (2009). Maturity levels for interoperability in digital government. *Government Information Quarterly*, *26*(1), 75–81. doi:10.1016/j.giq.2008.03.003

Hellberg, A. S., & Hedstrom, K. (2015). The story of the sixth myth of open data and open government. *Transforming Government: People. Process and Policy*, *9*(1), 35–51.

Hoque, M., Rajib, M. S. U., & Akter, M. (2016). Development of public sector accounting: Reformation and Challenges in Bangladesh. In *Australia Bangladesh Business Research Symposium*. Monash Business School.

Hoque, Z. (Ed.). (2015). *Making Governments Accountable: The Role of Public Accounts Committees and National Audit Offices*. Routledge.

Kalampokis, E., Tambouris, E., & Tarabanis, K. (2011). A classification scheme for open government data: Towards linking decentralized data. *International Journal of Web Engineering and Technology*, *6*(3), 266–285. doi:10.1504/IJWET.2011.040725

Kim, S., & Kim, D. (2003). South Korean public officials' perceptions of values, failure, and consequences of failure in e-government leadership. *Public Performance & Management Review*, *26*(4), 360–375. doi:10.1177/1530957603026004004

Klievink, B., & Janssen, M. (2009). Realizing joined-up government – Dynamic capabilities and stage models for transformation. *Government Information Quarterly*, *26*(2), 275–284. doi:10.1016/j.giq.2008.12.007

Layne, K., & Lee, J. (2001). Developing fully functional e-government: A four stage model. *Government Information Quarterly*, *18*(2), 122–136. doi:10.1016/S0740-624X(01)00066-1

Lee, G., & Kwak, Y. H. (2012). An open government model for social media-based public engagement. *Government Information Quarterly*, *29*(4), 492–503. doi:10.1016/j.giq.2012.06.001

Linders, D., & Wilson, S. C. (2011). What is open government? One year after the directive. *12th Annual International Conference on Digital Government Research*, 262 – 271. doi:10.1145/2037556.2037599

Maseh, E., & Katuu, S. (2017). The Kenyan Judiciary's open government initiative: Prospects and challenges. *Journal of Science and Technology Policy Management*, *8*(1), 76–94. doi:10.1108/JSTPM-04-2016-0007

Ministry of Finance of Macedonia (MoFM). (2017). *Public consultation for draft economic reform program 2017*. Retrieved on 3rd March, 2017 from http://www.finance.gov.mk/en/node/6198

Perez, C. C., Hernandez, A. M. L., & Bolivar, M. P. R. (2005). Citizens' access to on-line governmental financial information: Practices in the European Union countries. *Government Information Quarterly*, *22*(2), 258–276. doi:10.1016/j.giq.2005.02.002

Rajib, M. S. U., & Mou, N. Z. (2014). Ethical Issues of Qualitative Research. In J. Wang (Ed.), *Encyclopedia of Business Analytics and Optimization* (pp. 852–863). Hershey, PA: Business Science Reference; doi:10.4018/978-1-4666-5202-6.ch080

Rajib, M. S. U., Sajib, M. Q. U., & Hoque, M. (2017). Strengthening the Public Sector Accounting Through ICT: The Experience of a Developing Country. In H. Kaur, E. Lechman, & A. Marszk (Eds.), *Catalyzing Development through ICT Adoption*. Cham: Springer; doi:10.1007/978-3-319-56523-1_6

Romzek, B. S., & Dubnick, M. J. (1998). Accountability. In International Encyclopedia of Public Policy and Administration. Boulder, CO: Westview Press.

Sandoval-Almazan, R., & Gil-Garcia, J. R. (2016). Toward an integrative assessment of open government: Proposing conceptual lenses and practical components. *Journal of Organizational Computing and Electronic Commerce*, *26*(1-2), 170–192. doi:10.1080/10919392.2015.1125190

Siau, K., & Long, Y. (2005). Synthesizing e-government stage models – a meta-synthesis based on meta-ethnography approach. *Industrial Management & Data Systems*, *105*(4), 443–458. doi:10.1108/02635570510592352

Valdes, G., Solar, M., Astudillo, H., Iribarren, M., Concha, G., & Visconti, M. (2011). Conception, development and implementation of an e-government maturity model in public agencies. *Government Information Quarterly*, *28*(2), 176–187. doi:10.1016/j.giq.2010.04.007

Vries, M. D., & Nemec, J. (2013). Public sector reform: An overview of recent literature and research on NPM and alternative paths. *International Journal of Public Sector Management*, *26*(1), 4–16. doi:10.1108/09513551311293408

Wasike, B. (2016). FoIA in the age of "Open. Gov": An analysis of the performance of the freedom of information act under the Obama and Bush administrations. *Government Information Quarterly*, *33*(3), 417–426. doi:10.1016/j.giq.2016.05.001

World Bank (WB). (2013). *Governance in Bangladesh*. Retrieved from http://www.worldbank.org/en/country/bangladesh/brief/bangladesh-governance

World Bank (WB). (2015). *Tanzania - Open Government and Public Financial Management (OGPFM) Development Policy Operation Program Project*. Washington, DC: World Bank Group. Retrieved from http://documents.worldbank.org/curated/en/522551468300592178/Tanzania-Open-Government-and-Public-Financial-Management-OGPFM-Development-Policy-Operation-Program-Project

ENDNOTE

1 The native language of Bangladeshi people.

Section 4
Legal Barriers to OGI

Chapter 6
Prospects and Challenges of E-Government in Black Africa:
A Comparative Study of Nigeria and Cameroon

Floribert Endong
University of Calabar, Nigeria

ABSTRACT

Most scholars' perspectives on e-government development in Africa have tended to be monolithic. This has been irrespective of the fact that African nations have been adopting relatively different approaches to e-governance. Though the dominant tendency among them has been to struggle to have a certain amount of web presence through the creation of e-government web portals, each African country has designed its own (customized) e-government initiatives. It will therefore be very interesting to explore the extent to which the prospects and challenges of e-governance in Africa have been varying across countries. This chapter attempts to fill this gap in knowledge through a comparative study of e-government implementation in Nigeria and Cameroon. The chapter is divided into three main parts. The first part provides a conceptual definition and a brief history of e-government. The second part explores the phenomena of ICTs and e-governance in Africa while the last part provides a comparative perspective on the implementation of e-government in Nigeria and Cameroon.

DOI: 10.4018/978-1-5225-4987-1.ch006

INTRODUCTION

The Information and Communication Technologies (ICTs) have unarguably come to assume a central position in all aspects of human endeavors. Societal development and human progress have, in many respects, become highly dependent on them. This has been to the extent that, almost all developing nations are today investing huge resources and contracting various forms of partnerships with global influential institutions to (fully) acquire and apply these technologies (UNO 2014). As argued by Karisiddapa (2004), in order to achieve sustainable development, all nations – particularly the developing countries – must imperatively view the concept of ICT as "an essential knowledge". In the same line of argument, the *UN 2030 Agenda for Sustainable Development* enthuses that the proliferation of ICTs and global interconnectedness have great potential not only to accelerate human progress and to bridge the digital divide, but equally to "develop knowledge societies, as does scientific and technological innovation across areas as diverse as medicine and energy" (cited in United Nation Public Administration Network, 2016).

In view of all these prospects, ICTs have progressively been applied in socio-cultural, economic as well as political human endeavors. The application of ICTs in the political domain is vividly illustrated by the e-Government paradigm which has phenomenally become global and a clear imperative for sociopolitical and economic development. Like their western counterparts, most African nations have embraced this paradigm (electronic government) as an infallible elixir of some of their economic, social and political dilemmas. In effect, many of these African nations have progressively been regarding e-government as having the immense potential to (i) stimulate economic growth, (ii) democratize the political space and (iii) facilitate governance by enhancing institutional capacity and facilitating citizen participation in the policy-making process as well as by increasing transparency for better management of resources. According to many observers, ICTs have been massively appropriated by Black African countries as a tool to shape and transform relations between the government, the citizens and other major socio-political entities (Akunyili, 2010; Omeire & Omeire, 2014).

However, despite these prospects, the implementation of e-government initiatives in many Black African countries has most often faced varied and complex challenges. According to some recent studies, only about 15% of these initiatives are successes. Over 35% of them are complete failures while the remaining 50% are partial failures (Heeks 2008; Kenhago 2014). In the same line of argument, Abede and Dawit (2010) note that the use of ICTs to deliver e-government services in most African countries continues to be very minimal – compared to other parts of the world. This has largely been attributed to the fact that much of Africa continues to relatively be a "technological desert". Such a state of affairs has been facilitated by such factors as poor infrastructures, "insignificant" or low economic development, low literacy rate and a wide range of socio-cultural issues. As insightfully contended by both Afro-centric and Euro-centric scholars, most Black African countries' efforts towards e-governance are limited to a weak web presence, including few fully fledged e-government web portals. All these indexes tend to suggest that, although an amount of progress seems to have been made by African countries, "there is [still] a long way to go, to bridge not only the North–South divide when it comes to e-government services but also among the various sub-regions" (Abede & Dawit 2010, p.1). Africa continues to be rated among the last continents in terms of application of e-governance.

A critical look at the immense literature devoted to the prospects and challenges of e-governance in Africa reveals that, most researchers and authors tend to adopt either a purely nationalist perspective or a global/panoramic perspective on the issue. Most of them have a monolithic view on e-government paradigm in Africa; as they predominantly conceive the failures or/and successes of e-government initiatives to be somehow similar across African nations. However, it will be expedient to underline the fact that African nations have been adopting relatively – or slightly – different approaches to e-governance. Though the dominant tendency has been for them to attempt to have a certain amount of web presence through the creation of e-government web portals, each African country has designed its own (customized) e-Government initiatives. In tandem with this, the implementation of the paradigm has inevitably – and perhaps slightly – varied across countries. A clear indication of this reality is the fact that series of recent surveys carried out by global observers such as the UNO, the UNESCO and the Commonwealth among others have proven that African countries have various rankings in terms of the application of e-government (UN 2016). It will therefore be very interesting to explore the extent to which the prospects and challenges of e-governance in Africa have been varying across countries. This chapter attempts to fill this gap in knowledge through a comparative study of e-Government implementation in Nigeria and Cameroon. The chapter is divided into three main parts. The first part provides a conceptual definition and a brief history of e-government. The second part explores the phenomena of ICTs and e-governance in Africa while the last part provides a comparative perspective on the implementation of e-Government in Nigeria and Cameroon.

UNDERSTANDING AND TRACING THE ORIGIN OF E-GOVERNMENT

In simple terms, e-government could be defined as a methodology involving the use of information and communication technologies to enhance access to, and delivery of government services. The UNO (2008) defines the paradigm as the use of ICT to (i) promote more efficient and effective government, (ii) facilitate the accessibility of government services, (iii) allow greater public access to information, (iv) make governments more accountable to citizens. Two common features of e-Government are the automation and computerization of traditional paper-based procedures to ameliorate access to, and delivery of government services to citizens. A good number of definitions thus limit the concept of e-Government exclusively to internet-enabled applications or to service delivery; while others similarly confine it to relations between the government and the outside world. However, e-Government should be conceived as having a greater semantic sphere. Perhaps, the best way to define the concept will be to clearly identify its main domains. These domains include (i) e-administration (aimed at improving government processes), (ii) the provision of e-services to e-citizens and (iii) the building of external interactions (through the creation of an e-society). As clearly implied by the above itemization, these three domains may be said to represent the major aims of e-government.

E-administration focuses on improving the internal workings of the public sector, through initiatives bordering on the creation of strategic connections between the various (key) organs, data stores and agencies of government. Such connections may facilitate rapid and efficient investigations as well as the efficient formulation and implementation of government policies. Other e-administration initiatives may aim at reducing financial and time cost of administration as well as creating empowerment through transfer of resources, power and authority from their original locus to new locations. The e-service and e-citizens dimensions of e-Government have to do with initiatives that border on the relationship between government and the citizens. They include such projects as creating more effective (digitally driven) platforms to inform or talk to citizens. This entails providing details about government policies and public sector activities, in view of making public officials be more accountable for their decisions or actions as they affect the general public. The e-service and e-citizen concepts also relate to the creation of digitally assisted platforms that enable citizen to talk to their government. Such platforms have the potential to increase citizens' participation to government policies and democratization.

Finally, the e-society dimension of e-government has to do with initiatives that aim to improve relationship between governmental agencies and other national and international bodies such as NGOs, community and non-profit organizations as well as other private sector bodies. According to Ntiro (2000), they may, among other things, include projects aimed to improve interaction between government and businesses – for instance through the design of effective digitization frameworks. Other projects which are in line with e-society include the social and economic development of local communities as well as the creation of partnerships that will enable the grouping of social organizations to achieve social and economic objectives.

Based on the domains explored above, it may be observed that, in theory, e-government encompasses a wide range of interactions between the government and the society; even though most countries have tended to concentrate their efforts essentially in the application of ICTs in service delivery. Additionally, e-Government goes beyond the mere application of ICTs in the delivery of government services as it entails change in mind sets and work culture or novel procedures which may ultimately permit government agencies to serve the citizens in a better way. Indeed, the application of e-government enhances the capacity of government to be open to criticism. It equally enhances the institution of a new social contract between all stakeholders – or major social players – in a polity. It is in tandem with this thesis that most critics argue that e-governance is central to effective e-Government. As put by Kitaw (2006), "fundamental to seize the opportunities of e-Government in Africa is the genuine commitment and willingness of governments to induce transformational patterns towards being more citizen-centered" (p.55).

Institutions such as the UNO, the UNESCO and the Commonwealth Network of Information Technology and Development (COMNET-IT) have designed methodologies to determine the level of advancement of e-government application in countries of the world. These methodologies hinge on a variety of indexes or indicators, some of which include:

1. Plans for e-governance
2. Plans for the development and deployment of communities e-centers
3. The passing of cyber laws
4. The deregulation of telecommunications
5. Instances of public reaction to statements of direction, draft legislation and similar aspects of government policies
6. Websites of government agencies which provide information – beyond mere image building – to the general public

Besides these methodologies, global opinion molders such as the UNO, the World Economic Forum and the Commonwealth have designed and popularized specific indexes to measure e-Government development or related phenomena in world countries. A Kafkaesque example is UNO's e-Government Development Index (EGDI) which rests on three cardinal factors namely the availability of online services, telecommunication infrastructures and human capacity. In tandem with this, the concept of "e-Government readiness (of countries)" has equally been conceived. Measuring such a readiness takes into account factors such as (a) the country's levels of economic, (b) technological and (c) human resources development. Another major index (the Networked Readiness Index) has been conceived by the World Economic Forum.

It is popularly believed that e-Government originates from the advent of the Internet technology in the mid 1990s. From many observations, the paradigm is strongly inspired by business models, particularly in the domain of e-commerce. In effect, the remarkable success of the application of the ICTs in the area of good and service marketing has motivated many governments to envisage the deployment of digitally driven tools to enhance their capacity to deliver services to their respective citizens. The popular thinking has therefore been that, if the internet can be used to enable citizens or consumers to book a flight online, the same technology could be used to request a visa, a parking permit or to send in a tax form. Following this line of reasoning, the citizen could now technically be viewed as "an active consumer of public service, with borrowed private sector concepts, applied to public sector governance systems" (UNO, 2012, p.10). The advent and rapid spread of the internet and the mobile telephony have progressively pushed citizens to think of, and exploit new models of accessing even information and services. Citizens now expect their governments to provide them with such information and services through online platforms, making the concept of 'e-citizenship' to become prominent.

Despite the fact that most sources associate the emergence of e-Government with the advent of the World Wide Web in the nineties, some schools of thought beg to slightly differ. Such schools rather attribute the birth and popularization of the concept to a number of Information Technologies driven reforms in India right back in the seventies and eighties. According to these schools, the concept of e-governance was first introduced in India around the 1970s, when in-house government applications were developed in such areas as economic monitoring, planning and defense; and when the information technologies were also deployed to manage data intensive functions bordering on elections, census, tax and administration. These efforts were magnified in the eighties through a number of colossal projects executed by India's National Informatics Center (NIC). NIC actually developed information technology driven programs to connect all district headquarters in the country. It can therefore be observed that there is no consensus as to when exactly e-Government started.

Recent development in ICTs and the ever changing structures of societies – notably the emergence of the concept of smart cities– indicate that e-governance is bound to evolve. According to The Hague (2016), there are new paradigms such as the Internet of Things, Big Data analytics, blockchain and robots among others which are serious precursor signs that e-Government may – or needs to – be rethought and made to change from mere digitization of government service procedures to something more complex. The emergence of phenomena such as "data-ism" or "datafication" (the effect of the invasive application of combined computer, telecom and chip-technology in most aspects of our societies) could be seen as the prelude of the future emergence of a more digital society. This has serious implications for the application of e-governance. As The Hague (2016) puts it, the e-government community, government professionals, academics and industries should start thinking about turning "the tables from [the] digitalization present to [the] 'datafication' future". It is only in this way that governments can really "prepare for their new role in the ever more digital society and make sure this society is a better place for all of us to live in".

ICTS AND E-GOVERNMENT IN AFRICA

It is extremely difficult to trace the origin of e-Government in Africa. However, it can be observed that the concept has since the later part of the 1900s been the talk of the town in most African countries. Indeed, most – if not all –countries on the continent have since the 1990s, seen the paradigm (of e-government) as an elixir of progress and modernization. Precisely in 1996, African Ministers of planning and economic development (from states members of the ECA), adopted the African Information Society Initiative (AISA) which, among other provisions, recommends the implementation of projects which are in line with e-Government. The AISA framework stresses, for instance, on the need for African countries to develop and implement national policies and plans to promote ICT's adoption throughout key economic sectors and national administration (National Information and Communication Infrastructure strategies and plans-NICIs). It equally stresses the imperative of using ICTs to improve the effectiveness of government service delivery (ECA 1996). AISA has since then been the major framework used by ECA to work with African member States in the domain of the use of ICTs to promote economic and socio-cultural development in Africa.

Beside the AISA framework, African governments have adopted the *Charter for the Public Service in Africa* in 2001. This was done in Windhoek (Namibia) through African Ministers of Civil Service. The *Charter* makes explicit mention of African countries' commitment – or at least their ardent dreams – to harness the ICTs in order to upgrade or update processes and procedures in their respective civil services. The Preamble of the above mentioned *Charter* officially stipulates African countries' drive towards "modernizing administrative structures by mastering the new communication technologies, allowing to transform historically and politically motivated functions into sound business-like operations" (Windhoek Declaration, 2001). In its article 8, the Charter further expresses this drive thus:

The public service shall be organized along functional and decentralized lines designed to bring public management closer to the people and provide them with appropriate and accessible basic services. Physical proximity and accessibility can be achieved by the application of appropriate information and communication technologies (e-governance).

African countries' apparent commitment to make impressive strides towards e-Government has, to an extent, not only remained on paper. Visible moves and projects worth billions of Dollars have been undertaken by a number of African countries in recent times in view of attaining leadership positions in e-Government. In Mauritius Island for instance, the government has tremendously invested in education, ICT infrastructures and communications. The importance of ICTs in the socio-economic and political development of the country was viewed by the Mauritius government as early as 1990; as it set up an ICT promotion agency which in 1996 started initiating major e-government projects aimed at putting all Ministers on the web, thereby permitting citizens to have online access to relevant publications, acts and events (Kitaw 2006). Presently, the Mauritius government has an online portal and multiple websites which provide citizens with a variety of e-services segmented according to target persons. The Mauritius government website (gov.mu) has more than 100 e-services which are accessible online.

Additionally, the government has initiated the Contributions Network Project which connects Mauritian firms for tax payments to various government departments. The country's huge efforts have enabled it to improve its Human Capital Index and its Online Service Index (OSI). These efforts have brought the country immense dividends: recently it was rated the second leading African nation (after Tunisia) in the implementation of e-government. The Mauritius Island improved on its e-Government Development Index (EGDI) from 93rd (worldwide) in 2012 to 72nd in 2015 and to 58th in 2016 (UNPAN, 2016). Other good case studies in the continent include countries like South Africa, Morocco, Tunisia, Seychelles and Egypt which, according to a 2014 survey conducted by the UN, could be classified above the world average e-Government readiness – which is 0.402 (UNO, 2014).

Countries like Nigeria have similarly undertaken quite a number of impressive e-Government initiatives which have even earned them international acclaims. An egregious example is the "1-Gov.net" project initiated in 2006 by Nigeria's Galaxy Backbone (GBB) Ltd, a government company set up to provide ICT infrastructure and services to all Federal Government MDAs. Since its inception, the project has been ensuring that infrastructures and transversal applications be shared across MDAs, enabling huge savings. The project has provided a technological platform for e-government, as well as a comprehensive broadband policy and vision document which today provides broadband definition, performance indicators, incentives for investment, macroeconomic targets, deployment guidelines and citizens charter. The pertinence of the project caught the attention of the UNO resulting in GBB winning the United Nation Public Service Award in 2013.

The majority of e-Government initiatives undertaken by African countries have principally centered on enhancing ICTs infrastructures and increasing their Online Service Index (OSI). It has thus become a popular paradigm in most, if not all African countries to set up national ICT policies, automate administrative processes and create digitally driven platforms in view of engaging the citizens. Even countries such as Libya, the Democratic Republic of Congo and Bissau Guinea which, as of 2012, had no national websites; now enjoy a level of online presence (Abede & Dawit, 2010; UNO 2014). All these indexes point to the fact that most, if not all, African countries have keyed into the e-Government bandwagon. The indexes equally point to the fact that there is a remarkable progress in the implementation of e-Government in Africa even though the continent continues paradoxically to lag behind other parts of the world (particularly behind the west). Evidences strongly point to the fact that most governments within the continent now have at least a presence on the web with fully fledged e-Government web portals. Some of them like Rwanda, have since 2008, even gone to the extent of implementing some aspects of the Government-to-Any (G2X) model of e-Government delivery. Rwanda in particular has since 2008 designed online-services for the issuance of visas to foreigners as well as to foreign investors (Hafkin 2009).

Despite these efforts, most African countries have a very low e-Government Development Index. The average EGDI for the Continent is 0.2661 which is far below the world average of 0.4712 (UNO 2016). This slow spread of e-Government in Africa is attributable to multiple factors which particularly include low rate of literacy and the lack of political will to genuinely transform or reform governance into a citizen-center system in the respective countries. One notes for instance that, in view of improving their e-Government ranking, most African nations seem bent principally – nay essentially on investing enormously only in ICT infrastructures, without making concrete efforts towards changing mentalities in favor of good governance and sufficiently building the capacity of government personnel in the domain of ICT use. The ruling paradigm among most African governments seems therefore to consist in viewing ICTs alone as the key elixir of their problems in the domain of public service delivery; meanwhile, other factors such as trained personnel (high level of human capacity building), a citizen centric culture, the existence of defined business processes and a participatory design of services (which clearly have nothing to do with ICTs), are key to e-government.

Because of this myopic conception of e-Government, most African countries tend to confine their e-Government initiatives to web presence (Abede & Dawit 2010); meanwhile, as argued by many critics, this is just one of the initial or preliminary stages of the Government-to-citizen (G2C) model of e-Government delivery. African governments seem reluctant nay, slow to progress to the other two essential phases of this delivery model which include (i) using internet technology for government-citizen interaction (phase two) and (ii) using the web to facilitate citizens' transactions in government's institutions (phase three). African countries' concentration on the first stage of e-Government may partially explain their poor performance in the e-participation index (IPI). Despite few signs of progress in the continent in regard of e-participation activities, the UNO (2016) thinks that "more resources, technologies, and capacities, and robust national policies encouraging the use of public engagement e-tools are still needed to accelerate progress" in the continent. Only countries like Morocco and Tunisia seem to have made considerable progresses in the domain of e-participation.

Another serious challenge to e-government in Africa – as often highlighted by both exocentric and Afrocentric scholars – has been the persisting digital divide between Africa and the west (Abede & Dawit 2010; Fraser-Molekiti & Senghor 2010; UNO, 2016). Internet penetration in Africa is estimated to be around 26.5% compared to 70.5% and 87.7% respectively in Europe and America (Manor 2015). According to scholars, this divide has constituted a significant threat to e-participation in Black African countries. The recent survey conducted by the UNO revealed that citizens' participation to e-governance is actually very low in countries south of the Sahara. In effect, issues like lack of access to technology, poverty and inequality prevent people in Black African countries from taking full advantage of the potential of ICTs and e-governance for sustainable development. UNO's 2016 survey equally reveals that the persisting huge gap between African countries is shown by the fact that African countries averagely have an EGDI of 0.2882, against an average EGDI of 0.7241 for European countries. Additionally, Europe provides 10 times more services to the poor, persons with disabilities and older persons than Africa and Oceania (UNO 2016).

Despite the pertinence of these findings, it must be highlighted that, compared to the early parts of the 2000s, there has been some amount of improvement in internet penetration and mobile connectivity in African countries. Particular African countries such as Kenya and Nigeria have witnessed remarkable increase in internet penetration. Kenya can for instance boast of an internet penetration of 47.3% (Manor 2015). Additionally, as of 2009 over 40 percent of the population in the sub-Saharan Africa was already having access to mobile devices (Fraser-Molekiyi & Senghor, 2010). The 2016 ICT Development Survey conducted by the ITU revealed that though 29 out of 39 African countries belong to the "Least Connected Countries", a number of sub-Saharan countries witnessed a relatively considerable improvement from the IDI performance in preceding years. The ten top African countries in this ranking (including Mauritius, Seycheles, South Africa, Cape Verdes, Botswana, Ghana,

Namibia, Gabon and Kenya among others) registered an average improvement in their IDI values of 0.33 points (ITU 2016).

Furthermore, a number of recent studies reveal that smart phones are becoming cheaper and more accessible in many African countries. This augurs well for the development of mobile government in the continent. All the above mentioned indexes could rather be viewed as some of the prospects of e-participation in Africa. As enthused by Nohindra Raja, (founder of Icon Capital Partners), the increasing mobile connectivity witnessed in Black African countries actually points to the fact that, mobile governance (m-governance) will eventually surpass e-Governance in the near or remote future. He succinctly notes that:

We feel that eventually [the] mobile is going to overtake [the] electronic because of the penetration of mobiles. Africa has never had landlines in numbers comparable to other parts of the world. Today, most of the mobile devices are smartphones. It's surprising, looking at the per capita income, but the smartphones are overtaking the normal phones. And the way smartphones are becoming cheaper by the day, we feel mobile government is the future. (cited in Knowledge @ Wharton, 2016, p.45)

One could therefore conclude that the future of e-governance in Africa is not totally derisory for there are both challenges and prospects of the paradigm in the continent. The major challenges to the concept of e-governance in Africa include low literacy level (less than 40%), low access to ICTs, underdeveloped telecommunication infrastructures, low level of human capacity building (for both ICT users and administrators), widespread corruption and more especially the lack of political will to transform governance in African polities to a more transparent and citizen-centered process.

Despite the multiplicity and accentuation of these challenges, there exist a number of prospects; one of which is the growing mobile connectivity or rather the greater access to mobile devices such as smart phones in Africa. It has even been enthused by some scholars that mobile telephony could arguably be a serious route used by Africans to bridge the digital gap between them and their counterparts in other regions of the world (Akunyili 2010). This is so as the smartphones which are becoming more and more ubiquitous in Africa, integrate the abilities of both the personal computers (PC) and the mobile telephone. They enable their users to access the Internet and perform tasks that hitherto, could only be PC-aided. Ownership or lack of a PC has thus become a faulty index to gauge the level of digital divide between Africa and the rest of the world. It could be said that the remarkable proliferation of the smartphones in African countries is enabling access to the Internet and making the potential for e-participation brighter.

THE NIGERIAN AND CAMEROONIAN PERSPECTIVE

As earlier mentioned, researchers have tended to have a monolithic view of the prospects and challenges to e-Government development in Africa. Though this tendency is to an extent justifiable, one needs to underscore the fact that there are some little differences between individual African countries in terms of how they conceive and implement e-Governance. Such differences are attributable to the prevalence of varying political cultures as well as economic disparities between them (sub-Sahara countries). In fact, beside the regional disparities in terms of Internet penetration and mobile connectivity, there is the fact that the speed of democratization varies from country to country in the continent (Endong, 2017a,b; Nyamjoh 2013). These factors, to a relatively high extent, predispose African countries to be at varying stages of e-government application or development. As revealed by their differing rankings in the recent UNO's e-Government survey and ITU's IDI survey, some countries are making greater strides compared to their African counterparts; this for obvious reasons. One of these reasons, according to this author, is the level of democratization and political liberalism which clearly varies from one country to another in the continent. As earlier argued, e-Governance is more than the simplistic application of ICTs in governance as it entails a change in mind set and work culture mostly characterized by governments' openness to political criticism as well as the political will to integrate the common man in the decision making process. This is in line with the aphorism which stipulates that, the present digital revolution does not only multiply the citizens' possibilities to communicate and interact in an exponential fashion, but makes it possible nay imperative "to re-launch the classic idea of the individual at the center of the democratic e-society" (Asongwe 2013, p.160).

This key pre-requisite is still largely marginalized in most African countries' application of e-Government. Similarly to the concept of liberal democracy, the idea of effectively enabling e-participation is still subtly resisted or given selective attention by most government officials in Africa. This, as we shall discuss in the succeeding lines, constitutes one of the greatest points which differentiate Cameroon from Nigeria in the domain of e-Government development. Before delving into such an exercise, it will be expedient to highlight some similarities in the prospects of e-Government in Cameroon and Nigeria.

Similarities

It is important from the outset to underline the fact that comparing the prospects and problems of e-Government in Nigeria and Cameroon in a mathematic way, may necessitate broader methodological designs like those applied by the UNO (2016) and ITU (2016) in their various surveys on e-Government or ICT development. These methodological orientations fall outside the preview of this chapter. In this section, the author is mainly interested in highlighting a number of observable indexes which, to a reasonable extent, point to similarities or differences in approaches to e-Government implementation in the two countries as well as indicate similarities and differences in the prospects and challenges of the paradigm in the two countries. Attention is given first to the countries' efforts in the domain of ICT development and second to their e-Government efforts.

Efforts in the Domain of ICT Development

Comparatively, Nigeria and Cameroon could be said to have initiated a number of similar ICT development projects. Since the beginning of the 2000s, the two countries have embarked on relatively innovative ICT policies which have been responsible for a significant increase in the consumption of new information and communication technologies in their respective territories. In the domain of telecommunications for instance, Nigeria deregulated its cyberspace since 1992 and established procedures for the auctioning of Global System for Mobile (GSM) licenses in 2001. In this same year, Nigeria launched her National Information Technology Policy whose implementation has been ensured by the National Information Technology Development Agency (NITDA). This agency actually focused its strategies on creating a number of e-government models for the country in the areas of e-Administration, e-Judiciary, e-Healthcare, e-Taxation, and e-Education among others. According to government sources, the country's investments in ICT development in 2010 could be estimated at $ 18 billion, made up of $ 12 billion of Foreign Direct Investment and the rest coming from internal sources (Akunyili 2010).

A similar trend is observed in Cameroon where series of ICT policies were initiated as early as 1989 to make the country one of the early adopters of the GSM mobile platform in Africa (Nzepa & Keutchankeu 2012). The country created two bodies that have been very instrumental in the conception and implementation of its ICT development projects. These include its Telecommunications Regulatory Board (in 1998) and its National Agency for ICT (ANTI) (in 2001). The latter has led Cameroon's EGOV.CM project. This will be further discussed in the subsequent lines. The most recent moves towards ICT and e-Government development in Cameroon have been guided by two documents namely the Sector Strategy for Telecommunications and Communication Technologies 2005-2015 (MINPOSTEL, 2005), and the Growth and Employment Strategy Paper (GESP) (Republic of Cameroon, 2009). The first document highlights that Cameroon's sector strategy for telecommunication is based on the three following targets: (a) to refine the legal, regulatory and institutional framework; (b) increase service quality, quantity and affordability; and (c) increase the use of ICT and foster ICT enterprises (MINPOSTEL, 2005). The document equally provides a threefold strategy including: the development of policies aligned with the new environment; the adoption and implementation of those policies; and the elaboration of procedure to seek contributions from international cooperation partners and the private sector.

The GESP, for its part, highlights goals to be reached by the ICT sector by 2020. These goals include landline telephony coverage to 45% of the population, and mobile coverage to 65% of the population; provision of modern means of communication to 40 000 villages; and multiplication by 50 of the number of direct and indirect employment positions in the ICT sector (Republic of Cameroon, 2009, p. 63).

It can therefore be seen that a number of similar efforts have been made in Cameroon and Nigeria in the domain of ICT development. This various governmental efforts have brought about an increased in the consumption of ICTs in the two countries. The tele-density (number of telephone connections per every hundred inhabitants in a specific area) in both Nigeria and Cameroon has exponentially increased from the years the two countries deregulated their telecommunication sectors; and embarked on a wide range of other ICT policies. According to the Nigerian Communication Commission (cited in Adepetum, 2017), Nigeria has gone from 72 million active mobile telephone subscribers in 2009 to 154 million of active telephony users in December 2016. Similarly in Cameroon, mobile telephone penetration has increased from 50% in 2015 (Sindeu 2013) to 81% in 2016 (MINPOSTEL 2016). Internet penetration in the country has equally increased from 4% in 2012 (Nzepa & Keutchankeu 2012) to 18% in 2016.

Similarities in the degree of efforts made by the two countries could perhaps be further evidenced with the fact that, they are virtually in the same belt, in the ICT or e-government rankings done by major international observatories. In the 2016 ITU's survey, Nigeria was ranked 137th (with an IDI value of 2.72) while Cameroon was ranked 149th (with an IDI value of 2.16). Similarly, in the UNO's 2016 e-government survey, Nigeria was ranked 143rd (with an EGDI of 0.3291) while Cameroon was ranked 155th (with an EGDI of 0.2759). One realizes that though Nigeria leads Cameroon in all these categories, the gap between the ranks occupied by the two countries is relatively negligible. The two countries thus often appear in the same belt.

Efforts in the Domain of E-Government

Nigeria and Cameroon have equally initiated a number of similar E-Government projects. This can be illustrated with at least three examples bordering on the two countries' implementation of the G2G, G2C, G2E and G2B models of e-government delivery. First among these examples is Nigeria's Galaxy Backbone initiative (discussed earlier), which has had a Cameroonian replica in the name of EGOV.CM program. As earlier mentioned, the Galaxy Backbone project has been providing ICT infrastructures and services to all Federal Government agencies in Nigeria. The structure is responsible for the existence in Nigeria, of a technological platform for e-Government, as well as a comprehensive broadband policy and vision document which provides broadband definition, performance indicators, incentives for investment, macroeconomic targets, deployment guidelines and citizens charter. Similarly to the Galaxy Backbone project, Cameroon's EGOV.CM program has enabled a degree of access to government information and services. It has equally been providing IT support to the public administration reform program and has helped in promoting the objectives of national policies, providing an appropriate legal and regulatory environment (Asongwe 2012; Sindeu 2013).

There is equally a good number of similarities between the two countries in the amount of efforts made by the two governments in the domains of G2C and G2E service provision. The two governments have for instance put in place working mechanisms to institute electronic payments. This has been a remarkable shift from the old practice of relying on cash-and-carry approaches in payment of salaries. With the e-payment regime, workers in both countries receive their salaries through e-transactions. This makes the process faster, more reliable and less cumbersome.

In addition to this, government agencies and almost all ministerial services in the two countries have a degree of web presence. This has been facilitated through the creation of government portals with variety of websites through which citizen can access information about the activities of government's organs as well as apply for particular services to be rendered to them. In Nigeria for instance, candidates at such reputed exams as the national matriculation examination for admission into Nigerian institutions of higher learning simply need to visit a website few days after sitting the examination to have their results. Government has since computerized the process of administering the exam and of delivering the results. The marking of the exam scripts is computer-assisted while the results are made available in online platforms just few days after the exam. This contrasts with old practices which consisted of marking scripts manually and using surface mail service through the post office to get the candidates notified about their performances in the exam. The release of examination results in online platforms is just one example of e-services made available by the Nigerian government. Other government organs run websites through which information and e-services are provided.

A similar scenario is visible in Cameroon with the creation of the Cameroon Government Web Portal which has been a mechanism for publishing to, and interacting with Cameroon citizens and businesses. The portal is managed by CAMNET, the internet division of CAMTEL, Cameroon's public telecommunication agency. Since its inception in 2001, the portal has been a source of information on various activities of the Cameroonian government. Despite the fact that some observers have rated the quality of information and service provided through them as averagely poor (Tazo 2015), the portal represents a key e-government initiative by the Cameroon government. To an extent, it facilitates the provision of G2C and G2E services by the Cameroonian government.

Differences

Despite these similarities in the domains of ICT and e-Government development, there exist areas of differences. One of these areas is the varying level of democratic culture in the two countries. Though the two countries answer democratic, various indexes of authoritarianism are observable in their respective political spheres (BBC World Service Trust 2010; Crossriver Watch 2013; Hassam 2009; Ifreke 2017). These indexes of authoritarianism have, of course, been serious impediments to e-government, particularly e-participation. As earlier mentioned, the implementation of e-Government is highly dependent on government's political will to transform governance into a citizen-centered process, which implies government's enthusiastic embrace of liberal democracy. This full subscription to the civility of liberal democracy is yet to be observed in the two countries as freedom of expression is still under threat in the countries. Though reduced to a considerable amount, various forms of authoritarianism still prevail in Nigeria and Cameroon. However, the prevalence of authoritarianism seems more prevalent in Cameroon than Nigeria and this has been affecting the use of ICTs by citizens and businesses, indirectly posing a threat to e-participation in the Cameroonian republic (Endong 2017 a,b).

Contrarily to its Nigerian counterpart, the Cameroon government has in several occasions used very draconian methods of Internet censorship which have paralyzed citizens' expression of their opinions and positions on government policies through online platforms. Such draconian actions have been observed in 2011 and recently from 2016-2017 during the Anglophone Cameroon crisis, with the shutting down of the internet. In 2011, the internet black-out was general (it touched the whole country), while in 2016-2017 it exclusively targeted the two Anglophone regions of South-West and North-West were some English-speaking Cameroonians and their sympathizers were agitating against the imposition of French and some francophone traditions in the Anglophone system of education in the country . The 2016-2017 internet blackout therefore aimed at paralyzing citizens' expression of their anti-government feelings. It goes without saying that the internet blackout has had serious implications for e-government in Cameroon. It has for instance been a clear evidence of the Cameroonian government's non-readiness to wholly accept the idioms of freedom of expression and e-participation by its citizens. It has also shown the Cameroonian government's paradoxical attachment to authoritarianism despite its promulgation of various ICT and media bills which – on paper – promote freedom of expression and freedom of thought. Additionally, Cameroonian critics have equated the act (the government-provoked Internet blackout) with a kind of sabotage by Cameroon of its own digital economy. Such anti e-participation mechanisms have not (yet) been observed in Nigeria. Though the Nigerian government has, for security reasons, sometimes instituted seasonal and partial internet blackouts in the country, it has never embarked on a clear politically motivated internet blackout, to neutralize e-participation. One remembers that as part of its military strategy to combat Islamist insurgents (the Boko Haram terrorist group) in the north of the country in 2015, the Nigerian government instituted seasonal internet blackouts (Freedom House 2015), however, the acts were not politically motivated and did not aim to hamper e-participation. And so, it may be fair to argue that contrary to its Cameroonian counterpart, the Nigerian government has never shut down the internet in guise of disenabling digitally driven reactions to some of its (obnoxious) policies. This fact in itself could be considered one of the evidences suggesting that the political will to allow e-participation in particular and e-government in general seems lower in Cameroon, compared to Nigeria.

CONCLUSION

A monolithic perspective on the implementation of e-Government in Africa may not bring out some interesting details about the spread of the paradigm in the continent. Though African countries have been facing a number of similar challenges, their approaches to e-Government development have not always been the same. E-government is an extremely costly enterprise. Based on this, some African countries' low performance in ICT and e-Government rankings has had its roots in their limited economic power. The economic disparities and the varying level of democratization in African countries have caused ICT and e-Government development to vary from one country to the other in the continent. A case in point is the difference between Nigeria and Cameroon in the domain of e-Government implementation.

This chapter has attempted to show that though the two countries have made a number of similar efforts towards ICT and e-Government development, some areas of differences exist between them. Cameroon seems less ready for e-Government particularly compared to Nigeria. The country seems less politically prepared particularly when it comes to enabling e-participation by its citizens. This is so, given its constant shutting of the internet and other very draconian tactics deployed in guise of internet censorship. Such anachronistic procedures are incompatible with e-governance. They have not yet been observed in Nigeria. This constitutes a serious point of difference between Nigeria and Cameroon in the domain of e-Government development.

REFERENCES

Abede, R., & Dawit, D. (2010). An analysis of African e-Government service websites. *Government Information Quarterly*, *30*(31), 1–9.

Adepetum, A. (2017). Nigeria's teledensity increased by 2.27 in 2016. *The Guardian Business*. Retrieved June 14, 2017, from https://guardian.ng/business-services/nigerias-teledensity-increased-by-2-27-per-cent-in-2016/

Akunyili, D. (2010). *ICT and e-government in Nigeria: opportunities and challenges*. Paper presented at the World Congress on Information Technology.

Asongwe, P. N. (2013). E-Government and the Cameroon cybersecurity legislation 2010: Opportunities and challenges. *African Journal of Information and Communication*, *2*, 157–163.

BBC World Service Trust. (2010). *African Media Development Initiative. Cameroon country report context*. London: BBC World Service Trust.

CrossRiver Watch. (2013). We are not a flash in a pan – Agba Jalingo, founder CrossRiver Watch. *CrossRiver Watch*, *1*(6), 20–21.

Endong, F. P. C. (2017a). "Watchdogging" versus adversarial journalism by state-owned media: The Nigerian and Cameroonian experience. *IJELS: International Journal of English, Literature and Social Sciences*, *2*(2), 8–17.

Endong, F. P. C. (2017b). From dictatorship to African democracy: How has freedom of expression been improved in Nigeria and Cameroon? *Journal of Media Studies*, *31*(1), 1–17.

Fraser-Molekiti, G., & Senghor, D. (2010). *E-governance and citizen participation in West Africa: Challenges and opportunities*. Dakar: The Panos Institute & The United Nations Development Program.

Freedom House. (2015). *Freedom on the net 2015. Nigeria*. London: Freedom House.

Hafkin, N. I. (2009). *E-government in Africa: An overview of progress made and challenges*. Paper presented at the UNDESA/UNPAN Workshop on Electronic/Mobile Government in Africa.

Hassan, I.S. (2009, August 15). The fallacies of democracy and democratic dictatorship in Nigeria. *Kano Online*, 12-26.

Heeks, R. (2008). *The e-government for development information exchange*. Manchester, UK: Manchester Institute for Development Policy and Management.

Ifreke, I. (2017). *Bihari is trying to stifle freedom of expression- Soyinka*. Retrieved online http://dailypost.ng/2017/02/05/buhari-trying-stifle-freedom-expression-soyinka/

ITU. (2016). *ICT Development index 2016, Huwei*. ITU.

Karisiddappa, C. R. (2004). *Library and information science curriculum for developing countries*. Paper presented at IFLA General Conference and Council.

Kenhago, T. O. (2014). Successes and failures in e-government projects. *E-government for development*. Retrieved April 19, 2017 from http://www.egov4dev.org/success/case/camportal.shtml

Manor, I. (2015). Between two digital divides. *Exploring digital diplomacy*. Retrieved January 24, 2017, from https://digdipblog.com/2016/01/27/between-two-digital-divides/

Manor, I. (2015). In digital diplomacy, a narrowing digital divide. *Exploring digital diplomacy*. Retrieved January 24 from https://digdipblog.com/2015/01/19/divide/

MINPOSTEL. (2005). *Sector Strategy for Telecommunications and Information and Communication Technologies 2005- 2015*. Yaounde: Government Printers.

Ntiro, S. (2000). *eGovernment in Eastern Africa*. Dar-es Salam: KPMG.

Nzepa, N. O., & Keutchankeu, T. R. (2015). *Understanding what is happening in ICT in Cameroon. A supply-and-demand-side analysis of the ICT sector*. Cape Town, South Africa: Research ICT Africa.

Omiere, E., & Omiere, C. (2014). New wine in old wine skin: An exploration of major constraints to e-government implementation in Nigeria. *European Scientific Journal, 10*(14), 148–154.

Republic of Cameroon. (2009). *Growth and Employment Strategy Paper (GESP): Reference Framework for Government Action over the Period 2010-2020*. Yaounde: Government Printer.

Sindeu, E. (2013). *Implementation of e-government in Cameroon*. Paper presented at the 7th Annual E-Government Forum, Muyuno, Uganda.

The Windhoek Declaration. (2001). *African Charter on the Values and Principles of Public Service and the Administration*. Windhoek: African Ministers of Civil Service.

United Nation Public Administration Network. (2016). *Africa: UN e-Government survey ranks Mauritius 1st in Africa*. Retrieved May 27, 2017 from http://allafrica.com/stories/201608190714.html

UNO. (2008). *United Nations e-Government survey 2008: from e-Government to Connected Governance*. Washington, DC: UNO.

UNO. (2012). *United Nation e-government survey 2012*. Washington, DC: UNO.

UNO. (2014). *United Nation e-government survey 2014*. Washington, DC: UNO.

UNO. (2016). *United Nation e-Government survey 2016: E-government in support of sustainable development*. Washington, DC: UNO.

Wharton University (2016, August 23). Building e-governance in Africa: One pioneering company's approach. *Knowledge @ Wharton,* 43-49.

KEY TERMS AND DEFINITIONS

Digital Divide: This term refers to unequally in access to, and capabilities to use, information and communication technologies. Such inequalities are caused by economic and social factors. Most often, the term is used in reference to the uneven spread of the internet in the world illustrated by low internet penetration and low level of affordability of the internet in developing countries, compared to their western counterparts.

E-Governance: It is the application of Information and Communication technologies (ICT) for delivering a wide range of government services, for communication transactions and exchange of information among others.

Internet Penetration: The relationship between the number of internet users in each country and its demographic data.

Teledencity: Otherwise called telephone density, the term refers to the number of telephone connections for every hundred individuals living within a particular area. This number varies between countries and may also vary between rural and urban areas within a country.

Chapter 7
Data Organization as Structure for Collaborative Governance:
The Case of Implementation of Employment Guarantee Legislation in Rural India

Sharadindu Pandey
IIFM, India

Dhwani Sharma
Bhopal School of Social Science, India

ABSTRACT

NREGA is an employment guarantee legislation promulgated for the rural workers of India. It provides 100 days of employment in a year with a provision of unemployment allowance by implementing agencies. To monitor the legislation, a collaborative platform has been developed that is customized to the requirement of the multiple stakeholders (e.g., different governments, village bodies, beneficiaries, public, work engineers, etc.). A large amount of the data is generated on the platform. Despite this, it takes lot of time in complaint redressal and mostly it is done manually. The chapter attempts to explore ideas of how the collaborative platform could be made more effective by organizing the data such that the requirement of field-based variability can be minimized.

DOI: 10.4018/978-1-5225-4987-1.ch007

INTRODUCTION

In India, the right based rural employment scheme has been on ground to address the rural unemployment problem and development challenges. The scheme is promulgated as legislation known as National Rural Employment Guarantee Act, 2005 (NREGA). It provides the employment guarantee of 100 days to the village based individual. The rural workers may be engaged in the works like watershed management, rural connectivity, afforestation, land development etc. The scheme is financially supported by the union government and implemented by the state government. In India, the governance structure is at village, block, district and then state level. The key challenge of the structure is the orchestration of the right kind of role, information and participation of general public residing in the villages, elected representatives of village, block, district, state and national level and civil servants of village, block, and district and above. Despite of the fact that the use of information system is envisaged at the village level, the delay in the implementation of IT system and the challenges related to its robustness results in to the failed outcome. Various officials responsible for the governance often has solution to the problem, however for the want of robust and time bound information system, the concerns are not reaching to them.

Data organization is a concept where data is sent to the right authority for the disposal. The point where the data is generated remains buried there only due to absence of auto-data dissemination mechanism to the right authorities. The book chapter aims to bring out the limitation of the common data pool of the employment guarantee scheme of India. These limitations would be related to achievement of the legislative goals. The typical problems related to implementation of employment guarantee legislation are unavailability of the prescribed number of the work days made available to the beneficiaries, reduction of the work days due to slow progress at work and the convergence of this scheme with the other schemes of the union/ state government.

The chapter attempts to highlight that the data generated in the compliance of the monitoring specification needs to be disseminated to the concerned authority on the real time basis. Citizen's emersion is important for the collaborative governance. Rural governance in India has developed a portal by which the citizen's can convey their concerns to the authority. However, what if when the citizen's are not literate enough to convey the concerns through the portal. What if when the concerns are not properly addressed. How the chain the unaddressed issues are devised such as all the actors of the governance network occupy their roles and citizen's gets counselling, solution and satisfaction from the governance.

The chapter will discuss how the inter-organizational data organization is devised such as the outcome of the collaboration is linked with the drivers of the collaboration. Based on the field work carried out, social audit data and the stakeholder's complaint data accessible on portal, the critical instances are identified which reflect problem investigation modes, accountability mechanism developed and further data-reorganization requirement, which can ease the process of governance. During the field visit made at villages, it was observed that there is role conflict among monitoring authority who is mainly the elected representative at the district level and the implementation authority, which is the special executive authority responsible for the implementation of the rural development. District level monitoring and coordination authority was engaged with the district execution authority for the information update. A common villager is typically dependent upon the elected representative of the villages and staff for the redressal of their problems and concerns. There seems to be a substantial gap in the dissemination of the data related to complaints and concerns of the villagers to the empowered officials at various levels in the time bound manner.

IMPLEMENTATION OF NREGA LEGISLATION

The literature of the collaborative governance mentions the 'problem driven and opportunity driven' governance. The literature of the inter-organizational governance has some insights about what drives the particular type of organization structure. Usually bureaucratic organizations are driven by the career of the officers.

NREGAsoft: A Collaboration Platform

The offline and online version of this platform is provided to the implementing agencies. The platform is developed by the NIC (National Informatics centre), a government agency along with the MORD (Ministry of Rural Development), Government of India, which is the nodal agency of the legislative implementation. A customised interface is provided to the stakeholder. For example, primary beneficiaries may be illiterate villagers who can use this platform through voice and sound. State, district and village body has local language interface and Ministry does interface in English language. Following are the stakeholders of the IT platform:

1. Citizens
2. Village body called Gram Panchayat (GP), Block level body called Block Panchayat (BP) and district level body called Zila Panchayat (ZP)

3. Workers
4. District Programme coordinating body called DISHA, chaired by MP (Member of Parliament)
5. Banks
6. State Rural Development (RD) Department

Data entry in the software is done at village and block level. The platform envisages to provide access to create data on the platform. However, at village body level, there are only limited states where this platform is being used. There are various modules like Administrative, worker management, finance, work management, stores and inventory management, grievance redressal and cost estimation. These modules provide the management function, however, the challenge lies in the verifiability of the data entered. This is vital to investigate the complaint online only to save time in constituting investigating body and its field work.

NREGA Performance

See Table 1 and Table 2.

Challenges of Time Taken in Redressal

There is an instance where district representative who is also the elected member of the district informed the union level nodal ministry about irregularity being sustained in MNREGA implementation. The nodal ministry wrote to the state

Table 1. The summary of current performance of NREGA in India

National	
1.Total No. of Districts	685
2.Total No. of Blocks	6,863
3.Total No. of GPs	2,62,839
4.Total No. of Job Cards issued[In million]	124.9
5.Total No. of Workers [In million]	254.6
6.Total No. of Active Job Cards [In million]	66.1
7.Total No. of Active Workers [In million]	102.3
8.(i)SC worker (Dis-advantaged class) against active workers[%]	20.29
9.(ii)ST worker (Dis-advantaged class) against active workers[%]	16.58

Source: (Ministry of Rural Development, Government of India, 2017)

Table 2. The summary of 3 years progress of NREGA in India

National			
Progress	**FY 2016-2017**	**FY 2015-2016**	**FY 2014-2015**
1.SC person days % as of total person days	21.26	22.29	22.4
2.ST person days % as of total person days	17.61	17.8	16.97
3.Women Person days out of Total (%)	56.1	55.26	54.88
4.Average days of employment provided per Household	45.97	48.85	40.17
5.Average Wage rate per day per person(Rs.)	161.7	154.08	143.92
6.Total No of HHs completed 100 Days of Wage Employment	39,56,038	48,47,975	24,92,654
7.Total Households Worked[In Cr]	5.1146	4.8134	4.14
8.Total Individuals Worked[In Cr]	7.6505	7.2261	6.22
9.Differently abled persons worked	4,67,809	4,59,597	4,13,316
10.Number of GPs with NIL exp	19,938	39,469	39,531
11. .Number of Ongoing Works[In Lakhs]	96.13	86.94	68.21
12.Number of Completed Works[In Lakhs]	58.76	36.18	29.44
13. Percentage Utilization w.r.t. To fund release	104.01	101.43	95.84
14. Material(%)	26.29	25.81	28.03
15.Total Administration Expenditure[In Cr]	2,787.89	2,363.36	2,416.67
16.% payments generated within 15 days	43.99	36.92	26.85

Source: (Ministry of Rural Development, Government of India, 2017)

government for the comments which remained un-received for 2 years. After two years, a reminder was sent to the state government, which was answered this time and finally the corrective action of to pay from the state's exchequer was taken 4 years after which can considered a long delay. Here, there are two points of delay, one is response time taken by the state, accountability of the governance associated by it and legislative provisions available. The second is delay in time taken in actual redresssal of the complaint. NREGA act 2005 section 23 provides that programme officer or the block level officer is responsible for the wrong doing. The act also provides that if the problem involves many parties, the communication will be sent to all the parties with a copy to the complainant. Section 25 provides the penalty for the non-implementation by any person. All the steps are the part of the open data. The possible data organization challenge is using sequential mode of complaint redressal where at a time, one person or authority is contacted and remaining person and authority are not made the part of the process. The alternative system design mechanism is to system generated data dissemination and the distribution of the data to each party where all can see the response of each other. The programme officer or block officer will be able to address the complaint only if it is received to him through central or state agencies.

Now there is second incident where complaint is communicated to the state govt. in time. Section 27 of the act provides for the nodal govt. to ask any agency to investigate the matter. The nodal govt. found the investigative report and further asked the state govt. to take action against the responsible officers. Now the issue is against the recovery of the amount. It is notable that in the previous example, the recovery was made by the state exchequer. The nodal govt. also has the right entrusted by the legislation to provides the suitable directions to the implementation agencies. Now the problem is that in one case recovery is made by the state agency and in another case, the recovery is made pending. It may be due to the change of the people involved in the process. The possible corrective action is to make the past corrective action as precedent or part of the standard operating procedure for the officers so that they can decide about the outcome happened in previous cases. The manual system does not provide convenience to reproduce all such instances. The implementing person may be enabled by IT to produce all such instances.

Accountability of Multiple Levels

Section 25 provides straight penal provisions for 'whosoever' contravening the provisions. It imposes monetary punishment on the officers. Now the challenge with this provision is that recovering the huge amount foregone due to corrupt or wrong practices. There are two ways to get over this problem. One is to get the recovery in-case the officials have amassed with them, other way is to avoid such situation by more frequent monitoring and to avoid the escalation of the situation. The second way is more effective, which requires proactive approach in monitoring. The present method used for monitoring is largely empirical and dis-continuous. There are two levels of monitoring, the one is internal which is conducted by the implementing agency and another is usually performed by the third party. District level monitoring and coordinating agencies are the back bone of the internal monitoring mechanism, which faces inherent tendencies of the conflict with the district level executing official due to various factors. Usually the beneficiaries of the scheme are the common villagers and the labourers who may not be able to articulate their problem well. They might be required the help of proxy complainant who can put their matter rightly before the officials. The agents of village level, block level, state assembly level and district-parliament level representative can better play the role of proxy complainants to have better view of grounding of the scheme. Presently these elective representatives are made part of a committee called DISHA where it can commonly work together. Now these representatives being outside the Government, the government cannot fix accountability norms for them. The secretary of this committee is the part of the Government and he/she is also the nodal person of the scheme implementation at the district level. The action of suspension, dismissal and registering for criminal case were mainly the actions, which were taken generally against the functionaries at the village level. There are instances where block level officers and well as Chief executive of district level special body for rural development were also suspended. There are instances where Rs. 1000 penalty was recovered from the block level officer. However, the instances of the complete recovery of the misappropriated money are very less. There needs a data organization mechanism where the actual compliance of the provisions can be recorded. The internal monitoring office which acquires the data from the same sources may not get the realistic picture. The internal monitoring body needs to develop the alternative sources of the data acquisition to cross check the claims of the compliance to prevent the mis-appropriation of the funds. The same person responsible for executing the programme and monitoring the implementation may give the realistic picture provided he is asked to collect the data from the alternate means also e.g. beneficiaries, banks etc. So far as the accountability of the elected representatives are concerned, it is fixed at the lowest level. The village head is suspended, got recovery notices and faced the FIR (Criminal case registration) also. At the district level, the action against the elected representatives are very less, which is only possible at the state govt. level.

Data Organization

Complaint system is already online. In many instances of the complaints, it took disproportionate amount of time requesting the state government, setting up the investigating body and the infield document verification by this body and acting upon the corrective mechanism. This is because, some of the states are not using the NREGA soft where manual system is prevailing. Practices also show that despite the provision of 7 days as complaint redressal time, it takes substantial time in redressing the complaints. For reducing this time, the collaborative platform need to have all data uploaded which is required for the field verification of the complaint. The complaints are typically related to the not issuing job cards. The response is that job card request has not been made in writing. It is clearly a communication problem. To address this problem, the Interactive Voice Response System (IVRS) has been started.

However, to verify the job demand, IVRS system needs to generate some reference number, which can be provided in the complaint and it can be determined that the job demand was infact made. The Second type of the complaint is to pay less than what is the rate fixed by the government. This may be due to reducing the number of the days as per work measurement done before. To verify these complaints, the criterion of work measurement may also be uploaded. So that in the eventuality of the unfair criterion, the investigating body can suggest the alternate criterion which could provide some remedy to the complainants. It is also observed that only that the tendency of provide the minimum data is available on the platform, which is just enough to solve the complaints may lead new complaints. There may the uniform parameters of the work quality measurements, which could also be uploaded on the site and verified openly. Any change in the rating of these quality parameters should show on real time basis. The present system of the independent monitoring is only providing the verification of the sample of the work, which may be biased in the circumstances in which samples are chosen and examined. The multimedia based wok quality data would make it possible to examine all the works verifiable by anybody. While study of the corrective actions, it was found that the recovery actions were put in place but data organization should be such as individual share of the recovery can be ascertained. For determining the individual share, all actions made by the individuals must be available online so that the open data based inquiry may be carried out once the problem is exposed. And for exposing the problems also, the open data is required. Presently, only the part of the issues is surfaced and that is due to informal investigation by the civil society members.

CONCLUSION

In the present NREGA implementation, the dis-incentive has been linked with the implementation outcomes. For bringing any transformation in the NREGA implementation and outcome, the variable incentives may also be linked with the outcome. There are village body and block level workers who show potential for enterprise but due to lack of support and incentives, many initiatives are unrealized. The success of the collaborative governance in open data scenario lies in the fact the components of the system support each other. A team based reward system may lead the village and block level employees to help the general body of the village to come up with more possibility of the work execution. There are instances, where simply there are no work proposal and due to lack of work, the legislative aim of hundred days' work offer to the rural workers is not achieved. In the NREGA legislation, the provision of the unemployment allowance is up-to the economic conditions of the implementing states, there are states, which have not provided for the unemployment allowance. The legislation also provides for convergence of MNREGA with other schemes of the government. However, there is legislative checks that a stipulated labour material ratio has to be maintained at all level. Presently, this ratio is 70:30. The convergence of the scheme requires the structural change in the incentive system of the other departments also. The collaboration platform of the other schemes should also be in sync with the NREGA. The present system of the data organization is such as easy triangulation of the data is not fully possible so that one can reach to the verifiable source of the information. Many states where NREGA soft is only partially implemented is increasing the burden of the complaint redressal body to go to the field and check the record. It causes lot of delay and executive efforts. The collaborative platform needs to be capacitated so that it could show the documents also along with the information for easy verifiability.

REFERENCES

Ministry of Rural Development, Government of India. (2017, May 7). Retrieved from http://www.nrega.nic.in/netnrega/home.aspx

ADDITIONAL READING

Ansell, C., & Gash, A. (2007). Collaborative governance in theory and practice. *Journal of Public Administration: Research and Theory*, 18.

Donahua, J. (2004). On Collaborative Governance. Harvard University Working paper no. 2. Retrieved May 7, 2017, from https://www.hks.harvard.edu/mrcbg/CSRI/publications/workingpaper_2_donahue.pdf on

Section 5
Organisational Barriers to OGI

Chapter 8
Conceptualizing Cyber-Security From EU Perspective

Ayse Kok
Bogazici University, Turkey

ABSTRACT

If the aim of the EU is the establishment of deeper cooperation with other nations within the context of cyber security in the future, platforms (e.g., the Task Force) should create an effective agenda that reflects the differences between the EU (soft power) and other countries such as China or Russia (hard power). Yet, there should not be any compromise in the principles and norms of these countries with regard to their Internet policies. Although this may sound too difficult to accomplish, it is not impossible given EU's increased emphasis on cybersecurity along with its evolving cybersecurity strategy.

DOI: 10.4018/978-1-5225-4987-1.ch008

INTRODUCTION

In 2004, ENISA (European Network and Information Security Agency) was founded in order to facilitate 'best' practice among Member States with regard to cyber security policies with regard to EU's Information Society agenda. In 2007, due to DDoS (Distributed Denial of Service) attacks on the public infrastructure of Estonia, the EU along with NATO and other related actors considered to change their approach. As a result, the EU's policy has been developed within the light of the Europe 2020 strategy. The European Cybersecurity Strategy (2013) and its Guidelines and Principles for Internet Resilience (March 2011) focus on the significance of global partnerships to address both military and civilian aspects of cyber security challenges.

According to EU Cybersecurity strategy, the Internet must be kept protected and 'open and free' based on the same values and principles that the EU considers for offline space (EU Cybersecurity Strategy). EU Cybersecurity Strategy and its Directive on Network and Information Security (NIS Directive) were published on 7 February 2013, to require the reporting of significant cyber incidents across all critical infrastructure sectors (NIS Directive 2013). For the first time, the EU tried to specify priorities with regard to the protection of cyberspace via means of this strategy as previously there was no coordination with regard to the construction of an effective security ecosystem for cyberspace (Klimburg & Tirmaa-Klaar 2011).

This paper will be structured as follows: After a brief overview of the conceptual landscape of the EU's cyber security development, the suggested tools for cyber security policy of EU will be explained. Next an overview of the EU's way of dealing with cyber security threats will be explained. The final section will provide recommendations for EU's cooperation with other states on cybersecurity in the future.

Concepts and Approaches of the EU's Cybersecurity Policy

The existing body of academic literature with regard to the EU's action in cybersecurity is scarce as most of the available work focuses on the US and other regions (Kshetri, 2013), with no in-depth theoretical analysis of EU's cyber security policy. Various approaches such as managerial and strategic (Libicki 2007, 2009; Clarke & Knake 2010), historical (Carr 2009) and 'other approaches that focus on terrorists (Wiemann 2006; Colarik 2006) have been used. While the emphasis of such approaches has been more on recent cyber threats and how to establish the 'cyber peace' (Clarke & Knake 2010), other theoretically and methodologically driven works used innovative mixed-method (Deibert et al. 2012), regulatory (Brown & Marsden 2007) and other approaches that try to evaluate the extent of securitization of cyber policy (Dunn, 2007, 2008; Bendrath *et* al. 2007).

Cyber power has been so far one of the most frequently used concepts with regard to cyber security (Klimburg and Tirmaa- Klaar 2011; Betz and Stevens 2011; Klimburg 2011; Nye, 2010; Kramer et al. 2009). While Nye (2010) defines cyber power as the ability to utilize the digital pace to create an influence and gain advantages in other operational contexts (2010, p.4) he makes a distinction between information and physical instruments, as well as soft and hard power in cyber space, and provides examples of how they can be used both outside (extra cyberspace power) and inside (intra cyberspace power) (See Table 1).

Other scholars such as Betz & Stevens (2011, p.44) acknowledge the fluidity of cyberspace and mention that and that various non-state and state actors, ranging from states to citizens, global networks and organizations, can have an influence at any point in time in order to exploit the possibilities offered by cyberspace. As a result, they conceptualize the cyber power in four distinct forms:

- **Compulsory**: This occurs when one cyberspace actor makes use of direct coercion to change the behavior of another actor (hard power such as attacks on FBI systems);
- **Institutional**: This refers to one of the actor's Indirect control via means of formal and informal institutions (soft power such as setting norms);
- **Structural**: This refers to a control type which aims to maintain the existing structures and enable or limit the actions of the actors with regard to those with whom they have a connection (soft power regarding how cyberspace can enable or limit the actions of actors);
- **Productive**: This refers to the definition of the 'fields of possibility' that limit or enable social action (soft power such as a states' construction of the 'hacker' as threat) via means of discourse.

According to Klimburg (2011), cyber power has the following other crucial aspects:

Table 1. Instruments of power in cyberspace

	Intra Cyber Space	Extra Cyber Space
Information Instruments	Soft: Set standards & norms	Soft: Public campaign to influence opinion
	Hard: Denial of Service Attacks	Hard: Attack SCADA systems
Physical Instruments	Soft: Infrastructure to support activists of human rights	Soft: Protests to name and shame cyber providers
	Hard: Government controls over enterprises	Hard: Cut cables or bomb routers

(Source: Nye, 2010)

1. Coordination of policy and operational aspects across governmental structures;
2. Policy coherency through international alliances and legal frameworks;
3. Cooperation among non-state cyber actors.

In opposition to Nye (2010), Klimburg (2011) asserts that the last one is the most significant one as most of the control is exerted by civil and business society due the nature of the cyberspace and the state's capability is restricted to indirect influence. Based on the Model of Integrated Capability (Klimburg & Tirmaa-Klaar 2011), Klimburg (2011) emphasizes the need for a holistic approach to cyber security, in other words a soft-power approach which is focused on the inward is fundamental for the creation of a 'whole of nation' of cyber capability' (2011, p.43). Although the Cybersecurity Strategy (2013) included some of these scholars' recommendations it is not certain whether 'hard' cyber power considered in EU's conventional national security terms is actually aligned with the EU's core values. This is a crucial point given the revelations of post-PRISM (e-spying) that certain EU Member States such as Sweden and UK were complicit in mass data surveillance of citizens in contravention of EU laws on data protection among 'friends' in Europe.

Within the light of this information, it can be argued that the EU needs a security policy based on resilience approach (Christou 2015) and a specific kind of soft cyber power based on Klimburg's three aspects including productive and institutional cyber power, rather than the conventional and hard cyber power often exercised by democratic and authoritarian states, based on the logic of cyber sovereignty. In the post-Snowden era, this is even more imperative as the consequences of a mindset of 'national security first' has been in sharp contrast with the vision of EU's open, safe and secure cyberspace. Within this regard, Dunn-Cavelty (2013, p.3) states that a special type of 'soft' power driven by core values and internal resilience should be developed by the EU to make sure that its normative vision with regard to the cyberspace's governance is obtained within the global arena.

The EU Approach to Cybersecurity

Over time as the EU's approach to cybersecurity evolved in an ad hoc and fragmented manner several strands of cybersecurity 'policy' emerged which can be categorized as in Table 2:

According to Robinson (2013), given the complexity of the cyber security domain, and the difficulty for the design of a coherent internal EU policy, these strands entail the following aspects:

Table 2.Strands of EU's cybersecurity policy

Policy Strand	Responsible Institution
Cybercrime and cyber attacks	Directorate General Justice and Home Affairs
Network and Information Security (NIS): a) Critical Infrastructure Protection (CIP) b) Critical and Information Infrastructure Protection (CIIP)	Directorate General Connect (previously DG Information Society)
A cyber defense element	European External Action Service (EEAS)

(Source: Robinson, 2013)

- Legal (enforcement),
- Economic (Internal Market)
- Security (CSDP)

Furthermore, the Cybersecurity Strategy also includes both the development of technological resources for cybersecurity and the establishment of policy for cyberspace in order for the EU to contribute to its the fundamental values. (Robinson, 2013):

Based on the normative foundation of the EU approach, the global Internet is regarded as a collective or public good which should be made accessible and available to all (EU Cybersecurity strategy 2013; European principles and guidelines 2011). So, the use of the Internet should only be constrained when instruments and measures are used to provide harm to others. An effective cybersecurity strategy should take as its basis the main norms as stated in EU's Charter with regard to its Fundamental Rights (EU Cybersecurity Strategy 2013). Thus, main EU values and norms are at the core of both online and offline activity, as stated in its Cybersecurity Strategy.

According to the EU Cybersecurity Strategy (2013), the governance model of its cybersecurity policy should be based on multi-stakeholderism which arises due to the complex interactions among several actors using and managing the Internet. Some states such as Iran, Russia, China or India held the opinion that due to the excessive power of the US. over the management of the Internet these countries themselves are under-represented in current Internet governance institutions such as the ICANN (Internet Corporation for Assigned Numbers and Names) or IGF (Forum for Internet Governance).

As any of these principles on EU cybersecurity policy cannot exist in a vacuum, a specific type of public-private partnership is supported under this multi-stakeholder umbrella. Therefore, while the appropriate forms and modes of governance (i.e. incentives) should be agreed by public authorities in consultation with related stakeholders, the private sector plays an important role in day-to-day governance of the Internet (European principles and guidelines 2011). If there is any global disagreement with regard to the role of technical standards, data protection, who should regulate the Internet, and the appropriate legal conventions for fighting cybercrime (e.g. the Budapest Convention), these can undermine any effort to develop a secure cyberspace for everyone. In the post-Snowden era, an increased support for the Governmental Advisory Committee in ICANN was provided by EU, by assigning it a greater decision-making role in policy on Internet governance.

Progress and Challenges of the EU Cybersecurity Strategy

As Robinson (2014) states, in comparison to the US, China or Russia, whose main focus is on a national security (threat) logic and hence deterrence and militarisation constitute their central strategy (hard power), the EU is focused on building resilience to enable fast recovery from cyber attacks, developing the required capacities to resist cyber attacks, and fighting cybercrime (soft power). For the EU, those priorities that focus on non-military aspects which aim to create partnerships for the development of an effective cybersecurity culture within and beyond the EU are more important that its military and intelligence infrastructure (Bendiek, 2014). include not only dialague, incentives, platforms for cooperation and coordination and voluntary arrangements (to ratify the Budapest Convention), but also more formal requirements, such as the suggested NIS Directive to protect both the privacy and data of its citizens. Yet, it is not known which of these instruments provide the EU with the opportunity to create effective productive (soft) and institutional cyber power.

With regard to the preparation of its Cyber Defence Policy Framework, the EU so far developed bilateral relationships through means of participation in international platforms such as the London conference and appropriate international fora (OECD, ICANN, ITU, IGF), as well as international organisations such as NATO.

On the other hand, there has been some issues with the CoE (Budapest) Convention on Cybercrime as it was not implemented by all Member States across Europe. Besides, some countries such as Russia and China oppose ratifying the Convention as they are concerned that national security culture would be undermined because Internet users in these countries are often the alleged source of many cybersecurity attacks (Goldsmith, 2011).

Being members of SCO (Shanghai Cooperation Organization), Russia, China, Tajikistan and Uzbekistan proposed in September, 2011 that the UN Secretary General should establish a dialogue about the new 'Code of Conduct for International Security' with the purpose of reaching an agreement on international norms of behavior for the Internet. Although at first sight, its main principles (Appendix) are in alignment with what is being advocated by the EU with regard to full respect for rights and freedoms in cyberspace, an in-depth look reveals that rather than supporting a multi-stakeholder approach to cybersecurity, the commitment to prevent other states from using core technologies to threaten other countries' security is underpinned by a sovereign logic of control rather than freedom (Gjelten, 2010).

The promotion of the UN to take a more active role in Internet governance, where China has much more influence and weight in terms of voting behavior, could lead to a potential separation of national Internet spaces, rather than multi-stakeholder governance. In addition to the perceived dominance of the US in controlling the Internet, given the SCO members' commitments to restrict information flows in case of any impact upon their security culture, the main concerns are about repressive regimes' excuses to restrict access to independent external news sources, as in the case of the Arab uprisings (Gjelten, 2010). As some scholars argue, this might also be used as a justification to develop draconian laws on access and dissemination of information which might threaten 'national security' (Healey 2011b; Bendiek 2014). Finally, the fact that states such as Russia and China which are seen to be at the center of cyber conflict do not support a commitment to control patriotic hackers is regarded as another concern. Besides, no Code calls for all states to sign up and be bound by the laws of armed conflict which raises many questions with regard to the legitimacy and proportionality of certain targets (Christou, 2015).

CONCLUSION

If the aim of the EU is the establishment of deeper cooperation with other nations within the context of cyber security in the future, platforms (e.g: the Task Force) should create an effective agenda that reflects the differences between the EU (soft power) and other countries such as China or Russia (hard power). Yet, there should not be any compromise in the principles and norms of these countries with regard to their Internet policies. Although this may sound as being too difficult to accomplish it is not impossible given EU's increased emphasis on cybersecurity along with its evolving cybersecurity strategy.

REFERENCES

Bendiek, A. (2014). *Tests of Partnership: Transatlantic Cooperation in Cyber Security, Internet Governance and Data Protection.* SWP Research Paper, RP5, March 2014, Berlin.

Bendrath, R., Eriksson, J., & Giacomello, G. (2010). From 'cyberterrorism' to 'cyberwar', back and forth: How the United States securitized cyberspace. In International Relations and Security in the Digital Age. London: Routledge.

Betz, D., & Stevens, T. (2011). *Cyberspace and the State: Towards a Strategy for Cyber-Power.* Oxon, UK: Routledge.

Brown, I., & Marsden, C. T. (2007). *Co-regulating Internet Security: the London Action Plan.* Retrieved in April 2016 from http://essex.academia.edu/ChrisMarsden/Papers/700007/Co-regulating_Internet_security_the_London_Action_Plan

Carr, J. (2009). *Inside Cyber Warfare: Mapping the Cyber Underworld.* O'Reilly Media.

Christou, G. (2015). *Cyber Security in the European Union: Resilience and Adaptability in Governance Policy.* Houndmills, UK: Palgrave Macmillan.

Clarke, R. A., & Knake, R. K. (2010). *Cyber War: The Threat to National Security and what to do about it.* New York: Harper Collins.

Colarik, A. M. (2006). *Cyber terrorism: Political and Economic Implications.* IGI Publishing. doi:10.4018/978-1-59904-021-9

Deibert, R. J., Palfrey, J. G., Rohozinski, R., & Zittrain, J. (Eds.). (2011). *Access Contested: Security, Identity and Resistance in Asian Cyberspace.* Cambridge, MA: MIT Press. doi:10.7551/mitpress/9780262016780.001.0001

Dunn, C. M. (2007). Cyber-Terror-Looming Threat or Phantom Menace? The Framing of the US Cyber-Threat Debate. *Journal of Information Technology & Politics, 4*(1), 19–35.

Dunn-Cavelty, M. (2008). Cyber-Security and Threat Politics: US efforts to secure the Information Age. London: Routledge.

Dunn-Cavelty, M. (2013). *A Resilient Europe for an Open, Safe and Secure Cyberspace* (Occasional Papers, No.23). The Swedish Institute of International Affairs.

European Commission. (2009). *Internet Governance: Next Steps*. Communication from the Commission from the European Parliament and the Council, Brussels, 18 June, COM (2009) 277 final. Author.

European Commission. (2013). *Cybersecurity Strategy of the EU: An Open, Safe and Secure Cyberspace*. Brussels, 7.2.13, JOIN (2013) 1 FINAL. Author.

European Cybercrime Centre. (n.d.). *First Year Report*. Retrieved from April 24, 2016, from https://www.europol.europa.eu/content/european-cybercrime-center-ec3-first-year-report

European Cybercrime Centre – one year on. (2014). European Commission, Press Release, Brussels, IP/14/129, 10 February 2014.

European Principles and Guidelines for Internet Resilience and Stability. (2011). Retrieved on April 11, 2016, from http://ec.europa.eu/danmark/documents/alle_emner/videnskabelig/110401_rapport_cyberangreb_ en.pdf

Gjelten, T. (2010). *Seeing the Internet as an 'Information Weapon'*. Retrieved on March 12, 2016, from http://www.npr.org/templates/story/story.php?storyId=130052701

Goldsmith, J. (2011). *Cybersecurity treaties: A Sceptical View*. Stanford University.

Healey, J. (2011a). *Comparing Norms for National Conduct in Cyberspace*. Retrieved on March 12, 2016, from http://www.acus.org

Healey, J. (2011b). *Breakthrough or Just Broken? China and Russia's UNGA Proposal on Cyber Norms*. Retrieved on April 12, 2016, from http://www.acus.org

Klimburg, A. (2011). Ruling the Domain: (Self) Regulation and the Security of the Internet. Austrian Institute for International Affairs.

Klimburg, A., & Tirmaa-Klaar, H. (2011). Cyber war and Cyber security: Challenges faced by the EU and its Member States. DG for External Policies, Policy Department, European Parliament.

Kramer, Starr, & Wentz (Eds.). (2010). Cyber Power and National Security. Washington, DC: National Defence UP.

Kshetri, N. (2013). *Cybercrime and Cybersecurity in the Global South*. Houndmills, UK: Palgrave Macmillan. doi:10.1057/9781137021946

Libicki, M. C. (2007). *Conquest in Cyberspace: National Security and Information Warfare*. New York: Cambridge University Press. doi:10.1017/CBO9780511804250

Libicki, M. C. (2009). *Cyber Deterrence and Cyber War*. Rand Corporation.

Ministry of Foreign Affairs of the People's Republic of China. (2011, September 13). *China, Russia and Other Countries Submit the Document of International Code of Conduct for Information Security to the United Nations*. Retrieved from http://www.fmprc.gov.cn/mfa_eng/wjb_663304/zzjg_663340/jks_665232/jkxw_665234/t858978.shtml

Mueller, M. L. (2010). *Networks and States: The Global Politics of the Internet*. M.I.T. Press. doi:10.7551/mitpress/9780262014595.001.0001

Nye, J. (2010). Cyber Power. Harvard Kennedy School, Belfer Center for Science and International Affairs.

Robinson, N. (2013). *The European Cyber Security Strategy: Too Big to Fail?* Available at: http://www.rand.org/bog/2013/02/the-european-cyber-security-strategy-too-big-to-fail.html

Robinson, N. (2014). *EU cyber-defence: a work in progress*. European Union Institute for Security Studies.

United Nations. (2010). *Report of the Group of Governmental Experts on Developments in the Field of Information and Telecommunications in the Context of International Security, A/65/201, Study Series 33*. UN.

Wiemann, G. (2006). *Cyberterrorism: How Real Is the Threat*. Washington, DC: United States Institute of Peace.

APPENDIX 1

International Code of Conduct for Information Security (SCO) (Ministry of Foreign Affairs of the People's Republic of China, 2011)

1. *To comply with the UN Charter and universally recognized norms governing international relations, which enshrine, inter alia, respect for the sovereignty, territorial integrity and political independence of all states, respect for human rights and fundamental freedoms, as well as respect for diversity of history, culture and social systems of all countries.*
2. *Not to use ICTs including networks to carry out hostile activities or acts of aggression and pose threats to international peace and security. Not to proliferate information weapons and related technologies.*
3. *To cooperate in combating criminal and terrorist activities which use ICTs including networks, and curbing dissemination of information which incites terrorism, secessionism, extremism or undermines other countries' political, economic and social stability, as well as their spiritual and cultural environment.*
4. *To endeavour to ensure the supply chain security of ICT products and services, prevent other states from using their resources, critical infrastructures, core technologies and other advantages, to undermine the right of the countries, which accepted this Code of Conduct, to independent control of ICTs, or to threaten other countries' political, economic and social security.*
5. *To reaffirm all states' rights and responsibilities to protect, in accordance with relevant laws and regulations, their information space and critical information infrastructure from threats, disturbance, attack and sabotage*
6. *To fully respect the rights and freedom in information space, including rights and freedom of searching for, acquiring and disseminating information on the premise of complying with relevant national laws and regulations.*
7. *To promote the establishment of a multilateral, transparent and democratic international management of the Internet to ensure an equitable distribution of resources, facilitate access for all and ensure a stable and secure functioning of the Internet.*
8. *To lead all elements of society, including its information and communication private sectors, to understand their roles and responsibilities with regard to information security, in order to facilitate the creation of a culture of information security and the protection of critical information infrastructures.*
9. *To assist developing countries in their efforts to enhance capacity-building on information security and to close the digital divide.*

10. *To bolster bilateral, regional and international cooperation, promote the United Nations' important role in formulation of international norms, peaceful settlement of international disputes, and improvement of international cooperation in the field of information security, and enhance coordination among relevant international organizations.*
11. *To settle any dispute resulting from the application of this Code through peaceful means and refrain from the threat or use of force.*

Chapter 9
A Discussion Paper on Cybersecurity Policies

Ayse Kok
Bogazici University, Turkey

ABSTRACT

This chapter presents various reasons for the insufficiency of externalities in terms of the inference of market failure with regard to the field cybersecurity policy, which is claimed to be necessary for government intervention. The main argument of this chapter is that cybersecurity market failures are much smaller than initially assumed, and as a result, more harm might be done by trying to correct them through naïve government regulation.

DOI: 10.4018/978-1-5225-4987-1.ch009

INTRODUCTION

Given the rapid changes in the field of computer networking its implications for our lives are uncertain. As a result, policy-makers differ in their views with regard to the regulatory action required in the field of cybersecurity.

Proponents of government intervention in cybersecurity assert that as market forces on their own cannot obtain the required level of security for the fulfilment of national security objectives regulation is necessary to establish the suitable level of cybersecurity (CSIS, 2008). Their rationale can be explained based on the economic concepts of public goods and market failure.

Those goods whose benefits are for all of society yet whose returns are difficult to capture for any individual are defined as public goods. For instance, without the incentives of the government, basic research could not be supplied by the market, so it counts as a public good. Similarly, cybersecurity is another such public good as market forces are not adequate.

According to Van Eeten and Bauer (2009), if social costs and benefits of security decisions are not correctly reflected in the incentives of the players in the value net due to externalities or public good aspects of security investments, there will be a systematic deviation from the social optimum. These authors claim that low security investments may lead to slower diffusion rates of IT uses and the related opportunity costs to society (Van Eeten and Bauer, 2009).

According to some policy analysts, a market failure can be inferred whenever an externality is observed. Yet, this inference would be a mistake as the observation of an externality is *not sufficient* on its own to infer a market failure despite the close relationship between externalities and market failure.

Within the light of economic literature, this paper purports to present various reasons for the insufficiency of externalities in terms of the inference of market failure with regard to the field cybersecurity policy which is claimed to be necessary for government intervention. The main argument of this paper is that cybersecurity market failures are much smaller than initially assumed and as a result, more harm might be done by trying to correct them through naïve government regulation.

The Externalities of Cybersecurity

The domains considered in this paper include infrastructure security, botnets and DDoS attacks, and espionage and consumer privacy

Infrastructure Security

According to the CSIS report (2008), in the case of a future conflict or crisis, "cyber infrastructure" is a potential target. This means that a system can be accessed by opponents to steal information, while the vulnerabilities of the public can be mapped via use of penetrable information systems for planning attacks. Yet, depriving the public of communications, electricity and financial services could damage the ability to provide a response to these attacks. So, it should be expected that exploiting vulnerabilities in cyber infrastructure will be part of any future conflict.

Rather than claiming an externality or a market failure, an efficient level of support should be provided to make these resources secure. Due to being naturally owned by the government some resources are not taken care of by the market. So, there can be discussion of market failure for these resources. As the internal government policy is not informed by the price system or by profit feedback mechanisms the hope is that a right policy would be in place. Yet, Deloitte's global report (2004) finds out that more than 85 percentage of the critical infrastructure in US is possessed by the private sector. So, the private sector should take the appropriate level of care for securing these resources.

In case the CSIS report provides correct claims about the nature of "cyber war", then an externality with regard to the establishment of security seems obvious for the resources in question. For example, when financial institutions take security precautions this external benefit will be received by everyone. According to Van Eeten and Bauer (2009), such externalities count as market failures. Given the high cost of ensuring full security, rational stakeholders will tolerate some level of security breaches (Van Eeten and Bauer, 2009). Yet, if social costs and benefits of security decisions are not correctly reflected in the incentives of the players in the value net due to externalities or public good aspects of security investments, such privately rational decisions will systematically deviate from the social optimum.

However, according to Van Eeten and Bauer (2009), from a market failure perspective, the infrastructure security externalities are inframarginal and hence irrelevant. In case of an important distortion, the companies would lose significant amounts of capital; so there is a strong incentive for taking precautions against such an event. Yet, it is not obvious that the *marginal* externality is very large at all. While there is evidence showing that firms that possess critical infrastructure have a significant level of security budget, evidence is not clear in terms of the existence of crucial, socially worthwhile security measures which are avoided to be taken by these firms.

One of the scholars who made a research about spending for security in the field of financial services industry was Powell (2001). According to Powell (2001), the optimality of a specific level of security spending cannot be known based on mere observation. Powell (2001) provided a survey evidence for how much security is valued by executives and a rise in security budget over the prior year was confirmed by 63 percent of the participant entities.

In their survey of 600 IT executives from several infrastructure companies located in seven different industries, Baker *et* al. (2009) asserted that even in the case of a recession, security still counts one of the main reasons for IT investment. In a similar vein, a report published by PricewaterhouseCoopers in 2010 which includes interviews with 12,840 executives found out that for 71 percent of companies the focus on data protection was increasing. On the other hand, according to Soo Hoo (2000), there is overinvestment in cybersecurity, which results in a lower marginal rate of return on investments in cyberscurity in comparison to other technology investments.

There is a scarcity of studies with regard to the precautions that firms are failing to implement within the existing body of literature. If there is an underinvestment in security on behalf of those companies that possess critical infrastructure, one reason might be that ignorance prevails about what other cost-effective precautions could be put in place rather than the incentive to invest. In other words, the question that should be asked is: If specific security practices that are not commonly implemented today by regulatory agencies were required, for which practices would they ask to improve welfare?

From a market failure perspective, the positive externality with regard to security is irrelevant as *it is not known* what else to do to improve infrastructure security. According to those whose concern is about infrastructure security, welfare could be improved based on evidence of the cost-effectiveness of some specific security precautions which are not so common today.

While the incentive for capital protection would be strong from the perspective of unregulated private companies, the case for regulated public utilities would be more complicated. It is not so obvious if an investment for sufficient security precautions would be undertaken by these companies. Assuming that the facilitation of network security counts as a form of capital maintenance, a substantial literature with regard to the rate-of-return for regulated monopolies can establish a basis. According to Ronen & Srinidhi (1989), as certain accounting rules for depreciation are crucial for identification of capital maintenance and purchase decisions for rate-of-return regulated monopolies these might not be rational for a competitive private company.

Westfield (1965) claimed that higher profits can be earned by rate-of-return regulated monopolists in case their suppliers collude to increase prices. Moreover, the assertion of Sherman (1992) was that even in the case of a positive marginal product of capital there can be a motivation for capital waste. An in-depth analysis of investment in security related procedures is not within this paper's scope as the investment behaviour of rate-of-return regulated monopolies is influenced by related specific regulations. Nevertheless, the case of an underinvestment in security by public utilities that would be irrelevant for unregulated companies is possible. If further analysis reveals that there is an underinvestment in security by these companies, this should be thought of as a government failure rather than a market failure. As Sherman (1992) asserted, these firms are created by the state, rather than the market in spite of their nominally private status.

It is a subtle task to make an inference for a market failure. Rather than claiming that there is definitively no market failure with regard to unregulated firms in the market for critical infrastructure, the argument should be that current evidence of a market failure is weak (Sherman, 1992). It would be misleading to naively apply some popular principles in case of a market failure as this would be much smaller than initially assumed. Additionally, there is also a risk of government failure which can be dealt with by suggesting a Pigovian or regulatory solution (Sherman, 1992).

Based on the Pigovian logic, a tax credit for security spending can be subsidised in order to make an adjustment for the external component of security spending. Although such a subsidy may not necessarily result in a significantly greater level of security; available personnel could be re-categorized as "security staff" and via use of some accounting tricks, the security budgets of companies can be increased (Sherman, 1992). While actual security could be increased due to some of the increased spending, this increase would be at a *socially* cost-ineffective level of price (Sherman, 1992). If those socially efficient practices which are neglected by private companies are not obvious, then it would be difficult to ask companies for their implementation. Mandating companies to implement socially cost- ineffective practices would be not rational.

Botnets and DDoS Attacks

The externalities concerning botnets constitute a market failure which needs collective action (Van Eeten & Bauer, 2009). A botnet is a network infected machines which are controlled by modern malware (malicious software) coders via use of viruses so that these machines get involved in distributed denial of service (DDoS) attacks or send spam. The botnet "herder" enable infected machines to divert lots of traffic to specific servers during a DDoS attack, so that those servers could not respond to official requests.

The emergence of botnets and related security issues can be explained to a great extent by the incentives implemented by ISPs (Internet Service Providers). Van Eeten & Bauer (2009) claim that the major source of the problem is end users because of their less spending on security in general. So, as botnets increase they increase costs on virtually other actors in the network. There are few incentives for ISPs in terms of the control of malware. Although ISPs can disconnect infected machines from their networks, there is no incentive for them to do so (Van Eeten & Bauer (2009). On the contrary, a disincentive exists due to the fact that disconnected customers try to access the help-lines and take up the time of call-centre staff so that additional costs incur on behalf of the ISPs (Van Eeten & Bauer, 2009).

As not all of the customers are infected to the same degree, the decision should be made by ISPs whether there should be limited access to the infected machines or whether some modest harm can be inflicted upon other users in the form of increased risk of infecting other machines or network congestion. ISPs internalize these modest harms in the form of policies and prices. Although a different bundle could be offered by the ISP, its offer would be the one creating most value and profit. To give a specific example, the ISP could shut down access for all infected users, which would result in increased level of support costs. To afford these support costs, prices could be raised for all users or each support incident can be subject to an individual charge. To the extent that ISPs allow infected users to continue using their networks, it appears to be socially efficient for uninfected users to tolerate infected users, the core belief is that consumers prefer the status quo arrangement.

The robust informal networks underpinning ISPs' interests is mentioned by Van Eeten & Bauer (2009) in their studies. An incentive mentioned by these scholars concerns the informal networks of trusted security personnel among ISPs, CSIRTS [Computer Security Incident Response Teams] and related organizations (Van Eeten & Bauer, 2009). In case of security incidents, staff contacts within this trust network would be preferred as these enabled a quick access to another ISP to take action on a case of abuse (Van Eeten & Bauer, 2009). Van Eeten & Bauer (2009) claim that required enforcement of norms would be in place at low social cost due to these informal connections. The informal contacts provide an alternative for cost savings because dealing with the fallout of a security incident which may often require going through time-consuming procedures to get off blacklists would now require less staff time (Van Eeten & Bauer, 2009). As a result, with regard to botnets, these informal norms are capable of efficiently internalizing the externalities among *ISPs*.

Given the indefinitely repeated interactions of informal networks such as monitoring, graduated sanctions etc. maintaining a common pool resource without any external enforcement is crucial (Ostrom, 1990).

Despite the lack of evidence with regard to the existence of a substantial market failure between end users on a single ISP or between ISPs; one such failure might exist between the infected users and the operators. Van Eeten and Bauer (2009) explained how one Georgian newspaper, during its exposure to a DDoS attack originating out of Russia during the 2008 invasion, had to transfer its operation to Blogger hosted on Google's infrastructure. The lesson to be taken is that a more cost-effective way to be protected against DDoS attacks would be to host one's site on a large shared grid. Taking into account modern techniques such as edge caching, this lower cost alternative seems to decrease the amount of issues in case of an exposure to DDoS attacks.

With regard to the harm arising due to botnets and other malware ISPs would be exposed to indirect liability under the assumption that given high transaction costs indirect liability is bolstered. Conventional economic analysis suggests that an explicit rule imposing indirect liability is not necessary in case the following conditions are simultaneously met (Van Eeten and Bauer, 2009):

- Direct actors such as employees, drivers, and merchants can easily be identified and their assets would suffice to pay for the damage caused.
- These actors can use contractual law to transfer responsibility to any party that might otherwise be a relevant target for indirect liability.

Once these conditions are fulfilled, indirect liability can be created by related parties via contractual means, which would be subject to some other lower level constraints.

A research was undertaken by the scholars Lichtman & Posner (2006) to find out whether the network of peering contracts among ISPs could provide a ground for ISPs so that they could allocate liability efficiently. These scholars asserted if contracting is done anyway, then at the margin there would be low transaction costs (Lichtman & Posner, 2006). Their conclusion was that liability could not be efficiently allocated by ISPs (Lichtman & Posner, 2006). Any network of contracts with a focus on cyber-security would be perpetually out of date, and it would not be possible to update such complicated interdependent security obligations given the number of parties involved and the complicated issues with regard to the related adjustments for the flow of payments (Lichtman & Posner, 2006). Yet, the possibility for informal enforcement of liability norms among ISPs was ignored in this research study.

As ISPs rely on informal interactions for the alignment of their interests and enforcement of good security practices on other ISPs this informal system can be conceptualized as an alternative legal system. Yet, due to being less formal than the legal system, it should not be considered as being inferior; on the contrary, as written contracts are not required in this informal network of relationships there is more flexibility so that threats to network security can be dealt more effectively. Rather than being a case of market failure, these DDoS attacks and botnets provide the market with the opportunity of coping with externalities efficiently. If ISPs were to limit access to every infected computer even in the case of internalization of these externalities, this would rise the costs of Internet and support unnecessarily. By assigning indirect liability to ISPs for the harm occurring due to botnets and other malware, the informal networks would be weakened so that conflicts among ISPs would be resolved. This, too, could have major welfare costs as it would raise the cost of dispute resolution among ISPs.

Espionage and Consumer Privacy

EU implemented strict regulations with regard to data protection and privacy, starting with the Data Protection Directive in 1998 and the Directive on Privacy and Electronic Communications in 2003.

Despite the apparently modest nature of this regulation, the existence of a substantial market failure within the context of data breaches is not obvious. A provision that requests from service providers for notification of any data breach to their clients is included within the terms of services. One such example is the Safe Harbour that enables American entities to affirm that they abide by the standards of the EU's Data Privacy Directive. While this program is directed toward companies that export services to the EU, other U.S. firms such as Google and Facebook implement is as well. Another example would be private Certifications such as Payment Card Industry (PCI) which requires companies processing credit card payments to comply with its data security standards including breach notifications.

The market allows to accommodate different preferences with regard to safety. Relatively insecure online services are part of the optimal stock of online services. In the presence of easily accessible online terms of service that can include a notification provision, required notification of data breaches can oversupply security services.

Finally, firms can also benefit from being good stewards of customer privacy. In 2006, Google was praised for its resistance towards a U.S. Department of Justice subpoena on pornographic search terms. Google succeeded in substantially limiting the subpoena's scope. This concern for corporate reputation put the Coase Theorem into action as a substantial portion of any data privacy externality is internalized by the market. The claim of a substantial market failure in terms of data privacy would be difficult to make if firms can announce in advance how customer data will be protected and how customers will be informed in case of any breaches.

Despite the modesty of the proposed regulations, welfare nevertheless can be weakened which can result in government failure. The portion of the extra cost that exceeds the value placed by consumers onto the added security is a welfare cost. This additional cost will raise service fees and discourage some users from consuming the product. Furthermore, high regulatory burdens disproportionately harm small businesses and start-ups. While well established companies can easily comply with security regulations, required resources to implement the legal requirements may not easily be available for a new online service. Consequentially, start-ups and small companies can be discouraged due to unnecessary regulations.

CONCLUSION

As market failure is a complex topic no conclusion should simply suggest that an externality, without government intervention, will lead to a market failure. Cybersecurity policy entails interesting set of cases in which research shows that the market failure is much smaller than it seems to be at first glance, if it exists at all.

Inappropriate government regulation, whether it is in the form of being too stringent or just misapplication, can result in significant welfare costs that are as real as those occurring due to market failure. The possibility of "government failure" should not be ignored by policy analysts. The following evidence should be provided by those who prefer an intervention into the Internet economy:

- An evidence of the existence of actual market failure rather than observable externalities,
- A regulatory solution that is likely to do more good than harm.

None of these appear to have been provided yet.

REFERENCES

Baker, S., Waterman, S., & Ivanov, G. (2009). *In the Crossfire: Critical Infrastructure in the Age of Cyber War*. Santa Clara, CA: McAfee. Retrieved from http://www.mcafee.com/us/resources/reports/rp-in-crossfire-criticalinfrastructure-cyber-war.pdf

Center for Strategic and International Studies (CSIS). (2008). *CSIS Commission on Cybersecurity for the 44th Presidency*. Retrieved from http://csis.org/files/media/csis/pubs/081208_securingcyberspace_44.pdf

Clarke, R. A., & Knake, R. K. (2010). *Cyber War: The Next Threat to National Security and What tonDo About It*. New York: Ecco Publishing.

Deloitte Touche Tohmatsu. (n.d.). *2004 Global Security Survey*. Retrieved from http://www.deloitte.com/assets/Dcom-Argentina/Local%20Assets/Documents/global_security.pdf

Lichtman, J., & Posner, E. (2006). Holding Internet Service Providers Accountable. *Supreme Court Economic Review, 14*(229).

Ostrom, E. (1990). *Governing the Commons: The Evolution of Institutions for Collective Action*. Cambridge, UK: Cambridge University Press. doi:10.1017/CBO9780511807763

Powell, B. (2001). Is Cybersecurity a Public Good? Evidence from the Financial Services Industry. In *Independent Institute Working Paper 57*. Oakland, CA: The Independent Institute. Retrieved from http://www.independent.org/pdf/working_papers/57_cyber.pdf

PricewaterhouseCoopers. (2010). *Respected—But Still Restrained: Findings from the 2011 Global State of Information Security Survey*. Retrieved from http://www.pwc.com/gx/en/information-securitysurvey/pdf/giss-2011-survey-report.pdf

Ronen, J., & Srinidhi, B. (1989). Depreciation Policies in Regulated Companies: Which Policies Are the Most Efficient? *Management Science*, *35*(5), 515–526. doi:10.1287/mnsc.35.5.515

Sherman, R. (1992). Capital Waste in the Rate-of-Return Regulated Firm. *Journal of Regulatory Economics*, *4*(2), 197–204. doi:10.1007/BF00157165

Soo Hoo, K. J. (2000). *How Much Is Enough? A Risk Management Approach to Computer Security* (Working paper). Stanford, CA: Consortium for Research on Information Security and Policy. Retrieved from http://iisdb.stanford.edu/pubs/11900/soohoo.pdf

Van Eeten, M., & Bauer, J. M. (2009). Emerging Threats to Internet Security: Incentives, Externalities and Policy Implications. *Journal of Contingencies and Crisis Management*, *17*(223).

Westfield, F. M. (1965). Regulation and Conspiracy. *The American Economic Review*, *55*(3), 424–444.

Related References

To continue our tradition of advancing academic research, we have compiled a list of recommended IGI Global readings. These references will provide additional information and guidance to further enrich your knowledge and assist you with your own research and future publications.

Adeyemo, O. (2013). The nationwide health information network: A biometric approach to prevent medical identity theft. In *User-driven healthcare: Concepts, methodologies, tools, and applications* (pp. 1636–1649). Hershey, PA: IGI Global. doi:10.4018/978-1-4666-2770-3.ch081

Adler, M., & Henman, P. (2009). Justice beyond the courts: The implications of computerisation for procedural justice in social security. In A. Martínez & P. Abat (Eds.), *E-justice: Using information communication technologies in the court system* (pp. 65–86). Hershey, PA: IGI Global. doi:10.4018/978-1-59904-998-4.ch005

Aflalo, E., & Gabay, E. (2013). An information system for coping with student dropout. In L. Tomei (Ed.), *Learning tools and teaching approaches through ICT advancements* (pp. 176–187). Hershey, PA: IGI Global. doi:10.4018/978-1-4666-2017-9.ch016

Ahmed, M. A., Janssen, M., & van den Hoven, J. (2012). Value sensitive transfer (VST) of systems among countries: Towards a framework. *International Journal of Electronic Government Research*, *8*(1), 26–42. doi:10.4018/jegr.2012010102

Aikins, S. K. (2008). Issues and trends in internet-based citizen participation. In G. Garson & M. Khosrow-Pour (Eds.), *Handbook of research on public information technology* (pp. 31–40). Hershey, PA: IGI Global. doi:10.4018/978-1-59904-857-4.ch004

Aikins, S. K. (2009). A comparative study of municipal adoption of internet-based citizen participation. In C. Reddick (Ed.), *Handbook of research on strategies for local e-government adoption and implementation: Comparative studies* (pp. 206–230). Hershey, PA: IGI Global. doi:10.4018/978-1-60566-282-4.ch011

Aikins, S. K. (2012). Improving e-government project management: Best practices and critical success factors. In *Digital democracy: Concepts, methodologies, tools, and applications* (pp. 1314–1332). Hershey, PA: IGI Global. doi:10.4018/978-1-4666-1740-7.ch065

Akabawi, M. S. (2011). Ghabbour group ERP deployment: Learning from past technology failures. In E. Business Research and Case Center (Ed.), Cases on business and management in the MENA region: New trends and opportunities (pp. 177-203). Hershey, PA: IGI Global. doi:10.4018/978-1-60960-583-4.ch012

Akabawi, M. S. (2013). Ghabbour group ERP deployment: Learning from past technology failures. In *Industrial engineering: Concepts, methodologies, tools, and applications* (pp. 933–958). Hershey, PA: IGI Global. doi:10.4018/978-1-4666-1945-6.ch051

Akbulut, A. Y., & Motwani, J. (2008). Integration and information sharing in e-government. In G. Putnik & M. Cruz-Cunha (Eds.), *Encyclopedia of networked and virtual organizations* (pp. 729–734). Hershey, PA: IGI Global. doi:10.4018/978-1-59904-885-7.ch096

Akers, E. J. (2008). Technology diffusion in public administration. In G. Garson & M. Khosrow-Pour (Eds.), *Handbook of research on public information technology* (pp. 339–348). Hershey, PA: IGI Global. doi:10.4018/978-1-59904-857-4.ch033

Al-Shafi, S. (2008). Free wireless internet park services: An investigation of technology adoption in Qatar from a citizens' perspective. *Journal of Cases on Information Technology*, *10*(3), 21–34. doi:10.4018/jcit.2008070103

Al-Shafi, S., & Weerakkody, V. (2009). Implementing free wi-fi in public parks: An empirical study in Qatar. *International Journal of Electronic Government Research*, *5*(3), 21–35. doi:10.4018/jegr.2009070102

Aladwani, A. M. (2002). Organizational actions, computer attitudes and end-user satisfaction in public organizations: An empirical study. In C. Snodgrass & E. Szewczak (Eds.), *Human factors in information systems* (pp. 153–168). Hershey, PA: IGI Global. doi:10.4018/978-1-931777-10-0.ch012

Aladwani, A. M. (2002). Organizational actions, computer attitudes, and end-user satisfaction in public organizations: An empirical study. *Journal of Organizational and End User Computing*, *14*(1), 42–49. doi:10.4018/joeuc.2002010104

Allen, B., Juillet, L., Paquet, G., & Roy, J. (2005). E-government and private-public partnerships: Relational challenges and strategic directions. In M. Khosrow-Pour (Ed.), *Practicing e-government: A global perspective* (pp. 364–382). Hershey, PA: IGI Global. doi:10.4018/978-1-59140-637-2.ch016

Alshawaf, A., & Knalil, O. E. (2008). IS success factors and IS organizational impact: Does ownership type matter in Kuwait? *International Journal of Enterprise Information Systems*, *4*(2), 13–33. doi:10.4018/jeis.2008040102

Ambali, A. R. (2009). Digital divide and its implication on Malaysian e-government: Policy initiatives. In H. Rahman (Ed.), *Social and political implications of data mining: Knowledge management in e-government* (pp. 267–287). Hershey, PA: IGI Global. doi:10.4018/978-1-60566-230-5.ch016

Amoretti, F. (2007). Digital international governance. In A. Anttiroiko & M. Malkia (Eds.), *Encyclopedia of digital government* (pp. 365–370). Hershey, PA: IGI Global. doi:10.4018/978-1-59140-789-8.ch056

Amoretti, F. (2008). Digital international governance. In A. Anttiroiko (Ed.), *Electronic government: Concepts, methodologies, tools, and applications* (pp. 688–696). Hershey, PA: IGI Global. doi:10.4018/978-1-59904-947-2.ch058

Amoretti, F. (2008). E-government at supranational level in the European Union. In A. Anttiroiko (Ed.), *Electronic government: Concepts, methodologies, tools, and applications* (pp. 1047–1055). Hershey, PA: IGI Global. doi:10.4018/978-1-59904-947-2.ch079

Amoretti, F. (2008). E-government regimes. In A. Anttiroiko (Ed.), *Electronic government: Concepts, methodologies, tools, and applications* (pp. 3846–3856). Hershey, PA: IGI Global. doi:10.4018/978-1-59904-947-2.ch280

Amoretti, F. (2009). Electronic constitution: A Braudelian perspective. In F. Amoretti (Ed.), *Electronic constitution: Social, cultural, and political implications* (pp. 1–19). Hershey, PA: IGI Global. doi:10.4018/978-1-60566-254-1.ch001

Amoretti, F., & Musella, F. (2009). Institutional isomorphism and new technologies. In M. Khosrow-Pour (Ed.), *Encyclopedia of information science and technology* (2nd ed.; pp. 2066–2071). Hershey, PA: IGI Global. doi:10.4018/978-1-60566-026-4.ch325

Andersen, K. V., & Henriksen, H. Z. (2007). E-government research: Capabilities, interaction, orientation, and values. In D. Norris (Ed.), *Current issues and trends in e-government research* (pp. 269–288). Hershey, PA: IGI Global. doi:10.4018/978-1-59904-283-1.ch013

Anderson, K. V., & Henriksen, H. Z. (2005). The first leg of e-government research: Domains and application areas 1998-2003. *International Journal of Electronic Government Research*, *1*(4), 26–44. doi:10.4018/jegr.2005100102

Anttiroiko, A. (2009). Democratic e-governance. In M. Khosrow-Pour (Ed.), *Encyclopedia of information science and technology* (2nd ed.; pp. 990–995). Hershey, PA: IGI Global. doi:10.4018/978-1-60566-026-4.ch158

Association, I. R. (2010). *Networking and telecommunications: Concepts, methodologies, tools and applications* (Vols. 1–3). Hershey, PA: IGI Global. doi:10.4018/978-1-60566-986-1

Association, I. R. (2010). *Web-based education: Concepts, methodologies, tools and applications* (Vols. 1–3). Hershey, PA: IGI Global. doi:10.4018/978-1-61520-963-7

Baker, P. M., Bell, A., & Moon, N. W. (2009). Accessibility issues in municipal wireless networks. In C. Reddick (Ed.), *Handbook of research on strategies for local e-government adoption and implementation: Comparative studies* (pp. 569–588). Hershey, PA: IGI Global. doi:10.4018/978-1-60566-282-4.ch030

Becker, S. A., Keimer, R., & Muth, T. (2010). A case on university and community collaboration: The sci-tech entrepreneurial training services (ETS) program. In S. Becker & R. Niebuhr (Eds.), *Cases on technology innovation: Entrepreneurial successes and pitfalls* (pp. 68–90). Hershey, PA: IGI Global. doi:10.4018/978-1-61520-609-4.ch003

Becker, S. A., Keimer, R., & Muth, T. (2012). A case on university and community collaboration: The sci-tech entrepreneurial training services (ETS) program. In Regional development: Concepts, methodologies, tools, and applications (pp. 947-969). Hershey, PA: IGI Global. doi:10.4018/978-1-4666-0882-5.ch507

Bernardi, R. (2012). Information technology and resistance to public sector reforms: A case study in Kenya. In T. Papadopoulos & P. Kanellis (Eds.), *Public sector reform using information technologies: Transforming policy into practice* (pp. 59–78). Hershey, PA: IGI Global. doi:10.4018/978-1-60960-839-2.ch004

Bernardi, R. (2013). Information technology and resistance to public sector reforms: A case study in Kenya. In *User-driven healthcare: Concepts, methodologies, tools, and applications* (pp. 14–33). Hershey, PA: IGI Global. doi:10.4018/978-1-4666-2770-3.ch002

Bolívar, M. P., Pérez, M. D., & Hernández, A. M. (2012). Municipal e-government services in emerging economies: The Latin-American and Caribbean experiences. In Y. Chen & P. Chu (Eds.), *Electronic governance and cross-boundary collaboration: Innovations and advancing tools* (pp. 198–226). Hershey, PA: IGI Global. doi:10.4018/978-1-60960-753-1.ch011

Borycki, E. M., & Kushniruk, A. W. (2010). Use of clinical simulations to evaluate the impact of health information systems and ubiquitous computing devices upon health professional work. In S. Mohammed & J. Fiaidhi (Eds.), *Ubiquitous health and medical informatics: The ubiquity 2.0 trend and beyond* (pp. 552–573). Hershey, PA: IGI Global. doi:10.4018/978-1-61520-777-0.ch026

Borycki, E. M., & Kushniruk, A. W. (2011). Use of clinical simulations to evaluate the impact of health information systems and ubiquitous computing devices upon health professional work. In *Clinical technologies: Concepts, methodologies, tools and applications* (pp. 532–553). Hershey, PA: IGI Global. doi:10.4018/978-1-60960-561-2.ch220

Buchan, J. (2011). Developing a dynamic and responsive online learning environment: A case study of a large Australian university. In B. Czerkawski (Ed.), *Free and open source software for e-learning: Issues, successes and challenges* (pp. 92–109). Hershey, PA: IGI Global. doi:10.4018/978-1-61520-917-0.ch006

Buenger, A. W. (2008). Digital convergence and cybersecurity policy. In G. Garson & M. Khosrow-Pour (Eds.), *Handbook of research on public information technology* (pp. 395–405). Hershey, PA: IGI Global. doi:10.4018/978-1-59904-857-4.ch038

Burn, J. M., & Loch, K. D. (2002). The societal impact of world wide web - Key challenges for the 21st century. In A. Salehnia (Ed.), *Ethical issues of information systems* (pp. 88–106). Hershey, PA: IGI Global. doi:10.4018/978-1-931777-15-5.ch007

Burn, J. M., & Loch, K. D. (2003). The societal impact of the world wide web-Key challenges for the 21st century. In M. Khosrow-Pour (Ed.), *Advanced topics in information resources management* (Vol. 2, pp. 32–51). Hershey, PA: IGI Global. doi:10.4018/978-1-59140-062-2.ch002

Bwalya, K. J., Du Plessis, T., & Rensleigh, C. (2012). The "quicksilver initiatives" as a framework for e-government strategy design in developing economies. In K. Bwalya & S. Zulu (Eds.), *Handbook of research on e-government in emerging economies: Adoption, e-participation, and legal frameworks* (pp. 605–623). Hershey, PA: IGI Global. doi:10.4018/978-1-4666-0324-0.ch031

Cabotaje, C. E., & Alampay, E. A. (2013). Social media and citizen engagement: Two cases from the Philippines. In S. Saeed & C. Reddick (Eds.), *Human-centered system design for electronic governance* (pp. 225–238). Hershey, PA: IGI Global. doi:10.4018/978-1-4666-3640-8.ch013

Camillo, A., Di Pietro, L., Di Virgilio, F., & Franco, M. (2013). Work-groups conflict at PetroTech-Italy, S.R.L.: The influence of culture on conflict dynamics. In B. Christiansen, E. Turkina, & N. Williams (Eds.), *Cultural and technological influences on global business* (pp. 272–289). Hershey, PA: IGI Global. doi:10.4018/978-1-4666-3966-9.ch015

Capra, E., Francalanci, C., & Marinoni, C. (2008). Soft success factors for m-government. In A. Anttiroiko (Ed.), *Electronic government: Concepts, methodologies, tools, and applications* (pp. 1213–1233). Hershey, PA: IGI Global. doi:10.4018/978-1-59904-947-2.ch089

Cartelli, A. (2009). The implementation of practices with ICT as a new teaching-learning paradigm. In A. Cartelli & M. Palma (Eds.), *Encyclopedia of information communication technology* (pp. 413–417). Hershey, PA: IGI Global. doi:10.4018/978-1-59904-845-1.ch055

Charalabidis, Y., Lampathaki, F., & Askounis, D. (2010). Investigating the landscape in national interoperability frameworks. *International Journal of E-Services and Mobile Applications*, *2*(4), 28–41. doi:10.4018/jesma.2010100103

Charalabidis, Y., Lampathaki, F., & Askounis, D. (2012). Investigating the landscape in national interoperability frameworks. In A. Scupola (Ed.), *Innovative mobile platform developments for electronic services design and delivery* (pp. 218–231). Hershey, PA: IGI Global. doi:10.4018/978-1-4666-1568-7.ch013

Chen, I. (2005). Distance education associations. In C. Howard, J. Boettcher, L. Justice, K. Schenk, P. Rogers, & G. Berg (Eds.), *Encyclopedia of distance learning* (pp. 599–612). Hershey, PA: IGI Global. doi:10.4018/978-1-59140-555-9.ch087

Chen, I. (2008). Distance education associations. In L. Tomei (Ed.), *Online and distance learning: Concepts, methodologies, tools, and applications* (pp. 562–579). Hershey, PA: IGI Global. doi:10.4018/978-1-59904-935-9.ch048

Chen, Y. (2008). Managing IT outsourcing for digital government. In A. Anttiroiko (Ed.), *Electronic government: Concepts, methodologies, tools, and applications* (pp. 3107–3114). Hershey, PA: IGI Global. doi:10.4018/978-1-59904-947-2.ch229

Chen, Y., & Dimitrova, D. V. (2006). Electronic government and online engagement: Citizen interaction with government via web portals. *International Journal of Electronic Government Research, 2*(1), 54–76. doi:10.4018/jegr.2006010104

Chen, Y., & Knepper, R. (2005). Digital government development strategies: Lessons for policy makers from a comparative perspective. In W. Huang, K. Siau, & K. Wei (Eds.), *Electronic government strategies and implementation* (pp. 394–420). Hershey, PA: IGI Global. doi:10.4018/978-1-59140-348-7.ch017

Chen, Y., & Knepper, R. (2008). Digital government development strategies: Lessons for policy makers from a comparative perspective. In H. Rahman (Ed.), *Developing successful ICT strategies: Competitive advantages in a global knowledge-driven society* (pp. 334–356). Hershey, PA: IGI Global. doi:10.4018/978-1-59904-654-9.ch017

Cherian, E. J., & Ryan, T. W. (2014). Incongruent needs: Why differences in the iron-triangle of priorities make health information technology adoption and use difficult. In C. El Morr (Ed.), *Research perspectives on the role of informatics in health policy and management* (pp. 209–221). Hershey, PA: IGI Global. doi:10.4018/978-1-4666-4321-5.ch012

Cho, H. J., & Hwang, S. (2010). Government 2.0 in Korea: Focusing on e-participation services. In C. Reddick (Ed.), *Politics, democracy and e-government: Participation and service delivery* (pp. 94–114). Hershey, PA: IGI Global. doi:10.4018/978-1-61520-933-0.ch006

Chorus, C., & Timmermans, H. (2010). Ubiquitous travel environments and travel control strategies: Prospects and challenges. In M. Wachowicz (Ed.), *Movement-aware applications for sustainable mobility: Technologies and approaches* (pp. 30–51). Hershey, PA: IGI Global. doi:10.4018/978-1-61520-769-5.ch003

Chuanshen, R. (2007). E-government construction and China's administrative litigation act. In A. Anttiroiko & M. Malkia (Eds.), *Encyclopedia of digital government* (pp. 507–510). Hershey, PA: IGI Global. doi:10.4018/978-1-59140-789-8.ch077

Ciaghi, A., & Villafiorita, A. (2012). Law modeling and BPR for public administration improvement. In K. Bwalya & S. Zulu (Eds.), *Handbook of research on e-government in emerging economies: Adoption, e-participation, and legal frameworks* (pp. 391–410). Hershey, PA: IGI Global. doi:10.4018/978-1-4666-0324-0.ch019

Ciaramitaro, B. L., & Skrocki, M. (2012). mHealth: Mobile healthcare. In B. Ciaramitaro (Ed.), Mobile technology consumption: Opportunities and challenges (pp. 99-109). Hershey, PA: IGI Global. doi:10.4018/978-1-61350-150-4.ch007

Comite, U. (2012). Innovative processes and managerial effectiveness of e-procurement in healthcare. In A. Manoharan & M. Holzer (Eds.), *Active citizen participation in e-government: A global perspective* (pp. 206–229). Hershey, PA: IGI Global. doi:10.4018/978-1-4666-0116-1.ch011

Cordella, A. (2013). E-government success: How to account for ICT, administrative rationalization, and institutional change. In J. Gil-Garcia (Ed.), *E-government success factors and measures: Theories, concepts, and methodologies* (pp. 40–51). Hershey, PA: IGI Global. doi:10.4018/978-1-4666-4058-0.ch003

Cropf, R. A. (2009). ICT and e-democracy. In M. Khosrow-Pour (Ed.), *Encyclopedia of information science and technology* (2nd ed.; pp. 1789–1793). Hershey, PA: IGI Global. doi:10.4018/978-1-60566-026-4.ch281

Cropf, R. A. (2009). The virtual public sphere. In M. Pagani (Ed.), *Encyclopedia of multimedia technology and networking* (2nd ed.; pp. 1525–1530). Hershey, PA: IGI Global. doi:10.4018/978-1-60566-014-1.ch206

D'Abundo, M. L. (2013). Electronic health record implementation in the United States healthcare industry: Making the process of change manageable. In V. Wang (Ed.), *Handbook of research on technologies for improving the 21st century workforce: Tools for lifelong learning* (pp. 272–286). Hershey, PA: IGI Global. doi:10.4018/978-1-4666-2181-7.ch018

Damurski, L. (2012). E-participation in urban planning: Online tools for citizen engagement in Poland and in Germany. *International Journal of E-Planning Research, 1*(3), 40–67. doi:10.4018/ijepr.2012070103 de Almeida, M. O. (2007). E-government strategy in Brazil: Increasing transparency and efficiency through e-government procurement. In M. Gascó-Hernandez (Ed.), *Latin America online: Cases, successes and pitfalls* (pp. 34–82). Hershey, PA: IGI Global. doi:10.4018/978-1-59140-974-8.ch002

de Juana Espinosa, S. (2008). Empirical study of the municipalitites' motivations for adopting online presence. In A. Anttiroiko (Ed.), *Electronic government: Concepts, methodologies, tools, and applications* (pp. 3593–3608). Hershey, PA: IGI Global. doi:10.4018/978-1-59904-947-2.ch262

de Souza Dias, D. (2002). Motivation for using information technology. In C. Snodgrass & E. Szewczak (Eds.), *Human factors in information systems* (pp. 55–60). Hershey, PA: IGI Global. doi:10.4018/978-1-931777-10-0.ch005

Demediuk, P. (2006). Government procurement ICT's impact on the sustainability of SMEs and regional communities. In S. Marshall, W. Taylor, & X. Yu (Eds.), *Encyclopedia of developing regional communities with information and communication technology* (pp. 321–324). Hershey, PA: IGI Global. doi:10.4018/978-1-59140-575-7.ch056

Devonshire, E., Forsyth, H., Reid, S., & Simpson, J. M. (2013). The challenges and opportunities of online postgraduate coursework programs in a traditional university context. In B. Tynan, J. Willems, & R. James (Eds.), *Outlooks and opportunities in blended and distance learning* (pp. 353–368). Hershey, PA: IGI Global. doi:10.4018/978-1-4666-4205-8.ch026

Di Cerbo, F., Scotto, M., Sillitti, A., Succi, G., & Vernazza, T. (2007). Toward a GNU/Linux distribution for corporate environments. In S. Sowe, I. Stamelos, & I. Samoladas (Eds.), *Emerging free and open source software practices* (pp. 215–236). Hershey, PA: IGI Global. doi:10.4018/978-1-59904-210-7.ch010

Diesner, J., & Carley, K. M. (2005). Revealing social structure from texts: Meta-matrix text analysis as a novel method for network text analysis. In V. Narayanan & D. Armstrong (Eds.), *Causal mapping for research in information technology* (pp. 81–108). Hershey, PA: IGI Global. doi:10.4018/978-1-59140-396-8.ch004

Dologite, D. G., Mockler, R. J., Bai, Q., & Viszhanyo, P. F. (2006). IS change agents in practice in a US-Chinese joint venture. In M. Hunter & F. Tan (Eds.), *Advanced topics in global information management* (Vol. 5, pp. 331–352). Hershey, PA: IGI Global. doi:10.4018/978-1-59140-923-6.ch015

Drnevich, P., Brush, T. H., & Luckock, G. T. (2011). Process and structural implications for IT-enabled outsourcing. *International Journal of Strategic Information Technology and Applications*, *2*(4), 30–43. doi:10.4018/jsita.2011100103

Dwivedi, A. N. (2009). *Handbook of research on information technology management and clinical data administration in healthcare* (Vols. 1–2). Hershey, PA: IGI Global. doi:10.4018/978-1-60566-356-2

Elbeltagi, I., McBride, N., & Hardaker, G. (2006). Evaluating the factors affecting DSS usage by senior managers in local authorities in Egypt. In M. Hunter & F. Tan (Eds.), *Advanced topics in global information management* (Vol. 5, pp. 283–307). Hershey, PA: IGI Global. doi:10.4018/978-1-59140-923-6.ch013

Eom, S., & Fountain, J. E. (2013). Enhancing information services through public-private partnerships: Information technology knowledge transfer underlying structures to develop shared services in the U.S. and Korea. In J. Gil-Garcia (Ed.), *E-government success around the world: Cases, empirical studies, and practical recommendations* (pp. 15–40). Hershey, PA: IGI Global. doi:10.4018/978-1-4666-4173-0.ch002

Esteves, T., Leuenberger, D., & Van Leuven, N. (2012). Reaching citizen 2.0: How government uses social media to send public messages during times of calm and times of crisis. In K. Kloby & M. D'Agostino (Eds.), *Citizen 2.0: Public and governmental interaction through web 2.0 technologies* (pp. 250–268). Hershey, PA: IGI Global. doi:10.4018/978-1-4666-0318-9.ch013

Estevez, E., Fillottrani, P., Janowski, T., & Ojo, A. (2012). Government information sharing: A framework for policy formulation. In Y. Chen & P. Chu (Eds.), *Electronic governance and cross-boundary collaboration: Innovations and advancing tools* (pp. 23–55). Hershey, PA: IGI Global. doi:10.4018/978-1-60960-753-1.ch002

Ezz, I. E. (2008). E-governement emerging trends: Organizational challenges. In A. Anttiroiko (Ed.), *Electronic government: Concepts, methodologies, tools, and applications* (pp. 3721–3737). Hershey, PA: IGI Global. doi:10.4018/978-1-59904-947-2.ch269

Fabri, M. (2009). The Italian style of e-justice in a comparative perspective. In A. Martínez & P. Abat (Eds.), *E-justice: Using information communication technologies in the court system* (pp. 1–19). Hershey, PA: IGI Global. doi:10.4018/978-1-59904-998-4.ch001

Fagbe, T., & Adekola, O. D. (2010). Workplace safety and personnel well-being: The impact of information technology. *International Journal of Green Computing*, *1*(1), 28–33. doi:10.4018/jgc.2010010103

Fagbe, T., & Adekola, O. D. (2011). Workplace safety and personnel well-being: The impact of information technology. In *Global business: Concepts, methodologies, tools and applications* (pp. 1438–1444). Hershey, PA: IGI Global. doi:10.4018/978-1-60960-587-2.ch509

Farmer, L. (2008). Affective collaborative instruction with librarians. In S. Kelsey & K. St.Amant (Eds.), *Handbook of research on computer mediated communication* (pp. 15–24). Hershey, PA: IGI Global. doi:10.4018/978-1-59904-863-5.ch002

Favier, L., & Mekhantar, J. (2007). Use of OSS by local e-administration: The French situation. In K. St.Amant & B. Still (Eds.), *Handbook of research on open source software: Technological, economic, and social perspectives* (pp. 428–444). Hershey, PA: IGI Global. doi:10.4018/978-1-59140-999-1.ch033

Fernando, S. (2009). Issues of e-learning in third world countries. In M. Khosrow-Pour (Ed.), *Encyclopedia of information science and technology* (2nd ed.; pp. 2273–2277). Hershey, PA: IGI Global. doi:10.4018/978-1-60566-026-4.ch360

Filho, J. R., & dos Santos, J. R. Junior. (2009). Local e-government in Brazil: Poor interaction and local politics as usual. In C. Reddick (Ed.), *Handbook of research on strategies for local e-government adoption and implementation: Comparative studies* (pp. 863–878). Hershey, PA: IGI Global. doi:10.4018/978-1-60566-282-4.ch045

Fletcher, P. D. (2004). Portals and policy: Implications of electronic access to U.S. federal government information services. In A. Pavlichev & G. Garson (Eds.), *Digital government: Principles and best practices* (pp. 52–62). Hershey, PA: IGI Global. doi:10.4018/978-1-59140-122-3.ch004

Fletcher, P. D. (2008). Portals and policy: Implications of electronic access to U.S. federal government information services. In A. Anttiroiko (Ed.), *Electronic government: Concepts, methodologies, tools, and applications* (pp. 3970–3979). Hershey, PA: IGI Global. doi:10.4018/978-1-59904-947-2.ch289

Forlano, L. (2004). The emergence of digital government: International perspectives. In A. Pavlichev & G. Garson (Eds.), *Digital government: Principles and best practices* (pp. 34–51). Hershey, PA: IGI Global. doi:10.4018/978-1-59140-122-3.ch003

Franzel, J. M., & Coursey, D. H. (2004). Government web portals: Management issues and the approaches of five states. In A. Pavlichev & G. Garson (Eds.), *Digital government: Principles and best practices* (pp. 63–77). Hershey, PA: IGI Global. doi:10.4018/978-1-59140-122-3.ch005

Gaivéo, J. M. (2013). Security of ICTs supporting healthcare activities. In M. Cruz-Cunha, I. Miranda, & P. Gonçalves (Eds.), *Handbook of research on ICTs for human-centered healthcare and social care services* (pp. 208–228). Hershey, PA: IGI Global. doi:10.4018/978-1-4666-3986-7.ch011

Garson, G. D. (1999). *Information technology and computer applications in public administration: Issues and trends*. Hershey, PA: IGI Global. doi:10.4018/978-1-87828-952-0

Garson, G. D. (2003). Toward an information technology research agenda for public administration. In G. Garson (Ed.), *Public information technology: Policy and management issues* (pp. 331–357). Hershey, PA: IGI Global. doi:10.4018/978-1-59140-060-8.ch014

Garson, G. D. (2004). The promise of digital government. In A. Pavlichev & G. Garson (Eds.), *Digital government: Principles and best practices* (pp. 2–15). Hershey, PA: IGI Global. doi:10.4018/978-1-59140-122-3.ch001

Garson, G. D. (2007). An information technology research agenda for public administration. In G. Garson (Ed.), *Modern public information technology systems: Issues and challenges* (pp. 365–392). Hershey, PA: IGI Global. doi:10.4018/978-1-59904-051-6.ch018

Gasco, M. (2007). Civil servants' resistance towards e-government development. In A. Anttiroiko & M. Malkia (Eds.), *Encyclopedia of digital government* (pp. 190–195). Hershey, PA: IGI Global. doi:10.4018/978-1-59140-789-8.ch028

Gasco, M. (2008). Civil servants' resistance towards e-government development. In A. Anttiroiko (Ed.), *Electronic government: Concepts, methodologies, tools, and applications* (pp. 2580–2588). Hershey, PA: IGI Global. doi:10.4018/978-1-59904-947-2.ch190

Ghere, R. K. (2010). Accountability and information technology enactment: Implications for social empowerment. In E. Ferro, Y. Dwivedi, J. Gil-Garcia, & M. Williams (Eds.), *Handbook of research on overcoming digital divides: Constructing an equitable and competitive information society* (pp. 515–532). Hershey, PA: IGI Global. doi:10.4018/978-1-60566-699-0.ch028

Gibson, I. W. (2012). Simulation modeling of healthcare delivery. In A. Kolker & P. Story (Eds.), *Management engineering for effective healthcare delivery: Principles and applications* (pp. 69–89). Hershey, PA: IGI Global. doi:10.4018/978-1-60960-872-9.ch003

Gil-Garcia, J. R. (2007). Exploring e-government benefits and success factors. In A. Anttiroiko & M. Malkia (Eds.), *Encyclopedia of digital government* (pp. 803–811). Hershey, PA: IGI Global. doi:10.4018/978-1-59140-789-8.ch122

Gil-Garcia, J. R., & González Miranda, F. (2010). E-government and opportunities for participation: The case of the Mexican state web portals. In C. Reddick (Ed.), *Politics, democracy and e-government: Participation and service delivery* (pp. 56–74). Hershey, PA: IGI Global. doi:10.4018/978-1-61520-933-0.ch004

Goldfinch, S. (2012). Public trust in government, trust in e-government, and use of e-government. In Z. Yan (Ed.), *Encyclopedia of cyber behavior* (pp. 987–995). Hershey, PA: IGI Global. doi:10.4018/978-1-4666-0315-8.ch081

Goodyear, M. (2012). Organizational change contributions to e-government project transitions. In S. Aikins (Ed.), *Managing e-government projects: Concepts, issues, and best practices* (pp. 1–21). Hershey, PA: IGI Global. doi:10.4018/978-1-4666-0086-7.ch001

Gordon, S., & Mulligan, P. (2003). Strategic models for the delivery of personal financial services: The role of infocracy. In S. Gordon (Ed.), *Computing information technology: The human side* (pp. 220–232). Hershey, PA: IGI Global. doi:10.4018/978-1-93177-752-0.ch014

Gordon, T. F. (2007). Legal knowledge systems. In A. Anttiroiko & M. Malkia (Eds.), *Encyclopedia of digital government* (pp. 1161–1166). Hershey, PA: IGI Global. doi:10.4018/978-1-59140-789-8.ch175

Graham, J. E., & Semich, G. W. (2008). Integrating technology to transform pedagogy: Revisiting the progress of the three phase TUI model for faculty development. In L. Tomei (Ed.), *Adapting information and communication technologies for effective education* (pp. 1–12). Hershey, PA: IGI Global. doi:10.4018/978-1-59904-922-9.ch001

Grandinetti, L., & Pisacane, O. (2012). Web services for healthcare management. In D. Prakash Vidyarthi (Ed.), *Technologies and protocols for the future of internet design: Reinventing the web* (pp. 60–94). Hershey, PA: IGI Global. doi:10.4018/978-1-4666-0203-8.ch004

Groenewegen, P., & Wagenaar, F. P. (2008). VO as an alternative to hierarchy in the Dutch police sector. In G. Putnik & M. Cruz-Cunha (Eds.), *Encyclopedia of networked and virtual organizations* (pp. 1851–1857). Hershey, PA: IGI Global. doi:10.4018/978-1-59904-885-7.ch245

Gronlund, A. (2001). Building an infrastructure to manage electronic services. In S. Dasgupta (Ed.), *Managing internet and intranet technologies in organizations: Challenges and opportunities* (pp. 71–103). Hershey, PA: IGI Global. doi:10.4018/978-1-878289-95-7.ch006

Gronlund, A. (2002). Introduction to electronic government: Design, applications and management. In Å. Grönlund (Ed.), *Electronic government: Design, applications and management* (pp. 1–21). Hershey, PA: IGI Global. doi:10.4018/978-1-930708-19-8.ch001

Gupta, A., Woosley, R., Crk, I., & Sarnikar, S. (2009). An information technology architecture for drug effectiveness reporting and post-marketing surveillance. In J. Tan (Ed.), *Medical informatics: Concepts, methodologies, tools, and applications* (pp. 631–646). Hershey, PA: IGI Global. doi:10.4018/978-1-60566-050-9.ch047

Hallin, A., & Lundevall, K. (2007). mCity: User focused development of mobile services within the city of Stockholm. In I. Kushchu (Ed.), Mobile government: An emerging direction in e-government (pp. 12-29). Hershey, PA: IGI Global. doi:10.4018/978-1-59140-884-0.ch002

Hallin, A., & Lundevall, K. (2009). mCity: User focused development of mobile services within the city of Stockholm. In S. Clarke (Ed.), Evolutionary concepts in end user productivity and performance: Applications for organizational progress (pp. 268-280). Hershey, PA: IGI Global. doi:10.4018/978-1-60566-136-0.ch017

Hallin, A., & Lundevall, K. (2009). mCity: User focused development of mobile services within the city of Stockholm. In D. Taniar (Ed.), Mobile computing: Concepts, methodologies, tools, and applications (pp. 3455-3467). Hershey, PA: IGI Global. doi:10.4018/978-1-60566-054-7.ch253

Hanson, A. (2005). Overcoming barriers in the planning of a virtual library. In M. Khosrow-Pour (Ed.), *Encyclopedia of information science and technology* (pp. 2255–2259). Hershey, PA: IGI Global. doi:10.4018/978-1-59140-553-5.ch397

Haque, A. (2008). Information technology and surveillance: Implications for public administration in a new word order. In T. Loendorf & G. Garson (Eds.), *Patriotic information systems* (pp. 177–185). Hershey, PA: IGI Global. doi:10.4018/978-1-59904-594-8.ch008

Hauck, R. V., Thatcher, S. M., & Weisband, S. P. (2012). Temporal aspects of information technology use: Increasing shift work effectiveness. In J. Wang (Ed.), *Advancing the service sector with evolving technologies: Techniques and principles* (pp. 87–104). Hershey, PA: IGI Global. doi:10.4018/978-1-4666-0044-7.ch006

Hawk, S., & Witt, T. (2006). Telecommunications courses in information systems programs. *International Journal of Information and Communication Technology Education, 2*(1), 79–92. doi:10.4018/jicte.2006010107

Helms, M. M., Moore, R., & Ahmadi, M. (2009). Information technology (IT) and the healthcare industry: A SWOT analysis. In J. Tan (Ed.), *Medical informatics: Concepts, methodologies, tools, and applications* (pp. 134–152). Hershey, PA: IGI Global. doi:10.4018/978-1-60566-050-9.ch012

Hendrickson, S. M., & Young, M. E. (2014). Electronic records management at a federally funded research and development center. In J. Krueger (Ed.), *Cases on electronic records and resource management implementation in diverse environments* (pp. 334–350). Hershey, PA: IGI Global. doi:10.4018/978-1-4666-4466-3.ch020

Henman, P. (2010). Social policy and information communication technologies. In J. Martin & L. Hawkins (Eds.), *Information communication technologies for human services education and delivery: Concepts and cases* (pp. 215–229). Hershey, PA: IGI Global. doi:10.4018/978-1-60566-735-5.ch014

Hismanoglu, M. (2011). Important issues in online education: E-pedagogy and marketing. In U. Demiray & S. Sever (Eds.), *Marketing online education programs: Frameworks for promotion and communication* (pp. 184–209). Hershey, PA: IGI Global. doi:10.4018/978-1-60960-074-7.ch012

Ho, K. K. (2008). The e-government development, IT strategies, and portals of the Hong Kong SAR government. In A. Anttiroiko (Ed.), *Electronic government: Concepts, methodologies, tools, and applications* (pp. 715–733). Hershey, PA: IGI Global. doi:10.4018/978-1-59904-947-2.ch060

Holden, S. H. (2003). The evolution of information technology management at the federal level: Implications for public administration. In G. Garson (Ed.), *Public information technology: Policy and management issues* (pp. 53–73). Hershey, PA: IGI Global. doi:10.4018/978-1-59140-060-8.ch003

Holden, S. H. (2007). The evolution of federal information technology management literature: Does IT finally matter? In G. Garson (Ed.), *Modern public information technology systems: Issues and challenges* (pp. 17–34). Hershey, PA: IGI Global. doi:10.4018/978-1-59904-051-6.ch002

Holland, J. W. (2009). Automation of American criminal justice. In M. Khosrow-Pour (Ed.), *Encyclopedia of information science and technology* (2nd ed.; pp. 300–302). Hershey, PA: IGI Global. doi:10.4018/978-1-60566-026-4.ch051

Holloway, K. (2013). Fair use, copyright, and academic integrity in an online academic environment. In *Digital rights management: Concepts, methodologies, tools, and applications* (pp. 917–928). Hershey, PA: IGI Global. doi:10.4018/978-1-4666-2136-7.ch044

Horiuchi, C. (2005). E-government databases. In L. Rivero, J. Doorn, & V. Ferraggine (Eds.), *Encyclopedia of database technologies and applications* (pp. 206–210). Hershey, PA: IGI Global. doi:10.4018/978-1-59140-560-3.ch035

Horiuchi, C. (2006). Creating IS quality in government settings. In E. Duggan & J. Reichgelt (Eds.), *Measuring information systems delivery quality* (pp. 311–327). Hershey, PA: IGI Global. doi:10.4018/978-1-59140-857-4.ch014

Hsiao, N., Chu, P., & Lee, C. (2012). Impact of e-governance on businesses: Model development and case study. In *Digital democracy: Concepts, methodologies, tools, and applications* (pp. 1407–1425). Hershey, PA: IGI Global. doi:10.4018/978-1-4666-1740-7.ch070

Huang, T., & Lee, C. (2010). Evaluating the impact of e-government on citizens: Cost-benefit analysis. In C. Reddick (Ed.), *Citizens and e-government: Evaluating policy and management* (pp. 37–52). Hershey, PA: IGI Global. doi:10.4018/978-1-61520-931-6.ch003

Hunter, M. G., Diochon, M., Pugsley, D., & Wright, B. (2002). Unique challenges for small business adoption of information technology: The case of the Nova Scotia ten. In S. Burgess (Ed.), *Managing information technology in small business: Challenges and solutions* (pp. 98–117). Hershey, PA: IGI Global. doi:10.4018/978-1-930708-35-8.ch006

Hurskainen, J. (2003). Integration of business systems and applications in merger and alliance: Case metso automation. In T. Reponen (Ed.), *Information technology enabled global customer service* (pp. 207–225). Hershey, PA: IGI Global. doi:10.4018/978-1-59140-048-6.ch012

Iazzolino, G., & Pietrantonio, R. (2011). The soveria.it project: A best practice of e-government in southern Italy. In D. Piaggesi, K. Sund, & W. Castelnovo (Eds.), *Global strategy and practice of e-governance: Examples from around the world* (pp. 34–56). Hershey, PA: IGI Global. doi:10.4018/978-1-60960-489-9.ch003

Imran, A., & Gregor, S. (2012). A process model for successful e-government adoption in the least developed countries: A case of Bangladesh. In F. Tan (Ed.), *International comparisons of information communication technologies: Advancing applications* (pp. 321–350). Hershey, PA: IGI Global. doi:10.4018/978-1-61350-480-2.ch014

Inoue, Y., & Bell, S. T. (2005). Electronic/digital government innovation, and publishing trends with IT. In M. Khosrow-Pour (Ed.), *Encyclopedia of information science and technology* (pp. 1018–1023). Hershey, PA: IGI Global. doi:10.4018/978-1-59140-553-5.ch180

Islam, M. M., & Ehsan, M. (2013). Understanding e-governance: A theoretical approach. In M. Islam & M. Ehsan (Eds.), *From government to e-governance: Public administration in the digital age* (pp. 38–49). Hershey, PA: IGI Global. doi:10.4018/978-1-4666-1909-8.ch003

Jaeger, B. (2009). E-government and e-democracy in the making. In M. Khosrow-Pour (Ed.), *Encyclopedia of information science and technology* (2nd ed.; pp. 1318–1322). Hershey, PA: IGI Global. doi:10.4018/978-1-60566-026-4.ch208

Jain, R. B. (2007). Revamping the administrative structure and processes in India for online diplomacy. In A. Anttiroiko & M. Malkia (Eds.), *Encyclopedia of digital government* (pp. 1418–1423). Hershey, PA: IGI Global. doi:10.4018/978-1-59140-789-8.ch217

Jain, R. B. (2008). Revamping the administrative structure and processes in India for online diplomacy. In A. Anttiroiko (Ed.), *Electronic government: Concepts, methodologies, tools, and applications* (pp. 3142–3149). Hershey, PA: IGI Global. doi:10.4018/978-1-59904-947-2.ch233

Jauhiainen, J. S., & Inkinen, T. (2009). E-governance and the information society in periphery. In C. Reddick (Ed.), *Handbook of research on strategies for local e-government adoption and implementation: Comparative studies* (pp. 497–514). Hershey, PA: IGI Global. doi:10.4018/978-1-60566-282-4.ch026

Jensen, M. J. (2009). Electronic democracy and citizen influence in government. In C. Reddick (Ed.), *Handbook of research on strategies for local e-government adoption and implementation: Comparative studies* (pp. 288–305). Hershey, PA: IGI Global. doi:10.4018/978-1-60566-282-4.ch015

Jiao, Y., Hurson, A. R., Potok, T. E., & Beckerman, B. G. (2009). Integrating mobile-based systems with healthcare databases. In J. Erickson (Ed.), *Database technologies: Concepts, methodologies, tools, and applications* (pp. 484–504). Hershey, PA: IGI Global. doi:10.4018/978-1-60566-058-5.ch031

Joia, L. A. (2002). A systematic model to integrate information technology into metabusinesses: A case study in the engineering realms. In F. Tan (Ed.), *Advanced topics in global information management* (Vol. 1, pp. 250–267). Hershey, PA: IGI Global. doi:10.4018/978-1-930708-43-3.ch016

Jones, T. H., & Song, I. (2000). Binary equivalents of ternary relationships in entity-relationship modeling: A logical decomposition approach. *Journal of Database Management, 11*(2), 12–19. doi:10.4018/jdm.2000040102

Juana-Espinosa, S. D. (2007). Empirical study of the municipalitites' motivations for adopting online presence. In L. Al-Hakim (Ed.), *Global e-government: Theory, applications and benchmarking* (pp. 261–279). Hershey, PA: IGI Global. doi:10.4018/978-1-59904-027-1.ch015

Jun, K., & Weare, C. (2012). Bridging from e-government practice to e-government research: Past trends and future directions. In K. Bwalya & S. Zulu (Eds.), *Handbook of research on e-government in emerging economies: Adoption, e-participation, and legal frameworks* (pp. 263–289). Hershey, PA: IGI Global. doi:10.4018/978-1-4666-0324-0.ch013

Junqueira, A., Diniz, E. H., & Fernandez, M. (2010). Electronic government implementation projects with multiple agencies: Analysis of the electronic invoice project under PMBOK framework. In J. Cordoba-Pachon & A. Ochoa-Arias (Eds.), *Systems thinking and e-participation: ICT in the governance of society* (pp. 135–153). Hershey, PA: IGI Global. doi:10.4018/978-1-60566-860-4.ch009

Juntunen, A. (2009). Joint service development with the local authorities. In C. Reddick (Ed.), *Handbook of research on strategies for local e-government adoption and implementation: Comparative studies* (pp. 902–920). Hershey, PA: IGI Global. doi:10.4018/978-1-60566-282-4.ch047

Kamel, S. (2001). *Using DSS for crisis management.* Hershey, PA: IGI Global. doi:10.4018/978-1-87828-961-2.ch020

Kamel, S. (2006). DSS for strategic decision making. In M. Khosrow-Pour (Ed.), *Cases on information technology and organizational politics & culture* (pp. 230–246). Hershey, PA: IGI Global. doi:10.4018/978-1-59904-411-8.ch015

Kamel, S. (2009). The software industry in Egypt as a potential contributor to economic growth. In M. Khosrow-Pour (Ed.), *Encyclopedia of information science and technology* (2nd ed.; pp. 3531–3537). Hershey, PA: IGI Global. doi:10.4018/978-1-60566-026-4.ch562

Kamel, S., & Hussein, M. (2008). Xceed: Pioneering the contact center industry in Egypt. *Journal of Cases on Information Technology*, *10*(1), 67–91. doi:10.4018/jcit.2008010105

Kamel, S., & Wahba, K. (2003). The use of a hybrid model in web-based education: "The Global campus project. In A. Aggarwal (Ed.), *Web-based education: Learning from experience* (pp. 331–346). Hershey, PA: IGI Global. doi:10.4018/978-1-59140-102-5.ch020

Kardaras, D. K., & Papathanassiou, E. A. (2008). An exploratory study of the e-government services in Greece. In G. Garson & M. Khosrow-Pour (Eds.), *Handbook of research on public information technology* (pp. 162–174). Hershey, PA: IGI Global. doi:10.4018/978-1-59904-857-4.ch016

Kassahun, A. E., Molla, A., & Sarkar, P. (2012). Government process reengineering: What we know and what we need to know. In *Digital democracy: Concepts, methodologies, tools, and applications* (pp. 1730–1752). Hershey, PA: IGI Global. doi:10.4018/978-1-4666-1740-7.ch086

Khan, B. (2005). Technological issues. In B. Khan (Ed.), *Managing e-learning strategies: Design, delivery, implementation and evaluation* (pp. 154–180). Hershey, PA: IGI Global. doi:10.4018/978-1-59140-634-1.ch004

Khasawneh, A., Bsoul, M., Obeidat, I., & Al Azzam, I. (2012). Technology fears: A study of e-commerce loyalty perception by Jordanian customers. In J. Wang (Ed.), *Advancing the service sector with evolving technologies: Techniques and principles* (pp. 158–165). Hershey, PA: IGI Global. doi:10.4018/978-1-4666-0044-7.ch010

Khatibi, V., & Montazer, G. A. (2012). E-research methodology. In A. Juan, T. Daradoumis, M. Roca, S. Grasman, & J. Faulin (Eds.), *Collaborative and distributed e-research: Innovations in technologies, strategies and applications* (pp. 62–81). Hershey, PA: IGI Global. doi:10.4018/978-1-4666-0125-3.ch003

Kidd, T. (2011). The dragon in the school's backyard: A review of literature on the uses of technology in urban schools. In L. Tomei (Ed.), *Online courses and ICT in education: Emerging practices and applications* (pp. 242–257). Hershey, PA: IGI Global. doi:10.4018/978-1-60960-150-8.ch019

Kidd, T. T. (2010). My experience tells the story: Exploring technology adoption from a qualitative perspective - A pilot study. In H. Song & T. Kidd (Eds.), *Handbook of research on human performance and instructional technology* (pp. 247–262). Hershey, PA: IGI Global. doi:10.4018/978-1-60566-782-9.ch015

Kieley, B., Lane, G., Paquet, G., & Roy, J. (2002). e-Government in Canada: Services online or public service renewal? In Å. Grönlund (Ed.), Electronic government: Design, applications and management (pp. 340-355). Hershey, PA: IGI Global. doi:10.4018/978-1-930708-19-8.ch016

Kim, P. (2012). "Stay out of the way! My kid is video blogging through a phone!": A lesson learned from math tutoring social media for children in underserved communities. In *Wireless technologies: Concepts, methodologies, tools and applications* (pp. 1415–1428). Hershey, PA: IGI Global. doi:10.4018/978-1-61350-101-6.ch517

Kirlidog, M. (2010). Financial aspects of national ICT strategies. In S. Kamel (Ed.), *E-strategies for technological diffusion and adoption: National ICT approaches for socioeconomic development* (pp. 277–292). Hershey, PA: IGI Global. doi:10.4018/978-1-60566-388-3.ch016

Kisielnicki, J. (2006). Transfer of information and knowledge in the project management. In E. Coakes & S. Clarke (Eds.), *Encyclopedia of communities of practice in information and knowledge management* (pp. 544–551). Hershey, PA: IGI Global. doi:10.4018/978-1-59140-556-6.ch091

Kittner, M., & Van Slyke, C. (2006). Reorganizing information technology services in an academic environment. In M. Khosrow-Pour (Ed.), *Cases on the human side of information technology* (pp. 49–66). Hershey, PA: IGI Global. doi:10.4018/978-1-59904-405-7.ch004

Knoell, H. D. (2008). Semi virtual workplaces in German financial service enterprises. In P. Zemliansky & K. St.Amant (Eds.), *Handbook of research on virtual workplaces and the new nature of business practices* (pp. 570–581). Hershey, PA: IGI Global. doi:10.4018/978-1-59904-893-2.ch041

Koh, S. L., & Maguire, S. (2009). Competing in the age of information technology in a developing economy: Experiences of an Indian bank. In S. Koh & S. Maguire (Eds.), *Information and communication technologies management in turbulent business environments* (pp. 326–350). Hershey, PA: IGI Global. doi:10.4018/978-1-60566-424-8.ch018

Kollmann, T., & Häsel, M. (2009). Competence of information technology professionals in internet-based ventures. In I. Lee (Ed.), *Electronic business: Concepts, methodologies, tools, and applications* (pp. 1905–1919). Hershey, PA: IGI Global. doi:10.4018/978-1-60566-056-1.ch118

Kollmann, T., & Häsel, M. (2009). Competence of information technology professionals in internet-based ventures. In A. Cater-Steel (Ed.), *Information technology governance and service management: Frameworks and adaptations* (pp. 239–253). Hershey, PA: IGI Global. doi:10.4018/978-1-60566-008-0.ch013

Kollmann, T., & Häsel, M. (2010). Competence of information technology professionals in internet-based ventures. In *Electronic services: Concepts, methodologies, tools and applications* (pp. 1551–1565). Hershey, PA: IGI Global. doi:10.4018/978-1-61520-967-5.ch094

Kraemer, K., & King, J. L. (2006). Information technology and administrative reform: Will e-government be different? *International Journal of Electronic Government Research, 2*(1), 1–20. doi:10.4018/jegr.2006010101

Kraemer, K., & King, J. L. (2008). Information technology and administrative reform: Will e-government be different? In D. Norris (Ed.), *E-government research: Policy and management* (pp. 1–20). Hershey, PA: IGI Global. doi:10.4018/978-1-59904-913-7.ch001

Lampathaki, F., Tsiakaliaris, C., Stasis, A., & Charalabidis, Y. (2011). National interoperability frameworks: The way forward. In Y. Charalabidis (Ed.), *Interoperability in digital public services and administration: Bridging e-government and e-business* (pp. 1–24). Hershey, PA: IGI Global. doi:10.4018/978-1-61520-887-6.ch001

Lan, Z., & Scott, C. R. (1996). The relative importance of computer-mediated information versus conventional non-computer-mediated information in public managerial decision making. *Information Resources Management Journal, 9*(1), 27–0. doi:10.4018/irmj.1996010103

Law, W. (2004). *Public sector data management in a developing economy*. Hershey, PA: IGI Global. doi:10.4018/978-1-59140-259-6.ch034

Law, W. K. (2005). Information resources development challenges in a cross-cultural environment. In M. Khosrow-Pour (Ed.), *Encyclopedia of information science and technology* (pp. 1476–1481). Hershey, PA: IGI Global. doi:10.4018/978-1-59140-553-5.ch259

Law, W. K. (2009). Cross-cultural challenges for information resources management. In M. Khosrow-Pour (Ed.), *Encyclopedia of information science and technology* (2nd ed.; pp. 840–846). Hershey, PA: IGI Global. doi:10.4018/978-1-60566-026-4.ch136

Law, W. K. (2011). Cross-cultural challenges for information resources management. In *Global business: Concepts, methodologies, tools and applications* (pp. 1924–1932). Hershey, PA: IGI Global. doi:10.4018/978-1-60960-587-2.ch704

Malkia, M., & Savolainen, R. (2004). eTransformation in government, politics and society: Conceptual framework and introduction. In M. Malkia, A. Anttiroiko, & R. Savolainen (Eds.), eTransformation in governance: New directions in government and politics (pp. 1-21). Hershey, PA: IGI Global. doi:10.4018/978-1-59140-130-8.ch001

Mandujano, S. (2011). Network manageability security. In D. Kar & M. Syed (Eds.), *Network security, administration and management: Advancing technology and practice* (pp. 158–181). Hershey, PA: IGI Global. doi:10.4018/978-1-60960-777-7.ch009

Marich, M. J., Schooley, B. L., & Horan, T. A. (2012). A normative enterprise architecture for guiding end-to-end emergency response decision support. In M. Jennex (Ed.), *Managing crises and disasters with emerging technologies: Advancements* (pp. 71–87). Hershey, PA: IGI Global. doi:10.4018/978-1-4666-0167-3.ch006

Markov, R., & Okujava, S. (2008). Costs, benefits, and risks of e-government portals. In G. Putnik & M. Cruz-Cunha (Eds.), *Encyclopedia of networked and virtual organizations* (pp. 354–363). Hershey, PA: IGI Global. doi:10.4018/978-1-59904-885-7.ch047

Martin, N., & Rice, J. (2013). Evaluating and designing electronic government for the future: Observations and insights from Australia. In V. Weerakkody (Ed.), *E-government services design, adoption, and evaluation* (pp. 238–258). Hershey, PA: IGI Global. doi:10.4018/978-1-4666-2458-0.ch014

Martinez, A. C. (2008). Accessing administration's information via internet in Spain. In F. Tan (Ed.), *Global information technologies: Concepts, methodologies, tools, and applications* (pp. 2558–2573). Hershey, PA: IGI Global. doi:10.4018/978-1-59904-939-7.ch186

Mbarika, V. W., Meso, P. N., & Musa, P. F. (2006). A disconnect in stakeholders' perceptions from emerging realities of teledensity growth in Africa's least developed countries. In M. Hunter & F. Tan (Eds.), *Advanced topics in global information management* (Vol. 5, pp. 263–282). Hershey, PA: IGI Global. doi:10.4018/978-1-59140-923-6.ch012

Mbarika, V. W., Meso, P. N., & Musa, P. F. (2008). A disconnect in stakeholders' perceptions from emerging realities of teledensity growth in Africa's least developed countries. In F. Tan (Ed.), *Global information technologies: Concepts, methodologies, tools, and applications* (pp. 2948–2962). Hershey, PA: IGI Global. doi:10.4018/978-1-59904-939-7.ch209

Means, T., Olson, E., & Spooner, J. (2013). Discovering ways that don't work on the road to success: Strengths and weaknesses revealed by an active learning studio classroom project. In A. Benson, J. Moore, & S. Williams van Rooij (Eds.), *Cases on educational technology planning, design, and implementation: A project management perspective* (pp. 94–113). Hershey, PA: IGI Global. doi:10.4018/978-1-4666-4237-9.ch006

Melitski, J., Holzer, M., Kim, S., Kim, C., & Rho, S. (2008). Digital government worldwide: An e-government assessment of municipal web sites. In G. Garson & M. Khosrow-Pour (Eds.), *Handbook of research on public information technology* (pp. 790–804). Hershey, PA: IGI Global. doi:10.4018/978-1-59904-857-4.ch069

Memmola, M., Palumbo, G., & Rossini, M. (2009). Web & RFID technology: New frontiers in costing and process management for rehabilitation medicine. In L. Al-Hakim & M. Memmola (Eds.), *Business web strategy: Design, alignment, and application* (pp. 145–169). Hershey, PA: IGI Global. doi:10.4018/978-1-60566-024-0.ch008

Meng, Z., Fahong, Z., & Lei, L. (2008). Information technology and environment. In Y. Kurihara, S. Takaya, H. Harui, & H. Kamae (Eds.), *Information technology and economic development* (pp. 201–212). Hershey, PA: IGI Global. doi:10.4018/978-1-59904-579-5.ch014

Mentzingen de Moraes, A. J., Ferneda, E., Costa, I., & Spinola, M. D. (2011). Practical approach for implementation of governance process in IT: Information technology areas. In N. Shi & G. Silvius (Eds.), *Enterprise IT governance, business value and performance measurement* (pp. 19–40). Hershey, PA: IGI Global. doi:10.4018/978-1-60566-346-3.ch002

Merwin, G. A. Jr, McDonald, J. S., & Odera, L. C. (2008). Economic development: Government's cutting edge in IT. In M. Raisinghani (Ed.), *Handbook of research on global information technology management in the digital economy* (pp. 1–37). Hershey, PA: IGI Global. doi:10.4018/978-1-59904-875-8.ch001

Meso, P., & Duncan, N. (2002). Can national information infrastructures enhance social development in the least developed countries? An empirical investigation. In M. Dadashzadeh (Ed.), *Information technology management in developing countries* (pp. 23–51). Hershey, PA: IGI Global. doi:10.4018/978-1-931777-03-2.ch002

Meso, P. N., & Duncan, N. B. (2002). Can national information infrastructures enhance social development in the least developed countries? In F. Tan (Ed.), *Advanced topics in global information management* (Vol. 1, pp. 207–226). Hershey, PA: IGI Global. doi:10.4018/978-1-930708-43-3.ch014

Middleton, M. (2008). Evaluation of e-government web sites. In G. Garson & M. Khosrow-Pour (Eds.), *Handbook of research on public information technology* (pp. 699–710). Hershey, PA: IGI Global. doi:10.4018/978-1-59904-857-4.ch063

Mingers, J. (2010). Pluralism, realism, and truth: The keys to knowledge in information systems research. In D. Paradice (Ed.), *Emerging systems approaches in information technologies: Concepts, theories, and applications* (pp. 86–98). Hershey, PA: IGI Global. doi:10.4018/978-1-60566-976-2.ch006

Mital, K. M. (2012). ICT, unique identity and inclusive growth: An Indian perspective. In A. Manoharan & M. Holzer (Eds.), *E-governance and civic engagement: Factors and determinants of e-democracy* (pp. 584–612). Hershey, PA: IGI Global. doi:10.4018/978-1-61350-083-5.ch029

Mizell, A. P. (2008). Helping close the digital divide for financially disadvantaged seniors. In F. Tan (Ed.), *Global information technologies: Concepts, methodologies, tools, and applications* (pp. 2396–2402). Hershey, PA: IGI Global. doi:10.4018/978-1-59904-939-7.ch173

Molinari, F., Wills, C., Koumpis, A., & Moumtzi, V. (2011). A citizen-centric platform to support networking in the area of e-democracy. In H. Rahman (Ed.), *Cases on adoption, diffusion and evaluation of global e-governance systems: Impact at the grass roots* (pp. 282–302). Hershey, PA: IGI Global. doi:10.4018/978-1-61692-814-8.ch014

Molinari, F., Wills, C., Koumpis, A., & Moumtzi, V. (2013). A citizen-centric platform to support networking in the area of e-democracy. In H. Rahman (Ed.), *Cases on progressions and challenges in ICT utilization for citizen-centric governance* (pp. 265–297). Hershey, PA: IGI Global. doi:10.4018/978-1-4666-2071-1.ch013

Monteverde, F. (2010). The process of e-government public policy inclusion in the governmental agenda: A framework for assessment and case study. In J. Cordoba-Pachon & A. Ochoa-Arias (Eds.), *Systems thinking and e-participation: ICT in the governance of society* (pp. 233–245). Hershey, PA: IGI Global. doi:10.4018/978-1-60566-860-4.ch015

Moodley, S. (2008). Deconstructing the South African government's ICT for development discourse. In A. Anttiroiko (Ed.), *Electronic government: Concepts, methodologies, tools, and applications* (pp. 622–631). Hershey, PA: IGI Global. doi:10.4018/978-1-59904-947-2.ch053

Moodley, S. (2008). Deconstructing the South African government's ICT for development discourse. In C. Van Slyke (Ed.), *Information communication technologies: Concepts, methodologies, tools, and applications* (pp. 816–825). Hershey, PA: IGI Global. doi:10.4018/978-1-59904-949-6.ch052

Mora, M., Cervantes-Perez, F., Gelman-Muravchik, O., Forgionne, G. A., & Mejia-Olvera, M. (2003). DMSS implementation research: A conceptual analysis of the contributions and limitations of the factor-based and stage-based streams. In G. Forgionne, J. Gupta, & M. Mora (Eds.), *Decision-making support systems: Achievements and challenges for the new decade* (pp. 331–356). Hershey, PA: IGI Global. doi:10.4018/978-1-59140-045-5.ch020

Mörtberg, C., & Elovaara, P. (2010). Attaching people and technology: Between e and government. In S. Booth, S. Goodman, & G. Kirkup (Eds.), *Gender issues in learning and working with information technology: Social constructs and cultural contexts* (pp. 83–98). Hershey, PA: IGI Global. doi:10.4018/978-1-61520-813-5.ch005

Murphy, J., Harper, E., Devine, E. C., Burke, L. J., & Hook, M. L. (2011). Case study: Lessons learned when embedding evidence-based knowledge in a nurse care planning and documentation system. In A. Cashin & R. Cook (Eds.), *Evidence-based practice in nursing informatics: Concepts and applications* (pp. 174–190). Hershey, PA: IGI Global. doi:10.4018/978-1-60960-034-1.ch014

Mutula, S. M. (2013). E-government's role in poverty alleviation: Case study of South Africa. In H. Rahman (Ed.), *Cases on progressions and challenges in ICT utilization for citizen-centric governance* (pp. 44–68). Hershey, PA: IGI Global. doi:10.4018/978-1-4666-2071-1.ch003

Nath, R., & Angeles, R. (2005). Relationships between supply characteristics and buyer-supplier coupling in e-procurement: An empirical analysis. *International Journal of E-Business Research, 1*(2), 40–55. doi:10.4018/jebr.2005040103

Nissen, M. E. (2006). Application cases in government. In M. Nissen (Ed.), *Harnessing knowledge dynamics: Principled organizational knowing & learning* (pp. 152–181). Hershey, PA: IGI Global. doi:10.4018/978-1-59140-773-7.ch008

Norris, D. F. (2003). Leading-edge information technologies and American local governments. In G. Garson (Ed.), *Public information technology: Policy and management issues* (pp. 139–169). Hershey, PA: IGI Global. doi:10.4018/978-1-59140-060-8.ch007

Norris, D. F. (2008). Information technology among U.S. local governments. In G. Garson & M. Khosrow-Pour (Eds.), *Handbook of research on public information technology* (pp. 132–144). Hershey, PA: IGI Global. doi:10.4018/978-1-59904-857-4.ch013

Northrop, A. (1999). The challenge of teaching information technology in public administration graduate programs. In G. Garson (Ed.), *Information technology and computer applications in public administration: Issues and trends* (pp. 1–22). Hershey, PA: IGI Global. doi:10.4018/978-1-87828-952-0.ch001

Northrop, A. (2003). Information technology and public administration: The view from the profession. In G. Garson (Ed.), *Public information technology: Policy and management issues* (pp. 1–19). Hershey, PA: IGI Global. doi:10.4018/978-1-59140-060-8.ch001

Northrop, A. (2007). Lip service? How PA journals and textbooks view information technology. In G. Garson (Ed.), *Modern public information technology systems: Issues and challenges* (pp. 1–16). Hershey, PA: IGI Global. doi:10.4018/978-1-59904-051-6.ch001

Null, E. (2013). Legal and political barriers to municipal networks in the United States. In A. Abdelaal (Ed.), *Social and economic effects of community wireless networks and infrastructures* (pp. 27–56). Hershey, PA: IGI Global. doi:10.4018/978-1-4666-2997-4.ch003

Okunoye, A., Frolick, M., & Crable, E. (2006). ERP implementation in higher education: An account of pre-implementation and implementation phases. *Journal of Cases on Information Technology, 8*(2), 110–132. doi:10.4018/jcit.2006040106

Olasina, G. (2012). A review of egovernment services in Nigeria. In A. Tella & A. Issa (Eds.), *Library and information science in developing countries: Contemporary issues* (pp. 205–221). Hershey, PA: IGI Global. doi:10.4018/978-1-61350-335-5.ch015

Orgeron, C. P. (2008). A model for reengineering IT job classes in state government. In G. Garson & M. Khosrow-Pour (Eds.), *Handbook of research on public information technology* (pp. 735–746). Hershey, PA: IGI Global. doi:10.4018/978-1-59904-857-4.ch066

Owsinski, J. W., & Pielak, A. M. (2011). Local authority websites in rural areas: Measuring quality and functionality, and assessing the role. In Z. Andreopoulou, B. Manos, N. Polman, & D. Viaggi (Eds.), *Agricultural and environmental informatics, governance and management: Emerging research applications* (pp. 39–60). Hershey, PA: IGI Global. doi:10.4018/978-1-60960-621-3.ch003

Owsiński, J. W., Pielak, A. M., Sęp, K., & Stańczak, J. (2014). Local web-based networks in rural municipalities: Extension, density, and meaning. In Z. Andreopoulou, V. Samathrakis, S. Louca, & M. Vlachopoulou (Eds.), *E-innovation for sustainable development of rural resources during global economic crisis* (pp. 126–151). Hershey, PA: IGI Global. doi:10.4018/978-1-4666-4550-9.ch011

Pagani, M., & Pasinetti, C. (2008). Technical and functional quality in the development of t-government services. In A. Anttiroiko (Ed.), *Electronic government: Concepts, methodologies, tools, and applications* (pp. 2943–2965). Hershey, PA: IGI Global. doi:10.4018/978-1-59904-947-2.ch220

Pani, A. K., & Agrahari, A. (2005). On e-markets in emerging economy: An Indian experience. In M. Khosrow-Pour (Ed.), *Advanced topics in electronic commerce* (Vol. 1, pp. 287–299). Hershey, PA: IGI Global. doi:10.4018/978-1-59140-819-2.ch015

Papadopoulos, T., Angelopoulos, S., & Kitsios, F. (2011). A strategic approach to e-health interoperability using e-government frameworks. In A. Lazakidou, K. Siassiakos, & K. Ioannou (Eds.), *Wireless technologies for ambient assisted living and healthcare: Systems and applications* (pp. 213–229). Hershey, PA: IGI Global. doi:10.4018/978-1-61520-805-0.ch012

Papadopoulos, T., Angelopoulos, S., & Kitsios, F. (2013). A strategic approach to e-health interoperability using e-government frameworks. In *User-driven healthcare: Concepts, methodologies, tools, and applications* (pp. 791–807). Hershey, PA: IGI Global. doi:10.4018/978-1-4666-2770-3.ch039

Papaleo, G., Chiarella, D., Aiello, M., & Caviglione, L. (2012). Analysis, development and deployment of statistical anomaly detection techniques for real e-mail traffic. In T. Chou (Ed.), *Information assurance and security technologies for risk assessment and threat management: Advances* (pp. 47–71). Hershey, PA: IGI Global. doi:10.4018/978-1-61350-507-6.ch003

Papp, R. (2003). Information technology & FDA compliance in the pharmaceutical industry. In M. Khosrow-Pour (Ed.), *Annals of cases on information technology* (Vol. 5, pp. 262–273). Hershey, PA: IGI Global. doi:10.4018/978-1-59140-061-5.ch017

Parsons, T. W. (2007). Developing a knowledge management portal. In A. Tatnall (Ed.), *Encyclopedia of portal technologies and applications* (pp. 223–227). Hershey, PA: IGI Global. doi:10.4018/978-1-59140-989-2.ch039

Passaris, C. E. (2007). Immigration and digital government. In A. Anttiroiko & M. Malkia (Eds.), *Encyclopedia of digital government* (pp. 988–994). Hershey, PA: IGI Global. doi:10.4018/978-1-59140-789-8.ch148

Pavlichev, A. (2004). The e-government challenge for public administration. In A. Pavlichev & G. Garson (Eds.), *Digital government: Principles and best practices* (pp. 276–290). Hershey, PA: IGI Global. doi:10.4018/978-1-59140-122-3.ch018

Penrod, J. I., & Harbor, A. F. (2000). Designing and implementing a learning organization-oriented information technology planning and management process. In L. Petrides (Ed.), *Case studies on information technology in higher education: Implications for policy and practice* (pp. 7–19). Hershey, PA: IGI Global. doi:10.4018/978-1-878289-74-2.ch001

Planas-Silva, M. D., & Joseph, R. C. (2011). Perspectives on the adoption of electronic resources for use in clinical trials. In M. Guah (Ed.), *Healthcare delivery reform and new technologies: Organizational initiatives* (pp. 19–28). Hershey, PA: IGI Global. doi:10.4018/978-1-60960-183-6.ch002

Pomazalová, N., & Rejman, S. (2013). The rationale behind implementation of new electronic tools for electronic public procurement. In N. Pomazalová (Ed.), *Public sector transformation processes and internet public procurement: Decision support systems* (pp. 85–117). Hershey, PA: IGI Global. doi:10.4018/978-1-4666-2665-2.ch006

Postorino, M. N. (2012). City competitiveness and airport: Information science perspective. In M. Bulu (Ed.), *City competitiveness and improving urban subsystems: Technologies and applications* (pp. 61–83). Hershey, PA: IGI Global. doi:10.4018/978-1-61350-174-0.ch004

Poupa, C. (2002). Electronic government in Switzerland: Priorities for 2001-2005 - Electronic voting and federal portal. In Å. Grönlund (Ed.), *Electronic government: Design, applications and management* (pp. 356–369). Hershey, PA: IGI Global. doi:10.4018/978-1-930708-19-8.ch017

Powell, S. R. (2010). Interdisciplinarity in telecommunications and networking. In *Networking and telecommunications: Concepts, methodologies, tools and applications* (pp. 33–40). Hershey, PA: IGI Global. doi:10.4018/978-1-60566-986-1.ch004

Priya, P. S., & Mathiyalagan, N. (2011). A study of the implementation status of two e-governance projects in land revenue administration in India. In M. Shareef, V. Kumar, U. Kumar, & Y. Dwivedi (Eds.), *Stakeholder adoption of e-government services: Driving and resisting factors* (pp. 214–230). Hershey, PA: IGI Global. doi:10.4018/978-1-60960-601-5.ch011

Prysby, C., & Prysby, N. (2000). Electronic mail, employee privacy and the workplace. In L. Janczewski (Ed.), *Internet and intranet security management: Risks and solutions* (pp. 251–270). Hershey, PA: IGI Global. doi:10.4018/978-1-878289-71-1.ch009

Prysby, C. L., & Prysby, N. D. (2003). Electronic mail in the public workplace: Issues of privacy and public disclosure. In G. Garson (Ed.), *Public information technology: Policy and management issues* (pp. 271–298). Hershey, PA: IGI Global. doi:10.4018/978-1-59140-060-8.ch012

Prysby, C. L., & Prysby, N. D. (2007). You have mail, but who is reading it? Issues of e-mail in the public workplace. In G. Garson (Ed.), *Modern public information technology systems: Issues and challenges* (pp. 312–336). Hershey, PA: IGI Global. doi:10.4018/978-1-59904-051-6.ch016

Radl, A., & Chen, Y. (2005). Computer security in electronic government: A state-local education information system. *International Journal of Electronic Government Research, 1*(1), 79–99. doi:10.4018/jegr.2005010105

Rahman, H. (2008). Information dynamics in developing countries. In C. Van Slyke (Ed.), *Information communication technologies: Concepts, methodologies, tools, and applications* (pp. 104–114). Hershey, PA: IGI Global. doi:10.4018/978-1-59904-949-6.ch008

Ramanathan, J. (2009). Adaptive IT architecture as a catalyst for network capability in government. In P. Saha (Ed.), *Advances in government enterprise architecture* (pp. 149–172). Hershey, PA: IGI Global. doi:10.4018/978-1-60566-068-4.ch007

Ramos, I., & Berry, D. M. (2006). Social construction of information technology supporting work. In M. Khosrow-Pour (Ed.), *Cases on information technology: Lessons learned* (Vol. 7, pp. 36–52). Hershey, PA: IGI Global. doi:10.4018/978-1-59140-673-0.ch003

Ray, D., Gulla, U., Gupta, M. P., & Dash, S. S. (2009). Interoperability and constituents of interoperable systems in public sector. In V. Weerakkody, M. Janssen, & Y. Dwivedi (Eds.), *Handbook of research on ICT-enabled transformational government: A global perspective* (pp. 175–195). Hershey, PA: IGI Global. doi:10.4018/978-1-60566-390-6.ch010

Reddick, C. G. (2007). E-government and creating a citizen-centric government: A study of federal government CIOs. In G. Garson (Ed.), *Modern public information technology systems: Issues and challenges* (pp. 143–165). Hershey, PA: IGI Global. doi:10.4018/978-1-59904-051-6.ch008

Reddick, C. G. (2010). Citizen-centric e-government. In C. Reddick (Ed.), *Homeland security preparedness and information systems: Strategies for managing public policy* (pp. 45–75). Hershey, PA: IGI Global. doi:10.4018/978-1-60566-834-5.ch002

Reddick, C. G. (2010). E-government and creating a citizen-centric government: A study of federal government CIOs. In C. Reddick (Ed.), *Homeland security preparedness and information systems: Strategies for managing public policy* (pp. 230–250). Hershey, PA: IGI Global. doi:10.4018/978-1-60566-834-5.ch012

Reddick, C. G. (2010). Perceived effectiveness of e-government and its usage in city governments: Survey evidence from information technology directors. In C. Reddick (Ed.), *Homeland security preparedness and information systems: Strategies for managing public policy* (pp. 213–229). Hershey, PA: IGI Global. doi:10.4018/978-1-60566-834-5.ch011

Reddick, C. G. (2012). Customer relationship management adoption in local governments in the United States. In S. Chhabra & M. Kumar (Eds.), *Strategic enterprise resource planning models for e-government: Applications and methodologies* (pp. 111–124). Hershey, PA: IGI Global. doi:10.4018/978-1-60960-863-7.ch008

Reeder, F. S., & Pandy, S. M. (2008). Identifying effective funding models for e-government. In A. Anttiroiko (Ed.), *Electronic government: Concepts, methodologies, tools, and applications* (pp. 1108–1138). Hershey, PA: IGI Global. doi:10.4018/978-1-59904-947-2.ch083

Riesco, D., Acosta, E., & Montejano, G. (2003). An extension to a UML activity graph from workflow. In L. Favre (Ed.), *UML and the unified process* (pp. 294–314). Hershey, PA: IGI Global. doi:10.4018/978-1-93177-744-5.ch015

Ritzhaupt, A. D., & Gill, T. G. (2008). A hybrid and novel approach to teaching computer programming in MIS curriculum. In S. Negash, M. Whitman, A. Woszczynski, K. Hoganson, & H. Mattord (Eds.), *Handbook of distance learning for real-time and asynchronous information technology education* (pp. 259–281). Hershey, PA: IGI Global. doi:10.4018/978-1-59904-964-9.ch014

Roche, E. M. (1993). International computing and the international regime. *Journal of Global Information Management, 1*(2), 33–44. doi:10.4018/jgim.1993040103

Rocheleau, B. (2007). Politics, accountability, and information management. In G. Garson (Ed.), *Modern public information technology systems: Issues and challenges* (pp. 35–71). Hershey, PA: IGI Global. doi:10.4018/978-1-59904-051-6.ch003

Rodrigues Filho, J. (2010). E-government in Brazil: Reinforcing dominant institutions or reducing citizenship? In C. Reddick (Ed.), *Politics, democracy and e-government: Participation and service delivery* (pp. 347–362). Hershey, PA: IGI Global. doi:10.4018/978-1-61520-933-0.ch021

Rodriguez, S. R., & Thorp, D. A. (2013). eLearning for industry: A case study of the project management process. In A. Benson, J. Moore, & S. Williams van Rooij (Eds.), Cases on educational technology planning, design, and implementation: A project management perspective (pp. 319-342). Hershey, PA: IGI Global. doi:10.4018/978-1-4666-4237-9.ch017

Roman, A. V. (2013). Delineating three dimensions of e-government success: Security, functionality, and transformation. In J. Gil-Garcia (Ed.), *E-government success factors and measures: Theories, concepts, and methodologies* (pp. 171–192). Hershey, PA: IGI Global. doi:10.4018/978-1-4666-4058-0.ch010

Ross, S. C., Tyran, C. K., & Auer, D. J. (2008). Up in smoke: Rebuilding after an IT disaster. In H. Nemati (Ed.), *Information security and ethics: Concepts, methodologies, tools, and applications* (pp. 3659–3675). Hershey, PA: IGI Global. doi:10.4018/978-1-59904-937-3.ch248

Ross, S. C., Tyran, C. K., Auer, D. J., Junell, J. M., & Williams, T. G. (2005). Up in smoke: Rebuilding after an IT disaster. *Journal of Cases on Information Technology*, *7*(2), 31–49. doi:10.4018/jcit.2005040103

Roy, J. (2008). Security, sovereignty, and continental interoperability: Canada's elusive balance. In T. Loendorf & G. Garson (Eds.), *Patriotic information systems* (pp. 153–176). Hershey, PA: IGI Global. doi:10.4018/978-1-59904-594-8.ch007

Rubeck, R. F., & Miller, G. A. (2009). vGOV: Remote video access to government services. In A. Scupola (Ed.), Cases on managing e-services (pp. 253-268). Hershey, PA: IGI Global. doi:10.4018/978-1-60566-064-6.ch017

Saekow, A., & Boonmee, C. (2011). The challenges of implementing e-government interoperability in Thailand: Case of official electronic correspondence letters exchange across government departments. In Y. Charalabidis (Ed.), *Interoperability in digital public services and administration: Bridging e-government and e-business* (pp. 40–61). Hershey, PA: IGI Global. doi:10.4018/978-1-61520-887-6.ch003

Saekow, A., & Boonmee, C. (2012). The challenges of implementing e-government interoperability in Thailand: Case of official electronic correspondence letters exchange across government departments. In *Digital democracy: Concepts, methodologies, tools, and applications* (pp. 1883–1905). Hershey, PA: IGI Global. doi:10.4018/978-1-4666-1740-7.ch094

Sagsan, M., & Medeni, T. (2012). Understanding "knowledge management (KM) paradigms" from social media perspective: An empirical study on discussion group for KM at professional networking site. In M. Cruz-Cunha, P. Gonçalves, N. Lopes, E. Miranda, & G. Putnik (Eds.), *Handbook of research on business social networking: Organizational, managerial, and technological dimensions* (pp. 738–755). Hershey, PA: IGI Global. doi:10.4018/978-1-61350-168-9.ch039

Sahi, G., & Madan, S. (2013). Information security threats in ERP enabled e-governance: Challenges and solutions. In *Enterprise resource planning: Concepts, methodologies, tools, and applications* (pp. 825–837). Hershey, PA: IGI Global. doi:10.4018/978-1-4666-4153-2.ch048

Sanford, C., & Bhattacherjee, A. (2008). IT implementation in a developing country municipality: A sociocognitive analysis. *International Journal of Technology and Human Interaction*, *4*(3), 68–93. doi:10.4018/jthi.2008070104

Schelin, S. H. (2003). E-government: An overview. In G. Garson (Ed.), *Public information technology: Policy and management issues* (pp. 120–138). Hershey, PA: IGI Global. doi:10.4018/978-1-59140-060-8.ch006

Schelin, S. H. (2004). Training for digital government. In A. Pavlichev & G. Garson (Eds.), *Digital government: Principles and best practices* (pp. 263–275). Hershey, PA: IGI Global. doi:10.4018/978-1-59140-122-3.ch017

Schelin, S. H. (2007). E-government: An overview. In G. Garson (Ed.), *Modern public information technology systems: Issues and challenges* (pp. 110–126). Hershey, PA: IGI Global. doi:10.4018/978-1-59904-051-6.ch006

Schelin, S. H., & Garson, G. (2004). Theoretical justification of critical success factors. In G. Garson & S. Schelin (Eds.), *IT solutions series: Humanizing information technology: Advice from experts* (pp. 4–15). Hershey, PA: IGI Global. doi:10.4018/978-1-59140-245-9.ch002

Scime, A. (2002). Information systems and computer science model curricula: A comparative look. In M. Dadashzadeh, A. Saber, & S. Saber (Eds.), *Information technology education in the new millennium* (pp. 146–158). Hershey, PA: IGI Global. doi:10.4018/978-1-931777-05-6.ch018

Scime, A. (2009). Computing curriculum analysis and development. In M. Khosrow-Pour (Ed.), *Encyclopedia of information science and technology* (2nd ed.; pp. 667–671). Hershey, PA: IGI Global. doi:10.4018/978-1-60566-026-4.ch108

Scime, A., & Wania, C. (2008). Computing curricula: A comparison of models. In C. Van Slyke (Ed.), *Information communication technologies: Concepts, methodologies, tools, and applications* (pp. 1270–1283). Hershey, PA: IGI Global. doi:10.4018/978-1-59904-949-6.ch088

Seidman, S. B. (2009). An international perspective on professional software engineering credentials. In H. Ellis, S. Demurjian, & J. Naveda (Eds.), *Software engineering: Effective teaching and learning approaches and practices* (pp. 351–361). Hershey, PA: IGI Global. doi:10.4018/978-1-60566-102-5.ch018

Seifert, J. W. (2007). E-government act of 2002 in the United States. In A. Anttiroiko & M. Malkia (Eds.), *Encyclopedia of digital government* (pp. 476–481). Hershey, PA: IGI Global. doi:10.4018/978-1-59140-789-8.ch072

Seifert, J. W., & Relyea, H. C. (2008). E-government act of 2002 in the United States. In A. Anttiroiko (Ed.), *Electronic government: Concepts, methodologies, tools, and applications* (pp. 154–161). Hershey, PA: IGI Global. doi:10.4018/978-1-59904-947-2.ch013

Seufert, S. (2002). E-learning business models: Framework and best practice examples. In M. Raisinghani (Ed.), *Cases on worldwide e-commerce: Theory in action* (pp. 70–94). Hershey, PA: IGI Global. doi:10.4018/978-1-930708-27-3.ch004

Shareef, M. A., & Archer, N. (2012). E-government service development. In M. Shareef, N. Archer, & S. Dutta (Eds.), *E-government service maturity and development: Cultural, organizational and technological perspectives* (pp. 1–14). Hershey, PA: IGI Global. doi:10.4018/978-1-60960-848-4.ch001

Shareef, M. A., & Archer, N. (2012). E-government initiatives: Review studies on different countries. In M. Shareef, N. Archer, & S. Dutta (Eds.), *E-government service maturity and development: Cultural, organizational and technological perspectives* (pp. 40–76). Hershey, PA: IGI Global. doi:10.4018/978-1-60960-848-4.ch003

Shareef, M. A., Kumar, U., & Kumar, V. (2011). E-government development: Performance evaluation parameters. In M. Shareef, V. Kumar, U. Kumar, & Y. Dwivedi (Eds.), *Stakeholder adoption of e-government services: Driving and resisting factors* (pp. 197–213). Hershey, PA: IGI Global. doi:10.4018/978-1-60960-601-5.ch010

Shareef, M. A., Kumar, U., Kumar, V., & Niktash, M. (2012). Electronic-government vision: Case studies for objectives, strategies, and initiatives. In M. Shareef, N. Archer, & S. Dutta (Eds.), *E-government service maturity and development: Cultural, organizational and technological perspectives* (pp. 15–39). Hershey, PA: IGI Global. doi:10.4018/978-1-60960-848-4.ch002

Shukla, P., Kumar, A., & Anu Kumar, P. B. (2013). Impact of national culture on business continuity management system implementation. *International Journal of Risk and Contingency Management, 2*(3), 23–36. doi:10.4018/ijrcm.2013070102

Shulman, S. W. (2007). The federal docket management system and the prospect for digital democracy in U S rulemaking. In G. Garson (Ed.), *Modern public information technology systems: Issues and challenges* (pp. 166–184). Hershey, PA: IGI Global. doi:10.4018/978-1-59904-051-6.ch009

Simonovic, S. (2007). Problems of offline government in e-Serbia. In A. Anttiroiko & M. Malkia (Eds.), *Encyclopedia of digital government* (pp. 1342–1351). Hershey, PA: IGI Global. doi:10.4018/978-1-59140-789-8.ch205

Simonovic, S. (2008). Problems of offline government in e-Serbia. In A. Anttiroiko (Ed.), *Electronic government: Concepts, methodologies, tools, and applications* (pp. 2929–2942). Hershey, PA: IGI Global. doi:10.4018/978-1-59904-947-2.ch219

Singh, A. M. (2005). Information systems and technology in South Africa. In M. Khosrow-Pour (Ed.), *Encyclopedia of information science and technology* (pp. 1497–1502). Hershey, PA: IGI Global. doi:10.4018/978-1-59140-553-5.ch263

Singh, S., & Naidoo, G. (2005). Towards an e-government solution: A South African perspective. In W. Huang, K. Siau, & K. Wei (Eds.), *Electronic government strategies and implementation* (pp. 325–353). Hershey, PA: IGI Global. doi:10.4018/978-1-59140-348-7.ch014

Snoke, R., & Underwood, A. (2002). Generic attributes of IS graduates: An analysis of Australian views. In F. Tan (Ed.), *Advanced topics in global information management* (Vol. 1, pp. 370–384). Hershey, PA: IGI Global. doi:10.4018/978-1-930708-43-3.ch023

Sommer, L. (2006). Revealing unseen organizations in higher education: A study framework and application example. In A. Metcalfe (Ed.), *Knowledge management and higher education: A critical analysis* (pp. 115–146). Hershey, PA: IGI Global. doi:10.4018/978-1-59140-509-2.ch007

Song, H., Kidd, T., & Owens, E. (2011). Examining technological disparities and instructional practices in English language arts classroom: Implications for school leadership and teacher training. In L. Tomei (Ed.), *Online courses and ICT in education: Emerging practices and applications* (pp. 258–274). Hershey, PA: IGI Global. doi:10.4018/978-1-60960-150-8.ch020

Speaker, P. J., & Kleist, V. F. (2003). Using information technology to meet electronic commerce and MIS education demands. In A. Aggarwal (Ed.), *Web-based education: Learning from experience* (pp. 280–291). Hershey, PA: IGI Global. doi:10.4018/978-1-59140-102-5.ch017

Spitler, V. K. (2007). Learning to use IT in the workplace: Mechanisms and masters. In M. Mahmood (Ed.), *Contemporary issues in end user computing* (pp. 292–323). Hershey, PA: IGI Global. doi:10.4018/978-1-59140-926-7.ch013

Stellefson, M. (2011). Considerations for marketing distance education courses in health education: Five important questions to examine before development. In U. Demiray & S. Sever (Eds.), *Marketing online education programs: Frameworks for promotion and communication* (pp. 222–234). Hershey, PA: IGI Global. doi:10.4018/978-1-60960-074-7.ch014

Straub, D. W., & Loch, K. D. (2006). Creating and developing a program of global research. *Journal of Global Information Management, 14*(2), 1–28. doi:10.4018/jgim.2006040101

Straub, D. W., Loch, K. D., & Hill, C. E. (2002). Transfer of information technology to the Arab world: A test of cultural influence modeling. In M. Dadashzadeh (Ed.), *Information technology management in developing countries* (pp. 92–134). Hershey, PA: IGI Global. doi:10.4018/978-1-931777-03-2.ch005

Straub, D. W., Loch, K. D., & Hill, C. E. (2003). Transfer of information technology to the Arab world: A test of cultural influence modeling. In F. Tan (Ed.), *Advanced topics in global information management* (Vol. 2, pp. 141–172). Hershey, PA: IGI Global. doi:10.4018/978-1-59140-064-6.ch009

Suki, N. M., Ramayah, T., Ming, M. K., & Suki, N. M. (2013). Factors enhancing employed job seekers intentions to use social networking sites as a job search tool. In A. Mesquita (Ed.), *User perception and influencing factors of technology in everyday life* (pp. 265–281). Hershey, PA: IGI Global. doi:10.4018/978-1-4666-1954-8.ch018

Suomi, R. (2006). Introducing electronic patient records to hospitals: Innovation adoption paths. In T. Spil & R. Schuring (Eds.), *E-health systems diffusion and use: The innovation, the user and the use IT model* (pp. 128–146). Hershey, PA: IGI Global. doi:10.4018/978-1-59140-423-1.ch008

Swim, J., & Barker, L. (2012). Pathways into a gendered occupation: Brazilian women in IT. *International Journal of Social and Organizational Dynamics in IT, 2*(4), 34–51. doi:10.4018/ijsodit.2012100103

Tarafdar, M., & Vaidya, S. D. (2006). Adoption and implementation of IT in developing nations: Experiences from two public sector enterprises in India. In M. Khosrow-Pour (Ed.), *Cases on information technology planning, design and implementation* (pp. 208–233). Hershey, PA: IGI Global. doi:10.4018/978-1-59904-408-8.ch013

Tarafdar, M., & Vaidya, S. D. (2008). Adoption and implementation of IT in developing nations: Experiences from two public sector enterprises in India. In G. Garson & M. Khosrow-Pour (Eds.), *Handbook of research on public information technology* (pp. 905–924). Hershey, PA: IGI Global. doi:10.4018/978-1-59904-857-4.ch076

Thesing, Z. (2007). Zarina thesing, pumpkin patch. In M. Hunter (Ed.), *Contemporary chief information officers: Management experiences* (pp. 83–94). Hershey, PA: IGI Global. doi:10.4018/978-1-59904-078-3.ch007

Thomas, J. C. (2004). Public involvement in public administration in the information age: Speculations on the effects of technology. In M. Malkia, A. Anttiroiko, & R. Savolainen (Eds.), *eTransformation in governance: New directions in government and politics* (pp. 67–84). Hershey, PA: IGI Global. doi:10.4018/978-1-59140-130-8.ch004

Treiblmaier, H., & Chong, S. (2013). Trust and perceived risk of personal information as antecedents of online information disclosure: Results from three countries. In F. Tan (Ed.), *Global diffusion and adoption of technologies for knowledge and information sharing* (pp. 341–361). Hershey, PA: IGI Global. doi:10.4018/978-1-4666-2142-8.ch015

van Grembergen, W., & de Haes, S. (2008). IT governance in practice: Six case studies. In W. van Grembergen & S. De Haes (Eds.), *Implementing information technology governance: Models, practices and cases* (pp. 125–237). Hershey, PA: IGI Global. doi:10.4018/978-1-59904-924-3.ch004

van Os, G., Homburg, V., & Bekkers, V. (2013). Contingencies and convergence in European social security: ICT coordination in the back office of the welfare state. In M. Cruz-Cunha, I. Miranda, & P. Gonçalves (Eds.), *Handbook of research on ICTs and management systems for improving efficiency in healthcare and social care* (pp. 268–287). Hershey, PA: IGI Global. doi:10.4018/978-1-4666-3990-4.ch013

Velloso, A. B., Gassenferth, W., & Machado, M. A. (2012). Evaluating IBMEC-RJ's intranet usability using fuzzy logic. In M. Cruz-Cunha, P. Gonçalves, N. Lopes, E. Miranda, & G. Putnik (Eds.), *Handbook of research on business social networking: Organizational, managerial, and technological dimensions* (pp. 185–205). Hershey, PA: IGI Global. doi:10.4018/978-1-61350-168-9.ch010

Villablanca, A. C., Baxi, H., & Anderson, K. (2009). Novel data interface for evaluating cardiovascular outcomes in women. In A. Dwivedi (Ed.), *Handbook of research on information technology management and clinical data administration in healthcare* (pp. 34–53). Hershey, PA: IGI Global. doi:10.4018/978-1-60566-356-2.ch003

Villablanca, A. C., Baxi, H., & Anderson, K. (2011). Novel data interface for evaluating cardiovascular outcomes in women. In *Clinical technologies: Concepts, methodologies, tools and applications* (pp. 2094–2113). Hershey, PA: IGI Global. doi:10.4018/978-1-60960-561-2.ch806

Virkar, S. (2011). Information and communication technologies in administrative reform for development: Exploring the case of property tax systems in Karnataka, India. In J. Steyn, J. Van Belle, & E. Mansilla (Eds.), *ICTs for global development and sustainability: Practice and applications* (pp. 127–149). Hershey, PA: IGI Global. doi:10.4018/978-1-61520-997-2.ch006

Virkar, S. (2013). Designing and implementing e-government projects: Actors, influences, and fields of play. In S. Saeed & C. Reddick (Eds.), *Human-centered system design for electronic governance* (pp. 88–110). Hershey, PA: IGI Global. doi:10.4018/978-1-4666-3640-8.ch007

Wallace, A. (2009). E-justice: An Australian perspective. In A. Martínez & P. Abat (Eds.), *E-justice: Using information communication technologies in the court system* (pp. 204–228). Hershey, PA: IGI Global. doi:10.4018/978-1-59904-998-4.ch014

Wang, G. (2012). E-democratic administration and bureaucratic responsiveness: A primary study of bureaucrats' perceptions of the civil service e-mail box in Taiwan. In K. Kloby & M. D'Agostino (Eds.), *Citizen 2.0: Public and governmental interaction through web 2.0 technologies* (pp. 146–173). Hershey, PA: IGI Global. doi:10.4018/978-1-4666-0318-9.ch009

Wangpipatwong, S., Chutimaskul, W., & Papasratorn, B. (2011). Quality enhancing the continued use of e-government web sites: Evidence from e-citizens of Thailand. In V. Weerakkody (Ed.), *Applied technology integration in governmental organizations: New e-government research* (pp. 20–36). Hershey, PA: IGI Global. doi:10.4018/978-1-60960-162-1.ch002

Wedemeijer, L. (2006). Long-term evolution of a conceptual schema at a life insurance company. In M. Khosrow-Pour (Ed.), *Cases on database technologies and applications* (pp. 202–226). Hershey, PA: IGI Global. doi:10.4018/978-1-59904-399-9.ch012

Whybrow, E. (2008). Digital access, ICT fluency, and the economically disadvantages: Approaches to minimize the digital divide. In F. Tan (Ed.), *Global information technologies: Concepts, methodologies, tools, and applications* (pp. 1409–1422). Hershey, PA: IGI Global. doi:10.4018/978-1-59904-939-7.ch102

Whybrow, E. (2008). Digital access, ICT fluency, and the economically disadvantages: Approaches to minimize the digital divide. In C. Van Slyke (Ed.), *Information communication technologies: Concepts, methodologies, tools, and applications* (pp. 764–777). Hershey, PA: IGI Global. doi:10.4018/978-1-59904-949-6.ch049

Wickramasinghe, N., & Geisler, E. (2010). Key considerations for the adoption and implementation of knowledge management in healthcare operations. In M. Saito, N. Wickramasinghe, M. Fuji, & E. Geisler (Eds.), *Redesigning innovative healthcare operation and the role of knowledge management* (pp. 125–142). Hershey, PA: IGI Global. doi:10.4018/978-1-60566-284-8.ch009

Wickramasinghe, N., & Geisler, E. (2012). Key considerations for the adoption and implementation of knowledge management in healthcare operations. In *Organizational learning and knowledge: Concepts, methodologies, tools and applications* (pp. 1316–1328). Hershey, PA: IGI Global. doi:10.4018/978-1-60960-783-8.ch405

Wickramasinghe, N., & Goldberg, S. (2007). A framework for delivering m-health excellence. In L. Al-Hakim (Ed.), *Web mobile-based applications for healthcare management* (pp. 36–61). Hershey, PA: IGI Global. doi:10.4018/978-1-59140-658-7.ch002

Wickramasinghe, N., & Goldberg, S. (2008). Critical success factors for delivering m-health excellence. In N. Wickramasinghe & E. Geisler (Eds.), *Encyclopedia of healthcare information systems* (pp. 339–351). Hershey, PA: IGI Global. doi:10.4018/978-1-59904-889-5.ch045

Wyld, D. (2009). Radio frequency identification (RFID) technology. In J. Symonds, J. Ayoade, & D. Parry (Eds.), *Auto-identification and ubiquitous computing applications* (pp. 279–293). Hershey, PA: IGI Global. doi:10.4018/978-1-60566-298-5.ch017

Yaghmaei, F. (2010). Understanding computerised information systems usage in community health. In J. Rodrigues (Ed.), *Health information systems: Concepts, methodologies, tools, and applications* (pp. 1388–1399). Hershey, PA: IGI Global. doi:10.4018/978-1-60566-988-5.ch088

Yee, G., El-Khatib, K., Korba, L., Patrick, A. S., Song, R., & Xu, Y. (2005). Privacy and trust in e-government. In W. Huang, K. Siau, & K. Wei (Eds.), *Electronic government strategies and implementation* (pp. 145–190). Hershey, PA: IGI Global. doi:10.4018/978-1-59140-348-7.ch007

Yeh, S., & Chu, P. (2010). Evaluation of e-government services: A citizen-centric approach to citizen e-complaint services. In C. Reddick (Ed.), *Citizens and e-government: Evaluating policy and management* (pp. 400–417). Hershey, PA: IGI Global. doi:10.4018/978-1-61520-931-6.ch022

Young-Jin, S., & Seang-tae, K. (2008). E-government concepts, measures, and best practices. In A. Anttiroiko (Ed.), *Electronic government: Concepts, methodologies, tools, and applications* (pp. 32–57). Hershey, PA: IGI Global. doi:10.4018/978-1-59904-947-2.ch004

Yun, H. J., & Opheim, C. (2012). New technology communication in American state governments: The impact on citizen participation. In K. Bwalya & S. Zulu (Eds.), *Handbook of research on e-government in emerging economies: Adoption, e-participation, and legal frameworks* (pp. 573–590). Hershey, PA: IGI Global. doi:10.4018/978-1-4666-0324-0.ch029

Zhang, N., Guo, X., Chen, G., & Chau, P. Y. (2011). User evaluation of e-government systems: A Chinese cultural perspective. In F. Tan (Ed.), *International enterprises and global information technologies: Advancing management practices* (pp. 63–84). Hershey, PA: IGI Global. doi:10.4018/978-1-60960-605-3.ch004

Zuo, Y., & Hu, W. (2011). Trust-based information risk management in a supply chain network. In J. Wang (Ed.), *Supply chain optimization, management and integration: Emerging applications* (pp. 181–196). Hershey, PA: IGI Global. doi:10.4018/978-1-60960-135-5.ch013

Compilation of References

Abede, R., & Dawit, D. (2010). An analysis of African e-Government service websites. *Government Information Quarterly*, *30*(31), 1–9.

Abraham, S. (2015, January 1). *Privacy vs transparency*. Retrieved July 19, 2017, from https://newint.org/features/2015/01/01/privacy-transparency

Acemoglu, D., Johnson, S., & Robbinson, J. (2002). Reversal of fortunes: Geography, and institutions in the making of the modern world income distribution. *The Quarterly Journal of Economics*, *118*(4), 1231–1294. doi:10.1162/003355302320935025

Acemoglu, D., & Robinson, J. (2010). Why is Africa poor? *Economic History of Developing Regions*, *25*(1), 21–20. doi:10.1080/20780389.2010.505010

Adam, C., & Dercon, S. (2009). The political economy of development: An assessment. *Oxford Review of Economic Policy*, *25*(2), 173–189. doi:10.1093/oxrep/grp020

Adepetum, A. (2017). Nigeria's teledensity increased by 2.27 in 2016. *The Guardian Business*. Retrieved June 14, 2017, from https://guardian.ng/business-services/nigerias-teledensity-increased-by-2-27-per-cent-in-2016/

Adhikari, P., Timoshenko, K., & Garseth-Nesbakk, L. (2012). Reforming central government accounting in diverse contexts: A three-country comparison. *International Journal of Public Sector Performance Management*, *2*(1), 44–60. doi:10.1504/IJPSPM.2012.048743

Adu, K. K., Dube, L., & Adjei, E. (2016). Digital preservation: The conduit through which open data, electronic government and the right to information are implemented. *Library Hi Tech*, *34*(4), 733–747. doi:10.1108/LHT-07-2016-0078

Africa, S. (2009). *Well-kept Secrets: The right of access to information and the South African intelligence services*. South Africa Institute for Global Dialogue and Friedrich-Ebert-Stiftung.

Akunyili, D. (2010). *ICT and e-government in Nigeria: opportunities and challenges*. Paper presented at the World Congress on Information Technology.

Amadi L., and Ekekwe, E. (2014). Corruption and development Administration in Africa: Institutional Approach. *African Journal of Political Science and International Relations*, *8*(6), 163–177. doi:10.5897/AJPSIR2013.0634

Amadi, L., & Imoh-Ita, I. (2017) Intellectual capital and environmental sustainability measurement nexus: a review of the literature. *Int. J. Learning and Intellectual Capital, 14*(2).

Andersen, K. V., & Henriksen, H. Z. (2006). E-government maturity models: Extension of the Layne and Lee model. *Government Information Quarterly*, *23*(2), 236–248. doi:10.1016/j.giq.2005.11.008

Andrain, C., & Apter, D. (1995). *Political Protest and Social Change*. New York University Press.

Appadurai, A. (1996). *Modernity at large: Cultural dimensions of globalization*. Minneapolis, MN: University of Minnesota Press.

Arcelus, J. (2014). Framework for useful transparency websites for citizens. *Proceedings of the 6th International Conference on Theory and Practice of Electronic Governance*, 83–86. http://doi.acm.org/10.1145/2463728.2463749

Asongwe, P. N. (2013). E-Government and the Cameroon cybersecurity legislation 2010: Opportunities and challenges. *African Journal of Information and Communication*, *2*, 157–163.

Baker, S., Waterman, S., & Ivanov, G. (2009). *In the Crossfire: Critical Infrastructure in the Age of Cyber War*. Santa Clara, CA: McAfee. Retrieved from http://www.mcafee.com/us/resources/reports/rp-in-crossfire-criticalinfrastructure-cyber-war.pdf

Barboza, D. (2012a, October 25). *Family of Wen Jiabao Holds a Hidden Fortune in China*. Retrieved from http://www.nytimes.com/2012/10/26/business/global/family-of-wen-jiabao-holds-a-hidden-fortune-in-china.html

Barboza, D. (2012b, October 26). Obtaining Financial Records in China. *The New York Times*. Retrieved from https://www.nytimes.com/2012/10/27/business/global/obtaining-financial-records-in-china.html

Batke, J., Breuer, J., & Matthias, S. (2016, November 22). *Open government in China: bound to improve, within bounds - MERICS China Blog*. Retrieved June 2, 2017, from http://blog.merics.org/en/blog-post/2016/11/22/open-government-in-china-bound-to-improve-within-bounds/

Baum, C., & Di Maio, A. (2000). *Gartner's four phases of E-government model.* GartnerGroup. Retrieved on 2 April, 2017 from https://www.gartner.com/doc/317292/gartners-phases-egovernment-model

BBC World Service Trust. (2010). *African Media Development Initiative. Cameroon country report context*. London: BBC World Service Trust.

Bearfield, D., & Bowman, A. (2016). Can You Find It on the Web? An Assessment of Municipal E-Government Transparency. American Review of Public Administration, 1-17.

Bendiek, A. (2014). *Tests of Partnership: Transatlantic Cooperation in Cyber Security, Internet Governance and Data Protection*. SWP Research Paper, RP5, March 2014, Berlin.

Bendrath, R., Eriksson, J., & Giacomello, G. (2010). From 'cyberterrorism' to 'cyberwar', back and forth: How the United States securitized cyberspace. In International Relations and Security in the Digital Age. London: Routledge.

Bertot, J. C., Jaeger, P. T., & Grimes, J. M. (2007). Promoting transparency and accountability through ICTs, social media, and collaborative e-government. *Transforming Government: People. Process and Policy*, *6*(1), 78–91.

Betz, D., & Stevens, T. (2011). *Cyberspace and the State: Towards a Strategy for Cyber-Power*. Oxon, UK: Routledge.

Bevan, G., & Hood, C. (2006). What's measured is what matters: Targets and gaming in the English public health care system. *Public Administration*, *84*(3), 517–538. doi:10.1111/j.1467-9299.2006.00600.x

Bhabba, H. (1994). *The location of culture*. New York: Routledge.

Birdsal, N. (2005). Why Inequality Matters in a Globalizing World. In *WIDER Annual Lecture*. Washington, DC: Center for Global Development.

Bogdanovi'c-Dini'c, S., Veljkovi'c, N., & Stoimenov, L. (2014). How open are public government data? an assessment of seven open data portals. In M. P. Rodríguez-Bolívar (Ed.), *Measuring E-government Efficiency, Public Administration and Information Technology* (Vol. 5, pp. 25–44). Springer New York. doi:10.1007/978-1-4614-9982-4_3

Bovaird, T. (2007). Beyond engagement and participation: User and community coproduction in public services. *Public Administration Review*, *67*(5), 846–860. doi:10.1111/j.1540-6210.2007.00773.x

Bovens, M. (2007). Analysing and assessing accountability: A conceptual framework. *European Law Journal*, *13*(4), 447–468. doi:10.1111/j.1468-0386.2007.00378.x

Bovens, M., Goodin, R. E., & Schillemans, T. (2014). *The Oxford handbook of public accountability*. Oxford University Press.

Bratton, M., & Van de Walle, N. (1994). Neopatrimonial regimes and political. *Transitions in Africa World Politics, 46*(4), 453-489.

Brown, I., & Marsden, C. T. (2007). *Co-regulating Internet Security: the London Action Plan*. Retrieved in April 2016 from http://essex.academia.edu/ChrisMarsden/Papers/700007/Co-regulating_Internet_security_the_London_Action_Plan

Cannataci, J., Zhao, B., & Bonnici, J. P. M. (2016). *Privacy, free expression and transparency: redefining their new boundaries in the digital age*. UNESCO. Retrieved from http://unesdoc.unesco.org/images/0024/002466/246610E.pdf

Carr, J. (2009). *Inside Cyber Warfare: Mapping the Cyber Underworld*. O'Reilly Media.

Castells, M. (2012). *"El poder en la era de las redes sociales" en revista*. Nexos.

Cejudo, G. (2017). *Métrica del gobierno abierto*. CIDE- INAI.

Center for Strategic and International Studies (CSIS). (2008). *CSIS Commission on Cybersecurity for the 44th Presidency*. Retrieved from http://csis.org/files/media/csis/pubs/081208_securingcyberspace_44.pdf

Chandler, H. E. (1998). Towards open government: Official information on the web. *New Library World*, *99*(1144), 230–237. doi:10.1108/03074809810236784

Chen, Y. (2015). Privacy and Freedom of Information in China: Review through the Lens of Government Accountability. *European Data Protection Law Review*, *1*(4), 265–276. doi:10.21552/EDPL/2015/4/5

Chiara-Ubaldi, B. (2015). *Open Data: A Roadmap to Delivering Impact!* OECD.

Chin, J. (2013, June 28). *China Crows as Sex Tape Official Gets 13 Years*. Retrieved June 19, 2017, from https://blogs.wsj.com/chinarealtime/2013/06/28/china-crows-as-sex-tape-official-gets-13-years/

Chong, A., & Calderon, C. (2000). Causality and Feedback between Institutional Measures and Economic Growth. *Economics and Politics*, *12*(1), 69–81. doi:10.1111/1468-0343.00069

Christou, G. (2015). *Cyber Security in the European Union: Resilience and Adaptability in Governance Policy*. Houndmills, UK: Palgrave Macmillan.

Clarke, R. A., & Knake, R. K. (2010). *Cyber War: The Next Threat to National Security and What tonDo About It*. New York: Ecco Publishing.

Clarke, R. A., & Knake, R. K. (2010). *Cyber War: The Threat to National Security and what to do about it*. New York: Harper Collins.

Colarik, A. M. (2006). *Cyber terrorism: Political and Economic Implications*. IGI Publishing. doi:10.4018/978-1-59904-021-9

Collier, P., & Gunning, J. (1999a). Explaining African Economic Performance. *Journal of Economic Literature, 37*(1).

Collier, P., & Garg, A. (1999). Collier, Paul and Ashish Garg. (1999)."On Kin Groups and Wages in the Ghanaian Labour Market. *Oxford Bulletin of Economics and Statistics*, *61*(2), 131–151. doi:10.1111/1468-0084.00122

Collier, P., & Gunning, J. (1999, Summer). Why Has Africa Grown Slowly? *The Journal of Economic Perspectives*, *13*(3), 3–22. doi:10.1257/jep.13.3.3

CrossRiver Watch. (2013). We are not a flash in a pan – Agba Jalingo, founder CrossRiver Watch. *CrossRiver Watch, 1*(6), 20–21.

Dada, D. (2006). The failure of e-government in developing countries: A literature review. *The Electronic Journal on Information Systems in Developing Countries*, 26.

De Cock, C., & Bohm, S. (2007). Liberalist fantasies: Zizek and the impossibility of the open society. *Organization*, *14*(6), 815–836. doi:10.1177/1350508407082264

De Wite, B. (1999). The Past and Future Role of the European Court of Justice in the Protection of Human Rights. In *The EU and Human Rights* (pp. 859–898). Oxford, UK: Oxford University Press.

Deibert, R. J., Palfrey, J. G., Rohozinski, R., & Zittrain, J. (Eds.). (2011). *Access Contested: Security, Identity and Resistance in Asian Cyberspace*. Cambridge, MA: MIT Press. doi:10.7551/mitpress/9780262016780.001.0001

Deloitte Touche Tohmatsu. (n.d.). *2004 Global Security Survey.* Retrieved from http://www.deloitte.com/assets/Dcom-Argentina/Local%20Assets/Documents/global_security.pdf

Democracy Index. (n.d.) Retrieved from http://www.eiu.com/topic/democracy-index

Development Portfolio Management Group. (2017). *Open Government Partnership: Mid-Term Review*. University of Southern Carolina.

Di Maio, A. (2010). *Gartner group government maturity model*. Gartner Group.

Diallo, F., & Calland, R. (Eds.). (2013). *Access to Information in Africa: Law, Culture and Practice.* Brill Publishers.

Division for Public Administration and Development Management (DPADM). (2003). *UN Global E-government survey 2003*. United Nations and American Society for Public Administration. Retrieved on 5th January 2017 from https://publicadministration.un.org/egovkb/en-us/Reports/UN-E-Government-Survey-2003

Division for Public Administration and Development Management (DPADM). (2014). *United Nations E-government survey 2014: E-government for the future we want.* United Nations and American Society for Public Administration. Retrieved on 15th January from https://publicadministration.un.org/egovkb/en-us/Reports/UN-E-Government-Survey-2014

Division for Public Administration and Development Management (DPADM). (2016). *United Nations E-government survey 2016: E-governance in support for sustainable development.* United Nations and American Society for Public Administration. Retrieved on 4th April from https://publicadministration.un.org/egovkb/en-us/Reports/UN-E-Government-Survey-2016

Division for Public Administration and Development Management (DPADM). (2017). *Open Government data and services.* Retrieved on 1st January 2017 from https://publicadministration.un.org/en/ogd#popup

Dos Santos Brito, K., Silva Costa, M., Cardoso Garcia, V., & Romero de Lemos Meira, S. (2014) Experiences integrating heterogeneous government open data sources to deliver services and promote transparency in brazil. Computer Software and Applications Conference (COMPSAC), 2014 IEEE 38th Annual, 606–607.

Dunn, C. M. (2007). Cyber-Terror-Looming Threat or Phantom Menace? The Framing of the US Cyber-Threat Debate. *Journal of Information Technology & Politics*, *4*(1), 19–35.

Dunn-Cavelty, M. (2008). Cyber-Security and Threat Politics: US efforts to secure the Information Age. London: Routledge.

Dunn-Cavelty, M. (2013). *A Resilient Europe for an Open, Safe and Secure Cyberspace* (Occasional Papers, No.23). The Swedish Institute of International Affairs.

Endong, F. P. C. (2017a). "Watchdogging" versus adversarial journalism by state-owned media: The Nigerian and Cameroonian experience. *IJELS: International Journal of English, Literature and Social Sciences*, *2*(2), 8–17.

Endong, F. P. C. (2017b). From dictatorship to African democracy: How has freedom of expression been improved in Nigeria and Cameroon? *Journal of Media Studies*, *31*(1), 1–17.

European Commission. (2009). *Internet Governance: Next Steps*. Communication from the Commission from the European Parliament and the Council, Brussels, 18 June, COM (2009) 277 final. Author.

European Commission. (2013). *Cybersecurity Strategy of the EU: An Open, Safe and Secure Cyberspace*. Brussels, 7.2.13, JOIN (2013) 1 FINAL. Author.

European Cybercrime Centre – one year on. (2014). European Commission, Press Release, Brussels, IP/14/129, 10 February 2014.

European Cybercrime Centre. (n.d.). *First Year Report*. Retrieved from April 24, 2016, from https://www.europol.europa.eu/content/european-cybercrime-center-ec3-first-year-report

European Principles and Guidelines for Internet Resilience and Stability. (2011). Retrieved on April 11, 2016, from http://ec.europa.eu/danmark/documents/alle_emner/videnskabelig/110401_rapport_cyberangreb_ en.pdf

Evans, A. M., & Campos, A. (2013). Open government initiatives: Challenges of citizen participation. *Journal of Policy Analysis and Management*, *32*(1), 172–185. doi:10.1002/pam.21651

Evans, J., & Rauch, J. (2000). Bureaucratic Structure and Bureaucratic Performance in Less Developed Countries. *Journal of Public Economics*, *75*(1), 49–71. doi:10.1016/S0047-2727(99)00044-4

Fafchamps, M., Gunning, J. W., & Oostendorp, R. (1998). *Inventories, Liquidity and Contractual Risk in African Manufacturing Journal of Economic Perspectives*. Department of Economics, Stanford University.

Ferguson, J. (2006). Decomposing Modernity: History and Hierarchy after Development. Department of Anthropology University of California, Irvine.

Forsythe, M. (2015, June 11). Zhou Yongkang, Ex-Security Chief in China, Gets Life Sentence for Graft. *The New York Times*. Retrieved from https://www.nytimes.com/2015/06/12/world/asia/zhou-yongkang-former-security-chief-in-china-gets-life-sentence-for-corruption.html

Forsythe, M., & Stevenson, A. (2017, May 30). The Billionaire Gadfly in Exile Who Stared Down Beijing. *The New York Times*. Retrieved from https://www.nytimes.com/2017/05/30/world/asia/china-guo-wengui.html

Fraser-Molekiti, G., & Senghor, D. (2010). *E-governance and citizen participation in West Africa: Challenges and opportunities*. Dakar: The Panos Institute & The United Nations Development Program.

Freedom House. (2015). *Freedom on the net 2015. Nigeria*. London: Freedom House.

Garside, J., Harding, L., Watt, H., Pegg, D., Bengtsson, H., & Bowers, S. … Hopkins, N. (2016). What are the Panama Papers? A guide to history's biggest data leak. *The Guardian*. Available at https://www.theguardian.com/news/2016/apr/03/what-you-need-to-know-about-the-panamapapers

Giddens, A. (1999). *Runaway World: How Globalization is Reshaping our Lives*. London: Profile.

Gjelten, T. (2010). *Seeing the Internet as an 'Information Weapon'*. Retrieved on March 12, 2016, from http://www.npr.org/templates/story/story.php?storyId=130052701

Gobierno municipal. (2016). *Micrositio del Ayuntamiento de Ciudad Juárez*. Retrieved from http://mi.juarez.gob.mx/mijuarez/tech

Goëta, S., & Davies, T. (2016). The Daily Shaping of State Transparency: Standards, Machine-Readability and the Configuration of Open Government Data Policies. *Science & Technology Studies*, *29*(4), 10–30.

Goldsmith, J. (2011). *Cybersecurity treaties: A Sceptical View*. Stanford University.

Gómez-Peña, G. (1996). *The new world border: Prophecies, poems and loqueras for the end of the century*. San Francisco, CA: City Lights.

Gottschalk, P. (2009). Maturity levels for interoperability in digital government. *Government Information Quarterly*, *26*(1), 75–81. doi:10.1016/j.giq.2008.03.003

Gould, D., & Mukendi, T. (1989). Bureaucratic Corruption in Africa: Causes. *Consequences and Remedies International Journal of Public Administration*, *12*(3), 427–457. doi:10.1080/01900698908524633

Government of India. (2012, March 17). National Data Sharing and Accessibility Policy (NDSAP) 2012. *Gazette of India*.

Government of India. (n.d.a). *Open Data Government Platform India*. Retrieved from https://data.gov.in/

Government of India. (n.d.b). *National Data Sharing and Accessibility Policy (NDSAP)*. Retrieved from https://india.gov.in/national-data-sharing-and-accessibility-policy-ndsap

Hafkin, N. I. (2009). *E-government in Africa: An overview of progress made and challenges*. Paper presented at the UNDESA/UNPAN Workshop on Electronic/Mobile Government in Africa.

Hansson, K., Belkacem, K., & Ekenberg, L. (2015). Open Government and Democracy: A Research Review. *Social Science Computer Review*, *33*(5), 540–555. doi:10.1177/0894439314560847

Hassan, I.S. (2009, August 15). The fallacies of democracy and democratic dictatorship in Nigeria. *Kano Online*, 12-26.

Healey, J. (2011a). *Comparing Norms for National Conduct in Cyberspace*. Retrieved on March 12, 2016, from http://www.acus.org

Healey, J. (2011b). *Breakthrough or Just Broken? China and Russia's UNGA Proposal on Cyber Norms*. Retrieved on April 12, 2016, from http://www.acus.org

Heeks, R. (2008). *The e-government for development information exchange*. Manchester, UK: Manchester Institute for Development Policy and Management.

Hellberg, A. S., & Hedstrom, K. (2015). The story of the sixth myth of open data and open government. *Transforming Government: People. Process and Policy*, *9*(1), 35–51.

Höchtl, J., Parycek, P., & Schöllhammer, R. (2015). Big data in the policy cycle: Policy decision making in the digital era. *Journal of Organizational Computing and Electronic Commerce*, *26*, 1–2, 147–169.

Holsti, O. (1969). *Content Analysis for the Social Sciences and Humanities*. Reading, MA: Addison-Wesley.

Hoque, M., Rajib, M. S. U., & Akter, M. (2016). Development of public sector accounting: Reformation and Challenges in Bangladesh. In *Australia Bangladesh Business Research Symposium*. Monash Business School.

Hoque, Z. (Ed.). (2015). *Making Governments Accountable: The Role of Public Accounts Committees and National Audit Offices*. Routledge.

Horsley, J. P. (2016, April 28). *China's FOIA Turns Eight*. Retrieved June 22, 2017, from http://www.freedominfo.org/2016/04/chinas-foia-turns-eight/

Huang, Y. (2014, December 1). *The Anticorruption Campaign And Rising Suicides In China's Officialdom*. Retrieved July 13, 2017, from http://www.forbes.com/sites/yanzhonghuang/2014/12/01/the-anticorruption-campaign-and-rising-suicides-in-chinas-officialdom/

Huijboom, N., & Van der Broek, T. (2011). Open data: an international comparison of strategies. *European Journal of ePractice, 12*. Retrieved from http://www.epractice.eu/files/European%20Journal%20epractice%20Volume%2012_1.df

Hyden, G., Court, J., & Mease, K. (2003). *The Bureaucracy and Governance in 16 Developing Countries*. Overseas Development Institute (ODI) World Governance Survey Discussion Paper 7.

Ifreke, I. (2017). *Bihari is trying to stifle freedom of expression- Soyinka*. Retrieved online http://dailypost.ng/2017/02/05/buhari-trying-stifle-freedom-expression-soyinka/

INEGI. (2015). *Censo de población 2010*. INEGI.

ITU. (2016). *ICT Development index 2016, Huwei*. ITU.

Janssen, K. (2012). *Open government data: right to information 2.0 or its rollback version?* ICRI Working Paper.

Janssen, K. (2012). Open government data and the right to information: Opportunities and obstacles. *The Journal of Community Informatics*, *8*(2).

Janssen, M., Charalabidis, Y., & Zuiderwijk, A. (2012). Benefits, adoption barriers and myths of open data and open government. *Information Systems Management*, *29*(4), 258–268. doi:10.1080/10580530.2012.716740

Joseph, R. (1991). *Democracy and Prebendal Politics the Rise and Fall of Nigeria's Second Republic*. Spectrum Books Limited.

Kalampokis, E., Tambouris, E., & Tarabanis, K. (2011). A classification scheme for open government data: Towards linking decentralized data. *International Journal of Web Engineering and Technology*, *6*(3), 266–285. doi:10.1504/IJWET.2011.040725

Karisiddappa, C. R. (2004). *Library and information science curriculum for developing countries*. Paper presented at IFLA General Conference and Council.

Kendall, W. (1960). The "open society" and its fallacies. *The American Political Science Review*, *54*(4), 972–979.

Kenhago, T. O. (2014). Successes and failures in e-government projects. *E-government for development*. Retrieved April 19, 2017 from http://www.egov4dev.org/success/case/camportal.shtml

Kim, S., & Kim, D. (2003). South Korean public officials' perceptions of values, failure, and consequences of failure in e-government leadership. *Public Performance & Management Review*, *26*(4), 360–375. doi:10.1177/1530957603026004004

King, J. (2006). Openness and its discontents. In J. Dean, J. W. Anderson, & G. Lovink (Eds.), *Reformatting politics: Information technology and global civil society*. New York: Routledge.

Kitchin, R. (2013). *Four critiques of open data initiatives | Open Data Research Network*. Available at www.opendataresearch.org/tumblr/2013/four-critiques-open-data-initiatives

Klaas, B. (2016). *The Despot's Accomplice: How the West Is Aiding and Abetting the Decline of Democracy*. Oxford University Press.

Klievink, B., & Janssen, M. (2009). Realizing joined-up government – Dynamic capabilities and stage models for transformation. *Government Information Quarterly*, *26*(2), 275–284. doi:10.1016/j.giq.2008.12.007

Klimburg, A. (2011). Ruling the Domain: (Self) Regulation and the Security of the Internet. Austrian Institute for International Affairs.

Klimburg, A., & Tirmaa-Klaar, H. (2011). Cyber war and Cyber security: Challenges faced by the EU and its Member States. DG for External Policies, Policy Department, European Parliament.

Kramer, Starr, & Wentz (Eds.). (2010). Cyber Power and National Security. Washington, DC: National Defence UP.

Kshetri, N. (2013). *Cybercrime and Cybersecurity in the Global South*. Houndmills, UK: Palgrave Macmillan. doi:10.1057/9781137021946

Lasswell, H. (1948). Power and Personality. New York, NY: Academic Press.

Lathrop, D., & Ruma, L. (Eds.). (2010). Open government: Collaboration, transparency, and participation in practice. O'Reilly Media.

Layne, K., & Lee, J. (2001). Developing fully functional e-government: A four stage model. *Government Information Quarterly*, *18*(2), 122–136. doi:10.1016/S0740-624X(01)00066-1

Lee, G., & Kwak, Y. H. (2012). An open government model for social media-based public engagement. *Government Information Quarterly*, *29*(4), 492–503. doi:10.1016/j.giq.2012.06.001

Lee, I., & Anas, A. (1991). *Manufacturers' Responses to Infrastructure Deficiencies in Nigeria: Private Alternatives and Policy Options*. Washington, DC: World Bank.

Lessig, L. (2005). Open code and open societies. In J. Feller, B. Fitzgerald, S. A. Hissam, & K. R. Lakhani (Eds.), *Perspectives on free and open source software*. London: The MIT Press.

Libicki, M. C. (2007). *Conquest in Cyberspace: National Security and Information Warfare*. New York: Cambridge University Press. doi:10.1017/CBO9780511804250

Libicki, M. C. (2009). *Cyber Deterrence and Cyber War*. Rand Corporation.

Lichtman, J., & Posner, E. (2006). Holding Internet Service Providers Accountable. *Supreme Court Economic Review, 14*(229).

Linders, D., & Wilson, S. C. (2011). What is open government? One year after the directive. *12th Annual International Conference on Digital Government Research*, 262 – 271. doi:10.1145/2037556.2037599

Linz, J., & Stepan, A. (1996). Toward Consolidated Democracies Journal of Democracy 7.2 (14-33

Liu, H. (2016). Comparison Research on Open Government Data Websites in China——Base on the Investigation of Nine OGD Websites. In *Proceedings of the Doctoral Consortium at the 18th International Conference on Asia-Pacific Digital Libraries (ICADL 2016), and Asia-Pacific Forum of Information Schools (APIS 2016)*. Retrieved from http://icadl2016.org/apis/19_Liu.pdf

Liu, W. (2016, January 27). *Family Asset Audit Forces Chinese officials to File Genuine Report* (in Chinese). Retrieved July 20, 2017, from http://epaper.ynet.com/html/2016-01/27/content_180488.htm?div=0

Luhrmann, T. (1989). The Magic of Secrecy. *Ethos (Berkeley, Calif.)*, *17*(2), 131–165. doi:10.1525/eth.1989.17.2.02a00010

Manish, S. (2017, January 27). India improves rank in democracy index; civil liberties curtailed: EIU. *Business Standard.* Retrieved from http://mybs.in/2USj08G

Manor, I. (2015). Between two digital divides. *Exploring digital diplomacy.* Retrieved January 24, 2017, from https://digdipblog.com/2016/01/27/between-two-digital-divides/

Manor, I. (2015). In digital diplomacy, a narrowing digital divide. *Exploring digital diplomacy*. Retrieved January 24 from https://digdipblog.com/2015/01/19/divide/

Maseh, E., & Katuu, S. (2017). The Kenyan Judiciary's open government initiative: Prospects and challenges. *Journal of Science and Technology Policy Management*, *8*(1), 76–94. doi:10.1108/JSTPM-04-2016-0007

Mbakun, J. (1996). Bureaucratic corruption in Africa: The Futility of Cleanups. *Cato J, 16*(1).

Mduduzi, K. (2015). *The West Stole Africa's Wealth. Xilibris Press.*

Meijer, A., Curtin, D., & Hillebrandt, M. (2012). Open government: connecting vision and voice. In *International Review of Administrative Sciences* (pp. 10–29). London: SAGE.

Mercado-Lara, E., & Gil-Garcia, J. R. (2014). Open government and data intermediaries: The case of aiddata. In *Proceedings of the 15th Annual International Conference on Digital Government Research* (pp. 335–336). ACM. http://doi.acm.org/10.1145/2612733.2612789

Ministry of Finance of Macedonia (MoFM). (2017). *Public consultation for draft economic reform program 2017*. Retrieved on 3rd March, 2017 from http://www.finance.gov.mk/en/node/6198

Ministry of Foreign Affairs of the People's Republic of China. (2011, September 13). *China, Russia and Other Countries Submit the Document of International Code of Conduct for Information Security to the United Nations*. Retrieved from http://www.fmprc.gov.cn/mfa_eng/wjb_663304/zzjg_663340/jks_665232/jkxw_665234/t858978.shtml

Ministry of Rural Development, Government of India. (2017, May 7). Retrieved from http://www.nrega.nic.in/netnrega/home.aspx

MINPOSTEL. (2005). *Sector Strategy for Telecommunications and Information and Communication Technologies 2005- 2015*. Yaounde: Government Printers.

Minter, A. (2012, October 2). *In China, Mistresses and Corruption Go Hand in Hand*. Retrieved from https://www.bloomberg.com/view/articles/2012-10-02/in-china-mistresses-and-corruption-go-hand-in-hand

Moynihan, D. (1999). *The Science of Secrecy*. Retrieved from http://www.aaas.org/spp/secrecy/Presents/Moynihan.htm

Mueller, M. L. (2010). *Networks and States: The Global Politics of the Internet*. M.I.T. Press. doi:10.7551/mitpress/9780262014595.001.0001

Muller, J. (2013, March). Capitalism and Inequality, What the Right and Left Get Wrong. *Foreign Affairs*.

Narayan, D., Patel, R., Schafft, K., Rademacher, A., & Koch-Schulte, S. (2000). *Voices of the Poor: Can Anyone Hear Us?* Washington, DC: The World Bank. doi:10.1596/0-1952-1601-6

North, D. (1993). The New Institutional Economics and Development. *Economic History, 9*(8), 1-10.

NPR. (2014, March 2). *Corruption Blurs The Lines Of China's Mistress Culture*. Retrieved June 20, 2017, from http://www.npr.org/2014/03/02/284905579/corruption-blurs-the-lines-of-chinas-mistress-culture

Ntiro, S. (2000). *eGovernment in Eastern Africa*. Dar-es Salam: KPMG.

Nye, J. (2010). Cyber Power. Harvard Kennedy School, Belfer Center for Science and International Affairs.

Nzepa, N. O., & Keutchankeu, T. R. (2015). *Understanding what is happening in ICT in Cameroon. A supply-and-demand-side analysis of the ICT sector*. Cape Town, South Africa: Research ICT Africa.

Obama, B. (2010). *President Obama's Address to the United Nations General Assembly*. Available at http.//www.whitehouse.gov/the-press-office2010/09/23

OCDE. (2016). *Open Government Data Review of Mexico: Data Reuse for Public Sector Impact and Innovation*, OECD Digital Government Studies, OECD Publishing. Retrieved from http://www.keepeek.com/Digital-Asset-Management/oecd/governance/open-government-data-review-of-mexico_9789264259270-en#page158

Olayiwola, Akinwandc, Oluwatoyosi, & Ahmed. (2016). Open Data Portals in Africa: An Analysis of Open Government Data Initiatives. *African Journal of Library Archives and Information Science*, *26*(2), 97–106.

Omiere, E., & Omiere, C. (2014). New wine in old wine skin: An exploration of major constraints to e-government implementation in Nigeria. *European Scientific Journal*, *10*(14), 148–154.

Opengovguide. (2017). *Establish a law requiring public disclosure of income and assets by elected and senior public officials - Open Government Guide*. Retrieved July 18, 2017, from http://www.opengovguide.com/commitments/asset-disclosure/

Ostrom, E. (1990). *Governing the Commons: The Evolution of Institutions for Collective Action*. Cambridge, UK: Cambridge University Press. doi:10.1017/CBO9780511807763

Papińska-Kacperek, J., & Polańska, K. (2015). Open Government Data initiatives. *Collegium of Economic Analysis Annals*, (38), 191-202.

Parker, J. (2013, September 4). *The Privacy vs. Transparency Debate in China*. Retrieved June 13, 2017, from http://thediplomat.com/2013/09/the-privacy-vs-transparency-debate-in-china/

Pei, M. (2006). *China's trapped transition : the limits of developmental autocracy*. Cambridge, MA: Harvard University Press. doi:10.4159/9780674041981

Perez, C. C., Hernandez, A. M. L., & Bolivar, M. P. R. (2005). Citizens' access to on-line governmental financial information: Practices in the European Union countries. *Government Information Quarterly*, *22*(2), 258–276. doi:10.1016/j.giq.2005.02.002

Pieterse, J. N. (1994). Globalisation as hybridisation. *International Sociology*, *9*(2), 161–184. doi:10.1177/026858094009002003

Pieterse, J. N. (2010). *Development theory: Deconstructions / reconstructions* (2nd ed.). London: Sage Publications Ltd. doi:10.4135/9781446279083

Pikettey, T. (2014). *Capital in the Twenty First Century*. London: The Belknap Press of Harvard University Press Cambridge. doi:10.4159/9780674369542

Pollock, R. (2006). The value of the public domain. *IPPR*. Retrieved from http://www.ippr.org/publication/55/1526/thevalue-of-the-public-domain

Popper, K. (1962). *The open society and its enemies*. London: Routledge and Kegan Paul.

Posner, D., & Young, D. (2007). *The Institutionalization of Political Power in Africa. Journal of Democracy, 18*(3), 127–140.

Powell, B. (2001). Is Cybersecurity a Public Good? Evidence from the Financial Services Industry. In *Independent Institute Working Paper 57*. Oakland, CA: The Independent Institute. Retrieved from http://www.independent.org/pdf/working_papers/57_cyber.pdf

Pradhan, S. (1996). *Evaluating Public Spending*. World Bank Discussion Paper 323, Washington, DC.

PricewaterhouseCoopers. (2010). *Respected—But Still Restrained: Findings from the 2011 Global State of Information Security Survey.* Retrieved from http://www.pwc.com/gx/en/information-securitysurvey/pdf/giss-2011-survey-report.pdf

Qian, Z. (2012, April 9). Calls growing for national law to force officials to disclose full assets. *Global Times*. Retrieved July 18, 2017, from http://www.globaltimes.cn/content/703857.shtml

Rajib, M. S. U., & Mou, N. Z. (2014). Ethical Issues of Qualitative Research. In J. Wang (Ed.), *Encyclopedia of Business Analytics and Optimization* (pp. 852–863). Hershey, PA: Business Science Reference; doi:10.4018/978-1-4666-5202-6.ch080

Rajib, M. S. U., Sajib, M. Q. U., & Hoque, M. (2017). Strengthening the Public Sector Accounting Through ICT: The Experience of a Developing Country. In H. Kaur, E. Lechman, & A. Marszk (Eds.), *Catalyzing Development through ICT Adoption*. Cham: Springer; doi:10.1007/978-3-319-56523-1_6

Recursos. (2017, March 14). Retrieved from http://mxabierto.org/

Red Mexico Abierto. (2017). *Micositio de la oficina de Estrategia digital nacional del gobierno federal*. Retrieved from http://mxabierto.org/

Relyea, H., & Kolakowsk, M. (2007). *Cong. Research SERV., 97-71 GOV, Access TO Government Information in the United States, at CRS-2*. Retrieved from http://www.dtic.mil/dtic/tr/fulltext/u2/a470219.pdf

Republic of Cameroon. (2009). *Growth and Employment Strategy Paper (GESP): Reference Framework for Government Action over the Period 2010-2020*. Yaounde: Government Printer.

Robinson, N. (2013). *The European Cyber Security Strategy: Too Big to Fail?* Available at: http://www.rand.org/bog/2013/02/the-european-cyber-security-strategy-too-big-to-fail.html

Robinson, N. (2014). *EU cyber-defence: a work in progress*. European Union Institute for Security Studies.

Romzek, B. S., & Dubnick, M. J. (1998). Accountability. In International Encyclopedia of Public Policy and Administration. Boulder, CO: Westview Press.

Ronen, J., & Srinidhi, B. (1989). Depreciation Policies in Regulated Companies: Which Policies Are the Most Efficient? *Management Science*, *35*(5), 515–526. doi:10.1287/mnsc.35.5.515

Rosenau, J. (1997). Complexities and Contradictions of Globalization. *Current History (New York, N.Y.)*, *96*(613).

Rossi, I., Pop, L., Clementucci, F., & Sawaqed, L. (2012). *Using Asset Disclosure for Identifying Politically Exposed Persons*. Retrieved June 6, 2017, from https://openknowledge.worldbank.org/handle/10986/26790

Sandoval-Almazan, R., & Gil-Garcia, J. R. (2016). Toward an integrative assessment of open government: Proposing conceptual lenses and practical components. *Journal of Organizational Computing and Electronic Commerce*, *26*(1-2), 170–192. doi:10.1080/10919392.2015.1125190

Schlesinger, D., Henochowicz, A., & Wang, Y. (2016, March 17). *Why Xi Jinping's Media Controls Are 'Absolutely Unyielding'*. Retrieved July 16, 2017, from https://foreignpolicy.com/2016/03/17/why-xi-jinpings-media-controls-absolutely-unyielding-censorship-china-economy-speech/

Scott, R. (2004). Institutional Theory: Contributing to a Theoretical Research Program. In *Great Minds in Management: The Process of Theory Development*. Oxford, UK: Oxford University Press.

Sherman, R. (1992). Capital Waste in the Rate-of-Return Regulated Firm. *Journal of Regulatory Economics*, *4*(2), 197–204. doi:10.1007/BF00157165

Shim, D. C., & Eom, T. H. (2008). E-government and anti-corruption: Empirical analysis of international data. *International Journal of Public Administration*, *31*(3), 298–316. doi:10.1080/01900690701590553

Siau, K., & Long, Y. (2005). Synthesizing e-government stage models – a meta-synthesis based on meta-ethnography approach. *Industrial Management & Data Systems*, *105*(4), 443–458. doi:10.1108/02635570510592352

Simmel, G. (1950). The Secret and the Secret Society. In K. H. Wolff (Ed.), *The Sociology of Georg Simmel* (pp. 330–344). Glencoe, IL: The Free Press.

Sindeu, E. (2013). *Implementation of e-government in Cameroon*. Paper presented at the 7th Annual E-Government Forum, Muyuno, Uganda.

Soo Hoo, K. J. (2000). How Much Is Enough? A Risk Management Approach to Computer Security (Working paper). Stanford, CA: Consortium for Research on Information Security and Policy. Retrieved from http://iisdb.stanford.edu/pubs/11900/soohoo.pdf

Stiglitz, J. (1999). *On Liberty, the Right to Know, and Public Discourse: The Role of Transparency in Public Life*. Oxford Amnesty Lecture, Oxford, UK. Retrieved from http://derechoasaber.org.mx/documentos/pdf0116.pdf

Stiglitz, J. (2016). Globalization and its New Discontents. *Project Syndicate*. Available at https://www.projectsyndicate.org/default/library/c198d0035bc7db1aa409717cf4020935.square.pgitemprop=thumbnail

Stiglitz, J. (2004). *The Post Washington Consensus*. The Initiative for Policy Dialogue.

Straubhaar, J. (1991). Beyond media imperialism: Asymmetrical interdependence and cultural proximity. *Critical Studies in Mass Communication*, *8*(1), 29–38. doi:10.1080/15295039109366779

Susan, F. (2014, December 23). *How China Classifies State Secrets*. Retrieved July 18, 2017, from http://thediplomat.com/2014/12/how-china-classifies-state-secrets/

The Windhoek Declaration. (2001). *African Charter on the Values and Principles of Public Service and the Administration*. Windhoek: African Ministers of Civil Service.

Thelen, K. (1999). Historical Institutionalism in Comparative Politics. *The American Political Science Review*, *2*(1), 369–404. doi:10.1146/annurev.polisci.2.1.369

Thelwall, M. (2009). Introduction to webometrics: Quantitative web research for the social sciences. *Synthesis Lectures on Information Concepts, Retrieval, and Services, 1*(1), 1-116.

Tiezzi, S. (2015, August 14). *The Tianjin Explosion, As Chronicled on Chinese Social Media*. Retrieved July 17, 2017, from http://thediplomat.com/2015/08/the-tianjin-explosion-as-chronicled-on-chinese-social-media/

Tomlinson, J. (1999). *Globalization and Culture. University of Chicago Press.*

Transparency International. (n.d.). *Corruption Perceptions Index*. Retrieved from https://www.transparency.org/research/cpi/overview

Ubaldi, B. (2013). Open government data: Towards empirical analysis of open government data initiatives. *OECD Working Papers on Public Governance*, (22), 0-1.

United Nation Public Administration Network. (2016). *Africa: UN e-Government survey ranks Mauritius 1st in Africa.* Retrieved May 27, 2017 from http://allafrica.com/stories/201608190714.html

United Nations. (2010). *Report of the Group of Governmental Experts on Developments in the Field of Information and Telecommunications in the Context of International Security, A/65/201, Study Series 33*. UN.

UNO. (2008). *United Nations e-Government survey 2008: from e-Government to Connected Governance*. Washington, DC: UNO.

UNO. (2012). *United Nation e-government survey 2012*. Washington, DC: UNO.

UNO. (2014). *United Nation e-government survey 2014*. Washington, DC: UNO.

UNO. (2016). *United Nation e-Government survey 2016: E-government in support of sustainable development*. Washington, DC: UNO.

Valdes, G., Solar, M., Astudillo, H., Iribarren, M., Concha, G., & Visconti, M. (2011). Conception, development and implementation of an e-government maturity model in public agencies. *Government Information Quarterly*, *28*(2), 176–187. doi:10.1016/j.giq.2010.04.007

Valenzuela, R. (2015). La transparencia colaborativa: una herramienta para gobierno abierto. Buen Gobierno para que la democracia funcione, (18), 2-18.

Van Eeten, M., & Bauer, J. M. (2009). Emerging Threats to Internet Security: Incentives, Externalities and Policy Implications. *Journal of Contingencies and Crisis Management, 17*(223).

Vernon, R. (1976). The "great society" and the "open society": Liberalism in Hayek and Popper. *Canadian Journal of Political Science, 9*(2), 261–276. doi:10.1017/S0008423900043717

Vries, M. D., & Nemec, J. (2013). Public sector reform: An overview of recent literature and research on NPM and alternative paths. *International Journal of Public Sector Management, 26*(1), 4–16. doi:10.1108/09513551311293408

Wasike, B. (2016). FoIA in the age of "Open. Gov": An analysis of the performance of the freedom of information act under the Obama and Bush administrations. *Government Information Quarterly, 33*(3), 417–426. doi:10.1016/j.giq.2016.05.001

Weber, M. (1968). Economy and Society: An Outline of Interpretive Sociology. Berkeley, CA: University of California Press.

Wedel, J. (2009). *Shadow Elite: How the World's New Power Brokers Undermine Democracy, Government, and the Free Market*. New York: Basic Books.

Wee, S.-L. (2014, April 18). China sentences activists for urging asset disclosure: Lawyer. *Reuters*. Retrieved from http://www.reuters.com/article/us-china-activists-idUSBREA3H04H20140418

Welch, E. (2012). The relationship between transparent and participative government: A study of local goverments. In *International Review of Administrative Sciences* (pp. 78–93). SAGE.

Wenjing, L. (2011). Approaching Democracy Through Transparency: A Comparative Law Study on Chinese Open Government Information. *American University International Law Review, 26*(4). Retrieved from http://digitalcommons.wcl.american.edu/auilr/vol26/iss4/4

Werbner, P., & Moddod, T. (Eds.). (1997). *Debating cultural hybridity: Multi-cultural identities and the politics of anti-racism*. London: Zed Books.

Westfield, F. M. (1965). Regulation and Conspiracy. *The American Economic Review, 55*(3), 424–444.

Wharton University (2016, August 23). Building e-governance in Africa: One pioneering company's approach. *Knowledge @ Wharton,* 43-49.

Wiemann, G. (2006). *Cyberterrorism: How Real Is the Threat.* Washington, DC: United States Institute of Peace.

Williams, S. (2002). Free as in freedom: Richard Stallman's crusade for free software. Sebastopol, CA: O'Reilly & Associates, Inc.

Wonderlich, J. (2010). *Ten Principles for Opening Up Government Information.* Washington, DC: Sunlight Foundation.

World Bank (WB). (2013). *Governance in Bangladesh.* Retrieved from http://www.worldbank.org/en/country/bangladesh/brief/bangladesh-governance

World Bank (WB). (2015). *Tanzania - Open Government and Public Financial Management (OGPFM) Development Policy Operation Program Project.* Washington, DC: World Bank Group. Retrieved from http://documents.worldbank.org/curated/en/522551468300592178/Tanzania-Open-Government-and-Public-Financial-Management-OGPFM-Development-Policy-Operation-Program-Project

Yang, G. (2015, February 4). *Calls grow for top down asset disclosures.* Retrieved June 12, 2017, from http://www.chinadaily.com.cn/opinion/2015-02/04/content_19490935.htm

Yimin, R. (2016, November 16). *The Story of Gang Huang and His Mistress* (in Chinese). Retrieved July 18, 2017, from http://eurcb.com/html/xinwen/zixuan/201611162330.html

Yiu, C. (2012). A right to data: Fulfilling the promise of open public data in the UK. *Policy Exchange Research.* Available at http://www.policyexchange.org.uk/publications/category/item/a-right-todata-fulfilling-the-promise-of-open-public-data-in-the-uk

You, P. (2012, October 28). *Those secrets that cannot be told (说的秘密(组图)).* Retrieved June 12, 2017, from http://www.aboluowang.com/2012/1028/265889.html

Young, C. (2000). Africa: Democratization, Cultural Pluralism, and the Challenge of Political Order. *Macalester International, 9.* Retrieved from http://digitalcommons.macalester.edu/macintl/vol9/iss1/7

Yu, H & Robinson, D. (2012). The New Ambiguity of "Open Government". *UCLA Law. Rev., 59.*

Yu, H., & Robinson, D. (2012). *The New Ambiguity of Open Government. In Law review Discourse, no. 59* (pp. 178–208). UCLA.

Zhou, H. (2003). *Open Government in China: Practice and Problems*. Retrieved July 18, 2017, from https://academiccommons.columbia.edu/catalog/ac:126700

Zuiderwijk, A., & Janssen, M. (2014b). The negative effects of open government data - investigating the dark side of open data. In *Proceedings of the 15th Annual International Conference on Digital Government Research* (pp. 147–152). ACM. http://doi.acm.org/10.1145/2612733.2612761

Zuiderwijk, A., & Janssen, M. (2014a). Barriers and development directions for the publication and usage of open data: A socio-technical view. In M. Gascó-Hernández (Ed.), *Open Government, Public Administration and Information Technology* (Vol. 4, pp. 115–135). Springer New York. doi:10.1007/978-1-4614-9563-5_8

About the Contributors

Ayse Kok has over 8 years of experience in the field of social, mobile and digital technologies both from a practitioner and from a researcher perspective. She participated in various projects in partnership with international organizations such as UN, NATO and the EU. Previously, she was working for an international bank in Turkey where she established the Digital Learning Unit and has been awarded by Brandon Hall- a leading global institute in L & D practices- in two different categories for her projects. Ayse also acted as an adjunct faculty member in her home town Turkey. Ayse attended various international conferences as a speaker and published several articles in both peer-reviewed journals and academic books. She is the first female graduate student for both MSc and MLitt degrees in her academic field in Oxford University where she also became a member of Oxford Educational Technology Research Group. She is also passionate about philanthropy and is the co-founder of the first non-for-profit Turkish MooC (http://www.UniversitePlus.com) which aims to revolutionize higher education in Turkey.

* * *

Luke. A. Amadi specialized in Development Studies from the University of Port Harcourt, Nigeria. He has several publications in scholarly journals.

Rupak Chakravarty is an Associate Professor in the Department of Library & Information Science, Panjab University, Chandigarh, India for more than 10 years. Specialization areas include: Application of ICT in libraries including library automation, Free Open Source Software (FOSS), digital library, digital reference service, library portal development. Other areas of specialization include: Management of Library & Information Centres, Information & Communication, Dewey Decimal Classification, Information Sources, Open Access, Institutional Repositories (IRs), Web 2.0, Library 2.0. Also serving as Mendeley Advisor at Chandigarh region. Worked as Assistant Librarian, Panjab University Library for more than five years as the Reference Librarian and at Periodicals.

Floribert Patrick C. Endong (PhD) is a research consultant in the humanities and social sciences. He is a reviewer and editor with many scientific journals in the social sciences. His current research interest focuses on international communication, digital media, media laws, international relations, culture and religious communication He is author of numerous peer-reviewed articles and book chapters in the above-mentioned areas of interest.

Mahfuzul Hoque is the professor of Accounting and Information Systems Department, University of Dhaka. He was the secretary of The Institute of Chartered Accounts of Bangladesh (ICAB). Before being the secretory of ICAB, he was the director of Learning and Professional Development of ICAB. He publishes many papers including articles in the renowned international Journal, Edited Book and international conference. He is the managing Editor of Japanese Management and International Studies.

Prince Ikechukwu Igwe holds a Ph.D in Political Science from the University of Port Harcourt, Nigeria with specialization in Development Studies. He has several publications in scholarly journals.

Md. Rajib is serving as an assistant professor at the Department of Accounting & Information Systems in Jahangirnagar University. He has teaching experience both in the country and in abroad. His articles have been published by the renowned international publishers. His research interest includes Public Sector Accounting, Open Government, Big Data, Research Methodology and others. He is working as the reviewer of different national and international periodicals. He is working as the panel member of MPhil and PhD thesis proposal evaluation and thesis evaluation board at different universities.

Bo Zhao is a senior research fellow at TILT (Tilburg Institute for Law, Technology and Society), Tilburg University, the Netherlands (Oct. 2017-), and was the STeP (Security, Technology and e-Privacy) research group at the Faculty of Law, University of Groningen, the Netherlands (Jan. 2014 - Sept. 2017). Originally trained as a legal philosopher, he has been living and working in the Netherlands since 2002. His research interest includes comparative data and privacy protection law, comparative defamation law, Internet Governance, and legal development in China. He was also a visiting scholar at Pennsylvania University Law School in 2012.

Index

A

accountability 1-4, 7-10, 14-15, 18-19, 22, 31, 33, 44, 71, 92-95, 102, 104, 134, 136-138
Asset Disclosure 33-34, 37-42, 45
authority 32, 37, 39, 43, 114, 133-134, 136

B

Balancing 44-45
Bangladesh 92-96, 98-102, 104-105
Bangladesh, 95-96, 99, 102, 104
Bureaucracy 3-4, 8-9, 15-21
bureaucratic secrecy 1, 3-4, 7-9, 15-19, 22

C

central government 42, 51
China 29, 31-33, 36-37, 39-44, 143, 147-149, 153
collaboration 21-22, 53, 64, 71, 97, 102, 105, 134, 140
collaborative governance 132-134, 139
computer networking 156
conceptual landscape 144
cybersecurity 143-149, 155-156, 158, 163

D

data organization 132-134, 136, 138-140
Democracy Index 68, 73, 75-76, 79, 87, 90
Developing democracies 1, 3, 6, 15, 21-22
developing nations 93, 112
development partners 93
Digital Divide 112, 120-121, 131
Disclosure of Private Life 34, 36, 44
donor agencies 93, 101

E

E-Governance 2, 10-12, 20, 22, 30, 111, 113, 115-118, 120-122, 128, 131
Emerging Economy 92
employment 16, 123-124, 132-133
EU 44, 143-144, 146-149, 162
expenditure 17, 98, 101, 104

F

financial management 92-94, 98, 100, 104-105

G

global partnerships 144
government data 2-4, 12, 14, 21, 32, 55, 64, 68-73, 79, 81, 83-84, 86, 90, 92-94, 99, 104
government intervention 155-156, 163

I

Inclusive Governance 4, 20, 22
India 68-76, 79, 84, 86-88, 90, 116, 132-134, 147

Information security 144, 153
infrastructure 17, 52, 93, 104-105, 117-118, 144, 148, 156-159, 161
internet networks 2
Internet Penetration 120, 122, 124, 131

L

liberal democracy 2, 10, 122, 126
local governments 38, 50-51, 55, 59-60, 64-65

M

market failure 155-159, 161-163
market forces 156
Member States 75, 117, 144, 146, 148

N

National Data Sharing and Accessibility Policy (NDSAP) 68-69, 86, 90
neo liberal 2-3, 11, 14
NREGA 132-136, 138-140

O

OGD Platform 68-69, 71-72, 90
Open Data 10, 12, 14, 21, 50-53, 55-57, 60, 62, 64-65, 68-74, 87-88, 90, 136, 139
Open Data Barometer 68, 73-74, 87
Open Government (OG) 1-3, 6-10, 12-13, 15, 19-20, 22, 29-34, 36-39, 42-45, 52-54, 61, 64-65, 68-69, 71-73, 79, 81, 83-84, 86, 90, 92-97, 99, 104-105
Open Government Data 2, 12, 32, 64, 68-69, 71-73, 79, 81, 83-84, 86, 90, 92-94, 99, 104

P

political space 3, 22, 112
poor performance 93, 120
poverty 6, 16-18, 93, 104, 120
Privacy Protection 29-31, 33-37, 41, 43-45
Proportionality 35, 43-44, 149
public administration 56, 61, 93, 99, 104, 112, 125
Public Financial Management (PFM) 92-94, 98, 100, 104-105
public infrastructure 144
Public Interest 32-34, 36, 41, 43-45
public organizations 51
public sector 2, 16-18, 22, 31, 37, 52, 55, 93, 114, 116

R

research platforms 92-93, 104
revenue 21, 98, 104

S

scholars 3, 6, 9, 18, 21, 30, 94, 104, 111, 113, 120-121, 145-146, 149, 158, 160-161
stakeholders 2, 94, 99, 104, 115, 132, 134, 148, 157
stockholders 93

T

Teledencity 124, 131
Transparency 1-4, 7-10, 12-14, 16, 18-22, 29-32, 34, 36-38, 42-44, 51, 53, 55, 61-62, 68, 70-71, 73, 86, 88, 92-93, 96-97, 99, 102, 104-105, 112

U

unemployment 132-133, 140
unemployment problem 133
United Nations 3-4, 10, 94, 99, 104
United States 2, 10, 12, 84

W

Web Analyzer 79, 87, 90
Webometrics 79, 90
websites 90, 94, 99, 104, 118-119, 125

Encyclopedia of
Information Science and Technology
Fourth Edition

www.ingramcontent.com/pod-product-compliance
Lightning Source LLC
LaVergne TN
LVHW061535290926
849162LV00004B/804